Religion and Rajput Women

Religion and Rajput Women

The Ethic of Protection in Contemporary Narratives

Lindsey Harlan

UNIVERSITY OF CALIFORNIA PRESS
Berkeley · Los Angeles · Oxford

University of California Press
Berkeley and Los Angeles, California

University of California Press, Ltd.
Oxford, England

© 1992 by
The Regents of the University of California

Library of Congress Cataloging-in-Publication Data

Harlan, Lindsey.
    Religion and Rajput women: the ethic of protection in contemporary narratives /
Lindsey Harlan.
        p.   cm.
    Includes bibliographical references and index.
    ISBN 0-520-07339-8 (alk. paper)
    1. Women, Rajput (Indic people)—Social conditions. 2. Women, Rajput (Indic
people)—Religion. 3. Caste—India—Rajasthan. 4. Social structure—India—Rajasthan.
5. Hinduism—India—Rajasthan—Customs and practices. 6. Rajasthan (India)—Social
conditions. 7. Rajasthan (India)—Religious life and customs.
I. Title.
DS432.R3H37   1991   91-2389
305.4'0954'4—dc20

Printed in the United States of America

1 2 3 4 5 6 7 8 9

For Neil and Martha Harlan
and
Robert Gay

Contents

Figures

Note on Transliteration and Pronunciation

I have chosen a system of transliteration that avoids diacritics and provides approximate pronunciation for readers uninitiated into the Sanskritic diacritical system. I have added diacritics in the glossary, which contains both untranslatable and frequently used terms. Diacritics remain in quotations, in the titles of English and French writings, and in the titles of texts written in Devanagari script. For the sake of easier recognition I have used common English spellings for proper names. There is considerable variation in the English and Hindi spellings of some of these names, particularly geographical names. I have adopted regularly used English spellings appearing on government maps and signs. Some of these conventional spellings are not direct transliterations of the Devanagari.

Also for easier recognition I have used the standard Hindi spellings where possible rather than Rajasthani spellings. As the text reveals, the women I interviewed speak different dialects (some Rajasthani, others non-Rajasthani), which means considerable variation in pronunciation, spelling, and word endings. I treat this complicated linguistic situation by using standard Hindi equivalents (many women spoke in standard Hindi during the interviews) except where no Hindi equivalent exists (e.g., the Rajasthani word *malipanau*) or where the Hindi equivalent is reasonably different from the Rajasthani (e.g., the Rajasthani *shrap* for the Hindi *shap*).

Transliteration conventions that bear special mention include the dropping of unpronounced final *a* and the rendering of the Hindi *r̥* as *ri*. The Rajasthani retroflex *ḷ* is rendered *l*, as it would appear in a Hindi equivalent (e.g., Rajasthani *kuḷ* is shown as the Hindi *kul*). The retroflex *ḍ* is written *r* (with no distinction made between this and the consonant *r*) and the retroflex *ḍh* is written *rh*. Nasals are represented as *n* and *m*, according to standard convention (see, for example, R. S. McGregor's *Outline of Hindi Grammar*). The Hindi *v* is represented as *v*, except where conventional spellings of proper names employ a *w*. The Persian *ph* is rendered *f* and *k̲* as *q*. Finally, both *ṣ* and *ś* are rendered in English as *sh*.

Acknowledgments

I owe a debt of gratitude to many people who helped me in various ways as I worked on this book. For their invaluable suggestions I thank my readers, Alf Hiltebeitel and Margaret Trawick, and my editor, Lynne Withey. For commenting on early drafts I thank Susan Wadley, Tom Havens, and Paul Courtright. I am indebted to Diana Eck, John Carman, and Stanley Tambiah for their encouragement of my research in its earliest stages and to Jack Hawley, David Wills, Dennis Hudson, Gary Green, and Gene Gallagher for their support while I was writing and revising. I am grateful to Veena Das for advice as I undertook fieldwork and for suggestions while we were fellows at Amherst. For many practical suggestions about working in Rajasthan, I thank Susanne Rudolph, Lloyd Rudolph, Joan Erdman, and Ann Gold. For first inspiring my interest in *kshatriya* mythology, I thank Daniel Ingalls, whose instruction in Sanskrit made my days as a graduate student exhausting and wonderful.

I shall always be grateful for the hospitality, kindness, and patience of those whom I interviewed. Special thanks are owed the royal houses of Udaipur, Jodhpur, Jaipur, Kota, and Jhalawar and the noble families of Amet, Ghanerao, Bedla, Kanor, Delwara, Salumbar, Bhainsrorgarh, Bari Sadri, Bansi, and Bassi. I also appreciate the help given me in India by Komal Kothari, Michael Mahar, Cynthia Packert, Fateh Singh and Indu, R. S. Ashiya, Laxmi Kumari Chundavat, N. T. Cauhan, Jonathan Stangroom, and Pauline Kolenda. For steadfast friendship, wonderful humor, and too much tea, I thank Honey, Chotu, and Manju along with their families.

I should like to express my gratitude for the financial support provided by Fulbright-Hays, Kennedy, and Copeland fellowships. I thank the American Institute of Indian Studies for facilitating my research in its early stages.

Last and most important, I thank my husband, Robert Gay, and my parents, Neil and Martha Harlan, for their love, encouragement, and kindness as I worked on this project.

Introduction

Dominated by the great Thar Desert, the state of Rajasthan is a land of sand and rocks, parched farms and dusty grazing grounds. Its horizon outlines long plains occasionally punctuated by abrupt, rugged hills. These hills bear testimony to the land's martial history, for strewn along their crests are crumbling battlements and fortresses from which wars were won and lost over centuries of conflict.

Before 1947, the date of Indian independence from the British, what is now Rajasthan was a collection of kingdoms. While the rulers of these kingdoms had to defer to British judgment in matters political, they retained their authority in matters economic and social; categorized as princely states, the kingdoms were not subject to direct British rule. Most of Rajasthan's kings belonged to the Rajput caste, whose traditional duties are fighting and ruling.[1] The word Rajput means "son (*putra*) of a king (*raja*)" and indicates the shared Rajput assumption that although not all caste members have been princes, all have descended from kings and so have inherited royal blood.

During a year and a half of fieldwork in Rajasthan, I studied the religious traditions of women belonging to this caste.[2] My purpose was to

1. An exception is the ruler of Bharatpur, who belongs to the Jat caste. On the fluidity of Rajput caste identity and social mobility, see Dirk H. A. Kolff, "The Rajput of Ancient and Medieval North India: a warrior ascetic" (paper presented at the Conference on Preservation of the Environment and Culture in Rajasthan, Rajasthan University, Jaipur, India, December 1987).

2. I performed this fieldwork in 1984–85 and returned for a few weeks in 1987–88 and again in 1989–90.

examine the ways in which Rajput devotional traditions reflect and influence relations between women's caste duties and gender roles. I wanted to understand how and when the foremost Rajput duty, the duty to protect a community, and the foremost female duty, the duty to protect a husband, take account of each other. Because throughout India and Indian history, Hindu tradition has articulated and sanctioned categories of caste and gender, I was interested in discovering the specific local sources of traditional authority governing the explicit and implicit decisions Rajput women make in interpreting, harmonizing, and reconciling caste and gender duties. My goals included understanding traditions Rajput women have inherited from the past and discovering if and how Rajput women have utilized and adapted past traditions to suit the contemporary circumstances facing the Rajput community.

To conduct this project I settled in at Udaipur, a small city in southwestern Rajasthan. Udaipur is the former capital of Mewar, a princely state whose royal line ranks first among the various royal households of Rajasthan.[3] Mewar gained this distinction as a result of the unceasing resistance it launched against Muslim invaders in pre-British days. Today Mewar retains the reputation of being the area of Rajasthan most resistant to social change.[4] The staunch conservatism of Udaipur's Rajput community shows in pronounced form a persistent tension between the Rajput desire to conserve tradition and the Rajput need to adapt to a changing world.

The tourist literature on the scattered sites important in Mewar history is filled with romantic testimonials to the courage and bravery of Mewar's Rajput soldiers. Not a few of these testimonials are cited from Colonel Tod's classic *Annals and Antiquities of Rajasthan*,[5] one of the more famous British reports on Indian culture from the early nineteenth century. Captivated by Mewar's martial history, Tod devotes about as much attention to Mewar as he does to all the other Rajput kingdoms combined—a fact that irritates many non-Mewaris to this day. He enthusiastically recounts tales exemplifying chivalry, honor, fondness for

3. For interesting observations on the Maharana's superior status in the 1940s, see Gayatri Devi's autobiography. Gayatri Devi and Santha Ram Rau, *A Princess Remembers* (Delhi: Vikas, 1984), 202–3.
4. Among the scholars who have noted this characteristic are Susanne Hoeber Rudolph and Lloyd I. Rudolph, "Rajputana Under British Paramountcy," in *Essays on Rajputana* (Delhi: Concept Publishing, 1984), 15. Rajput residents of Udaipur, Jodhpur, and Jaipur also confirm it. As one Jaipur resident summed it up, "Udaipur is more backward than other places."
5. James Tod, *Annals and Antiquities of Rajasthan*, 2 vols. (1829; reprint, Delhi: M. N. Publishers, 1978).

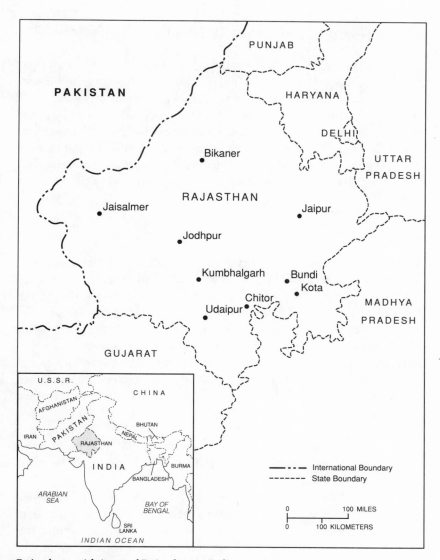

Rajasthan, with inset of Rajasthan in India.

opium, and weakness for women, traits he associates with Mewari Rajputs throughout their history.

Although sometimes disagreeing with Tod on the details of various battles or the subtler points of Rajput ritual and etiquette, the Mewari Rajputs I came to know readily refer to him as a masterful raconteur of their ancestral and cultural history.[6] Furthermore, while conceding that the circumstances in which Rajputs find themselves have changed dramatically, they believe that because they have inherited Rajput character, Tod's romantic depiction of Rajputs remains accurate. Keenly conscious and proud of their history, they want to preserve the values it exemplifies.

MEWAR

Throughout Udaipur and its environs are symbols of the past that Rajputs find so inspirational. The most prominent buildings in Udaipur are the enormous City Palace, situated high atop the steep banks of Lake Pichola, and the Lake Palace, a fairy-tale-like marble pleasure palace at the lake's center (fig. 1). Owing a portion of its fame to the James Bond film *Octopussy*, which was shot there in the early 1980s, the Lake Palace is now a moderately popular tourist resort. Although the City Palace contains a luxurious hotel and a well-appointed museum, it continues to house some members of the royal family, who also inhabit other stately residences. While some of these structures have been converted to attract tourists to Udaipur, they remain symbols of Rajput history and identity. Members of the Rajput community speak with pride of the invitations they have received to socialize with members of the royal family in these places.

Just as the Udaipur palaces represent both the mores of the old order and the advent of modern business, so the physical layout of Udaipur symbolizes the juxtaposition of tradition and innovation. Around the City Palace is the old city, in whose narrow alleyways are located the urban residences of the noblemen who once attended the Mewar court. Outside this area in the newer part of the city are the government buildings and the bustling Bapu Bazaar, where consumers can purchase goods ranging from fashionable Bombay apparel to stainless steel kitchen appliances.

Mediating this contrast are the animals and the people who travel

6. A town in modern Mewar is named after Tod. His work is available in English and Hindi.

1. The Lake Palace, Udaipur.

from one part of the city to the other. In the old and new cities alike there are languid camels pulling carts, lines of burros transporting construction materials, cows napping, pariah dogs (all of which bear a strong family resemblance), and of course everywhere people, usually on foot, sometimes on bicycles or in horse carts, less often in auto rickshaws or motor scooters, and only occasionally in automobiles. Some of the men are dressed in western trousers; many others wear turbans and dhotis, long pieces of cloth wound about the waist, pulled between the legs, and tucked into the waist in back. Some of the women wear saris, long the fashion elsewhere in India but relatively recent arrivals in Rajasthan; others don varieties of traditional Rajasthani dress, consisting chiefly of bright blouses, tight vests, and long flowing skirts.

The roads winding through Udaipur trace the peripheries of three large lakes, in which cart ponies and water buffalo seek refuge from the relentless desert sunshine. Around the city rise steep rocky hills with jagged peaks. Deteriorating along their ridges are ancient city walls and royal hunting blinds, from which kings and noblemen once hunted all manner of game, including tigers and wild boar.

Beyond these walls lie the arid plains of Mewar, plains ill suited to agriculture. They are dotted nonetheless with tiny wheat and corn plots inevitably bordered by crooked cactus fences, beyond which graze goats and sheep. Clustered nearby are little whitewashed houses. Most years the monsoon fails, and so the hot summer winds leave everything covered with thick yellow dust. During eight months of the year the daytime temperature often swells above a hundred degrees, which makes the water scarcity acutely troublesome.

Slicing through this barren landscape are a few single-lane highways, perhaps the most prominent signs of modernity. Along them travel trucks and buses, whose windshields are decorated with tinsel garlands draped over dashboard icons of Hindu deities. Once in a while an automobile speeds by, usually a taxi transporting tourists to such notable Mewar sites as Chitor and Kumbhalgarh, two of Mewar's former capitals (figs. 2, 3).[7] En route to anywhere are palaces and fortresses belonging to the erstwhile nobility. Those too expensive to maintain have been abandoned, but many are inhabited and remain the cultural focal point for residents of villages in which they are located and even for people in surrounding villages.

In sum, the juxtaposition of highway and fortress, trousers and dhotis, old and new, summarizes the transitional character of Mewari society. Trying to adapt to this changing world and yet conserve what they can of the old, Rajputs are particularly conscious of their status as Rajputs, as persons with royal blood. They cling to their sense of distinctiveness from members of other castes and maintain traditional status differentiations within their own caste community. They are distinctly aware of their "Rajputness."

CLASSES AND TRADITIONS

In Udaipur as elsewhere in Rajasthan, Rajputs understand themselves as belonging to one of three traditional classes. There are royal Rajputs, noble Rajputs, and ordinary Rajputs. The royal Rajputs ruled independent states, some of which, like Mewar, held vast territories. The heads of state were called *maharaja*s (great kings), except for the Mewari ruler, who was styled *maharana*, meaning the same thing, this status distinction marking his superiority over the other independent rulers. These royal titles are still very much in use.

Serving the maharajas were noblemen, to this day called *thakur*s or sometimes *raja*s, both terms meaning "king." Their families lived on

7. Spelling of Chitor varies widely on signs, maps, and texts; alternatives are Chittore, Chittor, Citaur, Chitaur.

2. Crenellated walls of the fortress at Kumbhalgarh, a former capital of Mewar.

3. The fortress at Kumbhalgarh; rugged Mewar terrain.

estates, *thikana*s, granted by the maharajas in return for military and administrative service. The *thikana*s consisted of a given number of villages, which the noblemen governed and taxed. When residing at their estates, the noblemen lived in palaces, which, if built in pre-British days, were usually protected by fortresses with tall crenellated walls. While attending their maharaja in his capital, however, they lived in rambling urban mansions (*haveli*s). Mewari noblemen spent up to six months a year living in their Udaipur households. Today, they remain distinctly aware of their privileged status as former advisors to the Maharana.

Finally, there are the ordinary, nonaristocratic Rajputs. While all Rajputs claim royal blood, some have been poor and powerless. The explanation all Rajputs give for this is primogeniture.[8] In traditional Rajput society the eldest son inherited his father's estate and title. Younger sons, potential threats to political stability, were encouraged to take their friends and followers, leave their brothers' kingdoms, and seek fortune by conquering their own lands or by entering into the service of a maharaja and winning from him a *thikana* grant. In turn, their younger sons set off to gain fortune and title; the prospects open to these second-generation younger sons were more limited than those that had been open to their fathers because they had fewer followers and other resources to take with them in their quests for power. Moreover, they had comparatively little to offer a maharaja in return for a *thikana*. Over a period of generations, youngest sons wound up with little or nothing at all and had to take up farming and living in small villages. These village Rajputs are referred to as "little brother" (*chota bhai*) Rajputs.

Despite the class differences represented by these three groups, Rajputs maintain that they are all related to one another, however distantly, either by descent or marriage. They openly acknowledge that the genealogies of all real Rajputs intersect somewhere or other.[9] Moreover, they consider all Rajputs members of a single, if scattered, Rajput community. This community is the entire Rajput caste, or *jati*, within which their daughters must be married.

Given the many political and status levels of Rajput society, I won-

8. Here as elsewhere my primary interest is not how things happened but how Rajputs understand them: not history, but its indigenous construction, grounds ethos. Doubtless primogeniture is partly responsible for creating *chota bhai* communities, but other factors, probably including upward caste mobility, enter the picture.

9. The force of this qualification is that there are many whom members of the Rajput community regard as impersonators, lower-caste persons trying to infiltrate their ranks through marriage. They believe the community is and must remain constant; only its generations can and should change.

dered at first if it would be possible to discover any truly common Rajput tradition. As I learned more about the Rajputs, however, I found
great continuity both of Rajput tradition and interpretation throughout
the rungs of the Rajput hierarchy. In talking with men and interviewing
women from royal, noble, and village households I found that Rajputs
at each level identify the same traditions as important to Rajputs. Thus
women from the three levels of society claim that all Rajput women
must perform the same religious functions, chief among which are worshiping Rajput *kuldevi*s (goddesses of the *kul*) and venerating family
*sati*s (women who have immolated themselves on their husbands' funeral pyres).[10] As I grew familiar with these traditions, it struck me that
women narrating *kuldevi* and *sati* stories often contextualized their stories by referring to well-known stories of Rajput heroines. Within a few
weeks of my arrival in Udaipur, I had learned many legends about the
various heroines admired throughout Rajput society. All Rajput women
knew these legends, though village women were often less clear on the
historical details of these stories than noble and royal women. Because
the Rajputs I met quite consistently identified traditions of *kuldevi*s,
*sati*s, and ancestral heroines (*virangana*s) as the ones most important
to Rajput women, and because the traditions provide several points of
access to the ethos of Rajput women, I have organized my investigation into caste duty and gender roles around analysis of these
traditions.[11]

Although the reasons for the importance of these traditions will
emerge in the chapters following, a few preliminary remarks about them
are in order. As concerning *kuldevi* worship, it is important to note that
the literature on Rajput tradition, by no measure vast, has paid scant
attention to the Rajput *kuldevi*. Though a number of prominent authors, some whose work I draw on, have analyzed the Rajput *kul* as a
kinship unit, no author has devoted serious study to the *kuldevi*, who is
the primary recipient of Rajput devotion and the primary emblem of
Rajput identity.

There is scholarship (some of it quite recent) that treats apparently
similar deities, including non-Rajput *kuldevi*s, who are worshiped by
groups in various parts of India. It can be roughly divided into four
categories: one comprising studies of deities, who are associated with

10. A *kul* is a kinship segmentation unit that I discuss in the following chapters.
11. I shall use other devotional traditions, especially those important to men, as context for these traditions. My ongoing book-length study of hero veneration treats many of
these more fully.

one or more groups;[12] another comprising studies of villages or regions, some of whose deities are said to be connected with a group or groups;[13] a third comprising studies of kingship, in which the legitimating aspect of deity worship is explored;[14] and a fourth comprising studies of folklore, in which deities and their communities are analyzed in passing.[15] Authors often refer to such deities as "tutelary deities" but give little explanation for why a deity is in fact a tutelary deity or how a tutelary deity differs from other deities. In most cases, providing such an explanation would require authors to digress substantially from the concerns that they explore. Thus they use the phrase as a rather imprecise convenience that refers to no indigenous category of divine protector. They posit a special relationship between a given deity and a particular group or groups but neither explore the nature of that relationship nor analyze it with reference to relationships between other tutelary deities and their affiliated groups.

The term "lineage deity" is somewhat more precise in that it specifies a kinship relationship but often does not specify the extent or nature of a "lineage," which might be a small or an extensive segmentary kinship unit. Scholars use the word to refer to very different levels of kinship organization and identity.[16]

When scholars do use the indigenous terms *kuldevi* or *kuldevta* (*kul* deity), they still face the matter of definition, for the term's meaning

12. Examples are Eveline Meyer, *Aṅkāḷaparmēcuvari* (Stuttgart: Steiner Verlag, 1986); Gilles Tarabout, *Sacrifier et donner à voir en pays Malabar* (Paris: Ecole Française d'Extrême-Orient, 1986); Alf Hiltebeitel, *The Cult of Draupadī*, vol. 1 (Chicago: University of Chicago Press, 1988); William Harman, *The Sacred Marriage of a Hindu Goddess* (Bloomington: Indiana University Press, 1989); C. J. Fuller, *Servants of the Goddess* (Cambridge: Cambridge University Press, 1984); Gananath Obeyesekere, *The Cult of the Goddess Pattini* (Chicago: University of Chicago Press, 1984); Olivier Herrenschmidt, "Le sacrifice du buffle en Andhra cotier," *Puruṣārtha* 5 (1981).

13. See Marie-Louise Reinich, *Les dieux et les hommes* (Paris: Mouton, 1979); Nicholas Dirks, *The Hollow Crown* (Cambridge: Cambridge University Press, 1987); Lynn Bennett, *Dangerous Wives and Sacred Sisters* (New York: Columbia University Press, 1983); Gerald Berreman, *Hindus of the Himalayas* (Berkeley: University of California Press, 1972); and Edgar Thurstan, "Komati" entry in *Castes and Tribes of Southern India* (Madras: Government Press, 1909).

14. For examples, articles from *Puruṣārtha* 10 (1986) by Dennis Vidal ("Le puits et le sanctuaire"), Jean-Claude Galey ("Totalité et hiérarchie"), and Henri Stern ("Le temple d'Eklingji et le royaume du Mewar [Rajasthan]"); France Bhattacharya, "La déesse et le royaume," *Puruṣārtha* 5 (1981); and Dirks, *Hollow Crown*.

15. Examples are Velcheru Narayana Rao, "Epics and Ideologies," in *Another Harmony*, ed. Stuart H. Blackburn and A. K. Ramanujan (Berkeley: University of California Press, 1986); Brenda Beck, *The Three Twins* (Bloomington: Indiana University Press, 1982); and Gene H. Roghair, *The Epic of Palnāḍu* (Oxford: Clarendon Press, 1982).

16. I first noted this variation during my frequent and often animated discussions with Veena Das at Amherst College in the spring of 1986.

varies from place to place and group to group. Thus with the borrowing of the word *kul*, we see that a divinity is conceptualized with reference to this particular kinship group. Often, however, the *kul* deity is not actually associated with a kinship group designated by the term *kul*. As we shall see, some Rajput *kuldevi*s are associated with *kul*s, and others are associated with smaller segmentary units. Elsewhere, deities deemed *kul* deities protect many different groups belonging to various *kul*s, sub-*kul*s, and castes.[17]

This study examines associations between *kuldevi*s—all Rajputs worship female, not male, *kul* deities—and their Rajput kinship groups. As it turns out, the notion conveyed by the term *kuldevi* is specific to the Rajasthani context. Understanding *kuldevi* tradition sheds abundant light on indigenous constructions of caste, kinship, and residency in Rajasthan; I believe that the same might well be true of *kul* deity traditions in other communities elsewhere in India.

Given the relative dearth of information on *kul* deities, it is perhaps not too surprising to find that no study has viewed *kuldevi* worship from the vantage point of women. In this study I show that Rajput men's and women's evaluations of the nature of *kuldevi* personality and of the meaning of *kuldevi* mythology vary dramatically. The sociological implications of this variance are important; focusing on *kuldevi* tradition reveals a number of crucial assumptions about the way women understand personal and familial obligations. For example, these assumptions challenge the traditional typification of North Indian wives as sociologically and religiously isolated from their natal religious traditions.[18]

As to *sati*s, I might mention that when I arrived in Rajasthan there existed no scholarly treatment of contemporary *satimata* veneration in this state. Those who had worked in Rajasthan had discussed the importance of commemorative *sati* stones and remarked that these monuments still play a part in the religious lives of some Rajasthanis.[19] No one, however, had investigated the tradition of veneration and discussed its paramount role in the religious lives of Rajputs today.[20] I was quite

17. See Hiltebeitel, *Cult of Draupadī*; Meyer, *Aṅkāḷaparmēcuvari*; and Roghair, *Epic of Palnāḍu*.

18. Also challenging this assumption are two papers presented at the conference, Women's Rites, Women's Desires, Harvard University, April 1988: William Sax, "Village Daughter, Village Goddess," 17; and Lindsey Harlan, "Kuldevi Tradition among Rajput Women," 15. Also see Bennett, *Dangerous Wives*, 169; and William Sax's manuscript, *Mountain Goddess* (forthcoming from Oxford University Press), passim.

19. See, for example, Ann Grodzins Gold, *Fruitful Journeys* (Berkeley: University of California Press, 1988).

20. Paul Courtright is working on a largely historical manuscript that will incorporate some contemporary materials (*The Goddess and the Dreadful Practice* [forthcoming from Oxford University Press]).

honestly surprised to find that *satimata* veneration remains a thriving tradition, though the practice of self-immolation has become almost extinct.[21]

These days few people interested in India are unaware that *sati* veneration is a living tradition. Since September 1987, when the young Rajput woman Rup Kanwar joined her husband on his cremation pyre in a small village in eastern Rajasthan, the Indian papers and magazines have been full of articles and editorials on *sati* immolation.[22] The controversy sparked by the case has drawn international attention, including coverage by the *New York Times*.[23] It recounts the flocking of Rajasthanis to the cremation site, which, to the dismay and indeed the outrage of many, has become a place of pilgrimage. In the first month after Rup Kanwar's death alone over two hundred thousand people visited her newly built shrine to pay respects and receive her blessing.

The case has catalyzed impassioned debates, both national and local, about the necessity for discouraging self-immolation through prosecuting accomplices and forbidding institutionally sponsored *sati* glorification. The controversy has been accompanied by large demonstrations organized by those who denounce the practice (with some Indian feminists at the forefront) or by those who support it (with some conservative Rajputs at the forefront). In short, as I found out firsthand on a recent trip back to India, *sati* veneration has become a politically salient and emotionally charged issue.

Given this explosive atmosphere, it is particularly important to understand the tradition of *sati* veneration as it has existed within the Rajput community. Although I find the idea of self-immolation horrifying, my purpose here is not to evaluate the contemporary national controversy politically and ethically. That extremely important task, now being pursued so vigorously in India, is in many ways beyond the limited scope and design of this study and would require a large and disruptive digression.[24] Rather, my task here is to give the best description of the Rajput tradition of veneration that I can, having revealed the intellectual

21. From literature and from discussions with ethnographers I conclude that Rajasthan retains the most widespread and thriving tradition of *sati* veneration in India.

22. Examples of substantial press treatment include Rajni Bakshi, "Shame," *Illustrated Weekly of India*, 4 Oct. 1987; Inderjit Bhadvar, "Militant Defiance," *India Today*, 31 Oct. 1987; *Manushi*, special double issue, nos. 42–43, September–December 1987; Ashis Nandy, "The Human Factor," *Illustrated Weekly of India*, 17 Jan. 1988; *Seminar* 342, "Sati: a symposium on widow immolation and its social context" (February 1988).

23. See Steven R. Weisman, "Indian Widow's Death at Pyre Creates Shrine," *New York Times*, 19 Sept. 1987.

24. Because the Kanwar incident took place after my departure from India I have no systematic field research on local reactions to it. For a historical overview of *sati* immolation, see V. N. Datta, *Sati* (Delhi: Manohar, 1988).

interests and motivations that brought me to consider the topic in the first place.

By way of introducing the heroine stories to be analyzed in my final chapters, I should say that not nearly enough work has been done by way of analyzing how specific groups of people construe popular narratives that are part of their culture. Often researchers have gathered narratives without benefiting from the direct interpretive commentary that indigenous narrators can give them.[25] Because I was interested in the heroic stories as possible repositories of moral paradigms, I was keenly interested in voluntary exegesis.

One thing that surprised me in the course of interviewing was that when women listed their favorite heroines, they almost invariably insisted on telling the stories about these heroines in full, even if they knew that I had heard the stories many times. Clearly they thought that I could not possibly understand who a heroine was unless I understood crucial features of her behavior. These could only be pointed out properly in the context of storytelling. The evaluative glosses that women volunteered and of course the usually very subtle variations that they narrated gave me a rich source of information about women's values. Moreover, because the two stories that dominated women's responses, the stories of Mira and Padmini, radically conflict at one level in the values they espouse, only the interpretive and evaluative comments women made gradually enabled me to understand the broader, more encompassing normative ideals that the stories share. Furthermore, the Mira and Padmini stories have conveniently served to illustrate in narrative form some basic resolutions of normative dilemmas discussed in the *kuldevi* and *sati* chapters.

THE RESEARCH PROCESS

I realize that the nuts-and-bolts details of the research process do not hold equal fascination for all readers. For those curious about the specifics of the interviewing schedule I undertook, I have provided a detailed account in appendix A, as well as the interview format itself, in appendix B.[26] What follows here is a more general description of my

25. An interesting exception is the new work by Linda Hess on oral *Ramayan*: "The Poet, the People, and the Western Scholar," *Theatre Journal* 40, no. 2 (May 1988): 236–53.

26. I thank Alf Hiltebeitel and Tom Havens for the suggestion and acknowledge the agreeable example of this approach provided by Brenda Beck, *Peasant Society in Koṅku* (Vancouver: University of British Columbia Press, 1972).

fieldwork, including a brief characterization of the interview and its rationale.

For reasons to be divulged shortly, I chose to focus my work on the nobility, the middle rung of the Rajput class hierarchy. I did not feel I could generalize in any competent way, however, if I limited my interviews to members of this class. Without interviewing members of the royal and *chota bhai* (little brother) classes, I would be uncertain what information I received characterized only the nobility and what information pertained to all Rajput women. Thus for purposes of establishing boundaries and providing context I interviewed women from all three Rajput classes.

When I interviewed *chota bhai* Rajputs I did so in a small Rajput-dominated village forty minutes' drive northwest of Udaipur (fig. 4). All but two of the families in this rocky little hamlet trace their ancestry to the ruling family of Kelwa, an important estate several hours' drive north of Udaipur. The remaining families are connected historically to Delwara (fig. 5), another prominent Mewar estate. There was among villagers a consensus that the ones who really know the Rajput traditions, including the religious traditions, are the "high" (*unce*, referring to royal or noble) Rajputs. Village Rajputs felt that the aristocracy naturally and best performs, preserves, and understands the Rajput traditions (figs. 6, 7). They appeared convinced that preserving high Rajput tradition requires the kind of social education only the nobility has received and that the Rajput tradition preserved in the village is but a pale reflection of what goes on in the homes of higher persons. There is certainly some truth to this perception: although the villagers have a limited familiarity with traditions common to all Rajputs, the Rajput traditions they observe are heavily contextualized and influenced by local customs and lore.[27] Though I became intrigued with these local customs and lore, I decided to direct the focus of this particular study to the basic traditions that Rajputs generally share.[28] Following the villagers' advice I turned to the aristocracy and used my village notes only for contextual comparison.

27. Gerald Berreman received similar advice from Himalayan villagers, who suggested he consult learned people instead of them (Berreman, *Hindus of the Himalayas*, 108).

28. I intend to focus on the specific village synthesis in coming articles. With little information on other Rajput villages, I lack the comparative basis that I gained in studying aristocratic women. Some religious traditions are similar to those described in Gold (*Fruitful Journeys*), but because the village I came to know is overwhelmingly Rajput, its *kuldevi* and *sati* traditions figure larger in village life than they do in Gold's case and in non-Rajput villages.

4. Rajput village woman in her courtyard.

In my focus on the nobility I have sometimes included substantiating information gleaned from interviews with women from royal households, who were either native to or had been married in major Rajasthani kingdoms.[29] I encountered great continuity of knowledge and belief among noblewomen and royal women. One reason for this is that many royal wives are born in noble households. Another is that both noble persons and royal persons have patronized, articulated, and interpreted Rajput tradition. They have performed the same religious functions on parallel political levels.

I made my decision to concentrate on noblewomen instead of royal women for two reasons. First, quite simply, the nobility is larger than the royalty and therefore provides a better sample of experience. Second, on balance, noblewomen have preserved their traditions more completely than have the royal women, many of whom live in fairly modern urbanized settings and spend much of their time away from Rajasthan in Delhi, Bombay, and abroad.[30]

Most of the noblewomen I interviewed are from Udaipur, yet because I wanted to understand not just the traditions of Mewar but those shared by Rajputs as a whole, I combined my work in Mewar with multiple visits to Jodhpur (northwestern Rajasthan) and Jaipur (northeastern Rajasthan). In this way I was able to discover traditional patterns illustrated by Udaipur households that are common to all noble households throughout Rajasthan. Furthermore, such an approach also enabled me to discern pattern variations.

Finally, while I was in Udaipur I not only interviewed women living in urban residences (whether *havelis* or modern houses) but also traveled to various estates (*thikanas*) whose fortresses or palaces were still occupied.[31] My purpose in visiting these places was to talk with women still living in estate households and to examine the division of traditional households into the *zanana* (female quarters) and *mardana* (male quarters).[32] Most urban households, even *havelis*, are no longer divided up

29. These kingdoms include Jodhpur, Jaipur, Kota, Jhalawar, and Bikaner, as well as Udaipur. Among the noblewomen some have husbands from very small states that were technically independent. Many such states are actually smaller and less powerful than the major *thikanas* attached to the large states; like them, these small states are aligned with and in many ways dependent on large neighboring states. The leaders of both often use the same titles (*rana, rao sahib,* etc.) and have similar status.

30. This is a relative distinction. Many royal women are conversant with Rajput traditions. Some observe them and are quite religious; others have knowledge but say travel or other priorities often intrude on observance.

31. These included Amet, Ghanerao, Bari Sadri, Bansi, and Kothariya, all prominent Mewar *thikanas*.

32. In some of these estates elderly women still live in the *zanana*, whereas younger women go back and forth between the parts of the household. Unlike the crowded urban

5. Delwara: a Solah Thikana.

this way. By investigating and diagraming the temples and shrines in male and female space within estates, I learned much about the origins of differences between male and female devotional traditions.[33]

At the very start of my research among the nobility, the biggest problem I faced was that of access. One cannot simply call up a princess and ask to come over.[34] At first, those few Rajput noblewomen I met through acquaintances were cordial, but most did not want to be interviewed. Some eventually explained that Rajput women despise chattiness and consciously cultivate social reserve toward those people they consider outsiders. Reserve, I was gradually to learn, is greatly valued by Rajput women, who understand it as the sine qua non of dignity.

Thus my initial meetings with Rajput women were often characterized by almost excruciating formality. I sat in *havelis* or *thikana* forts sipping tea, conversing politely, meeting relatives, confronting curious children, usually to find that, alas, no time remained for discussing matters related to my research. Sometimes this was accidental; often it was not. Only after I had met many members of the community and been in Udaipur for months observing daily affairs, participating in festivals, visiting pilgrimage sites, and dropping by for cups of tea did I find that the atmosphere had relaxed enough for informal chatting and open questioning.

When at last I began to interview, a number of women expressed true surprise at the nature of my questions. "You mean you actually want to know about *kuldevis!*" one woman exclaimed. She admitted that she had been sure that I was not interested in women's religious traditions and that I was really in Udaipur to find out about Rajput family problems.[35] She said that she had initially dodged an interview because a Rajput woman must always save face: even though she has problems, she must not complain about them. This woman added that her suspicion had been shared by others who were hesitating to be in-

residences, the spacious estate palaces clearly show the delineation of male and female space.

33. Men have usually worshiped *kuldevis* in temples located in the *mardana* or outside the household, and women have worshiped them in small, sometimes crude, *kuldevi* shrines in the *zanana*. This segregation of tradition has engendered standard variations in interpretations of *kuldevi* tradition.

34. The fact that many of those I interviewed lack phones turned out to be an advantage, as it made unannounced return visits possible.

35. At first some women feared that my interest was male alcohol abuse and its associated family problems. While women uphold alcohol consumption as a Rajput prerogative, many worry about excesses in consumption, which they often attribute to depression over declining Rajput values and fortune.

terviewed.[36] Once my real purpose was clear, almost all the women relaxed and obviously enjoyed the interview. Many considered themselves very religious and found it pleasant to talk about religious matters.[37]

Interviews were generally done in Hindi. Women who speak English, however, sometimes preferred to do so during the interview or to go back and forth between the two languages, which I often found myself doing as well. I conducted one hundred and seven interviews, of which seventy-seven were with aristocratic women, eight with members of royalty, and twenty-two with villagers. The narratives that women provided during these interviews were generally concise stories, often best known and recited by older women. Many of these women were worried that younger women and their children were uninterested in their narratives and too interested in storybooks and, even worse, in television, which arrived in Udaipur shortly after I did.[38]

Though I am uncertain as to the extent to which storytelling is on the decline (it would be interesting to reinterview women in a number of years to see if they grow more or less conversant with narratives as they mature), I am impressed by the extent to which women of all ages overwhelmingly stress the importance of preserving *parda*, the seclusion of women within the household. Rajput women often say that the mark of a Rajput woman is her unwillingness to "go out." Most women in Udaipur stay inside; they do not worship in local temples, shop in markets, or even enter voting booths. Interestingly enough, this norm of seclusion has not made them ignorant of religious customs in other parts of Rajasthan and beyond. The women in an aristocratic Rajput household tend to come from a variety of regional and financial backgrounds. The interview results and indeed the general history of Rajput marriage alliances demonstrate that *zanana*s have always been more cosmopolitan than *mardana*s. Each Rajput family has daughters-in-law familiar with religious and mythical traditions from their natal homes. Hence although each family has its own traditions known to all members, the women of the family also have knowledge of traditions from

36. Several women have confirmed the initial general suspicion of my motives, which in retrospect amuses them.

37. Most women, however, as members of the nobility and public persons, did not want their names attached to the information and opinions they provided. Having promised to protect their anonymity, I have identified only those women who gave me permission.

38. On recent social change in the Rajput community see Lindsey Harlan, "Social Change and Rajput Tradition" (paper presented at the Conference on Modern South Asian Religion, Social Science Research Council, Amherst College, August 1987).

6. Noblewomen approaching hero shrine at their *thikana*.

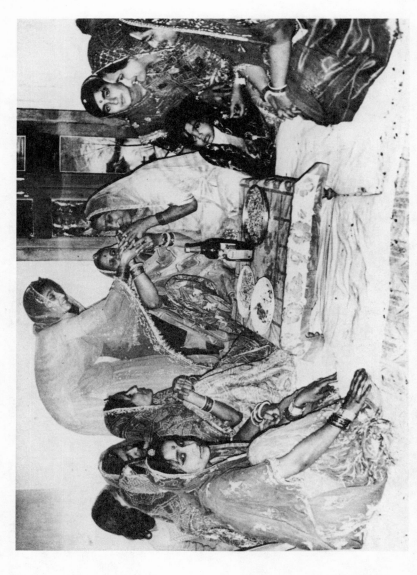

7. Drinking ceremony in an aristocratic Rajput wedding (from the wedding album of a Mewari *thakur*).

outside the family. Because of this, by talking to women of any major town, an interviewer can learn about traditions from all over Rajasthan.[39]

While every individual Rajput marriage introduces into a family a woman with a foreign background, on a macro level of analysis, intermarriage within the relatively small Rajput community tends to reinforce the same general norms throughout Rajasthan. Moreover, as mentioned above, while women bring in different traditions, they share the conviction that natal traditions should not subvert or supplant conjugal traditions.

A significant qualification to this point is that whereas Rajputs all over the state are aware of traditional Rajput norms and customs, those living in eastern Rajasthan, especially in or near Jaipur, have by and large taken up a more urbanized style of life than that still followed in the west. While the interview questions revealed attitudes shared by all Rajput women, the women I interviewed were largely those married into Mewari households. The results are therefore dominated by the experiences of women living in the conservative western part of the state.

Although the majority of information upon which I rely in this study comes from the interviews, I had other significant sources. Throughout my stay in Rajasthan, I made recurrent and often extended visits to urban and rural homes to chat informally and observe families in the midst of their daily routines. Many women from these homes graciously included me in family activities and social functions. Within this group were many noblewomen with whom I became sufficiently good friends to visit frequently, in fact even daily. They freely voiced their concerns about such matters as the cheapness of my jewelry and the ugliness of my freckles and sunglasses. From them I learned the intricacies of Rajput etiquette and protocol and also, little by little, the local gossip. At their homes I consumed countless quantities of tea and asked what I am sure amounts to thousands of questions, many of them surely annoying questions about details of ritual and etiquette. Two of these women invited me to stay at their *thikana* residences for extended visits. Although I visited many *thikana*s during my time in Rajasthan, my time in these old estates was particularly rich as it afforded many uninterrupted hours of discussion on religion and family history.

39. In Rajasthan, as elsewhere in India, marriage is typically patrilocal; brides live with their husbands in extended families. Rajputs tend to marry across long distances. Although most Mewari brides come from other regions in Rajasthan, a few come from more distant places like Himachal Pradesh, Madya Pradesh, and Orissa.

I also spent a lot of time with two other women, Honey and Chotu, who were then unmarried women in their middle twenties. Having taken an interest in my research early on, they volunteered their help in many ways, including arranging introductions, filling me in on the latest happenings, and occasionally joining me on excursions. They frequently kept me company during the lonely and hot afternoon hours when the rest of Udaipur was napping.[40]

The other types of information upon which I relied were informal conversations with Rajput men (who were often interested in their ancestral history and willing to narrate parts of it they thought relevant to my interests), discussions with non-Rajputs from different caste backgrounds about their perceptions of Rajput women, many visits to shrines and pilgrimage places that Rajput women said were important to them, and later, brief informal follow-up interviews with fifty women to test tentative conclusions before I headed back to the United States.[41]

Throughout my stay in Rajasthan I felt there was always more to learn; rare was the day that was not filled with new discoveries. Because the religious tradition of the area has been understudied and thus underrepresented in the literature on India, I found much in my research that contradicted general assumptions I had assembled during my years of study. I was continuously challenged by puzzles demanding solutions. Some of the puzzles that intrigued me most I have attempted to work out in this book.

This puzzle-solving project begins in the next chapter, which characterizes the Rajput community as a whole and then focuses more narrowly on the separate world of women. Its survey of the social and religious beliefs, norms, and responsibilities of Rajput women serves as background for the investigation of caste and gender duties conducted in remaining chapters.

40. These women were unusual. They were daughters in prominent and traditional families but worked together in an emporium managed by relatives. They explained that their families had allowed this work because they were unmarried and working with relatives. Now both have married and quit working outside the home. One married into a *thikana* near Jodhpur. The other moved to Kuwait with her new husband, who is from a prominent *thikana* in Gujarat, but then returned to Bombay during the airlift of Indian nationals after Iraq's invasion of Kuwait.

41. The results of these interviews concerning possession and dream appearances quantitatively confirmed the information about appearances by supernatural beings contained in chapters 2 through 5.

CHAPTER 1

Rajasthan and the Rajputs

The past looms large in the self-understanding of Rajputs living in all parts of Rajasthan. Most experience a persistent nostalgia for their former lifestyle and its privileges. Thus in Mewar when Rajput men gather together to sip scotch and socialize, they often speak of those days in which they ruled and hunted or those more remote times in which their ancestors ruled and waged war against one another.[1] Continually stirring memories of bygone days are the tiger skins and other hunting trophies on their walls, the coats of arms above their entryways, the hand-colored photographs of royalty in their parlors, and their various heirlooms—ivory-inlaid swords, elaborate bridles, the occasional silver throne.

Doubtless intensifying this nostalgia are the particular circumstances of Rajasthan's recent history. In 1947, when the princely states of Rajasthan were combined into a single political unit, the state of Rajasthan, Rajputs were simply not prepared for democracy.[2] In 1818, when the Rajput rulers signed treaties with the British, they had been able to continue as heads of their respective states. Their power to govern was often ambiguous, but it was by no means nominal. When 1947 arrived,

1. John Hitchcock uses the phrase "martial Rājpūt" to convey this political and military ethos in his study, "The Idea of the Martial Rājpūt," in *Traditional India*, ed. Milton Singer (Austin: University of Texas Press, 1959), 11. Also see Susanne Hoeber Rudolph and Lloyd I. Rudolph, "Rajput Adulthood," in *Essays on Rajputana* (Delhi: Concept Publishing, 1984), 179–80; and Gold, *Fruitful Journeys*, 24–25.
2. Rudolph and Rudolph, "Rajputana Under British Paramountcy," 3–4.

the institutional changes that had taken over a century to evolve elsewhere in India where there was direct British rule, now were implemented by the central Indian government immediately. To an overwhelming extent, the Rajputs had no part in the process of political transformation.[3] Hence Independence was for them a sudden and bewildering shock. They saw their way of life radically transformed in a very short time. Now, over forty years later, many still speak of themselves as hereditary rulers and so implicitly (or even explicitly) claim that they are the rightful rulers. In short, they are still adjusting.

Nevertheless, Rajput nostalgia has not always resulted in merely reactionary attitudes toward change. Many Rajputs say that their aristocratic and martial heritage has inspired them to adapt to the privations brought about by their loss of legal title and power. They feel that facing the future requires holding on to the values that helped their forebears face defeat in former days.[4] To take account of current Rajput constructions of caste and gender duties, it will be useful to become acquainted with the Rajput past and the ethos it has bequeathed.

GENEALOGY AND IDENTITY

Rajputs are keenly conscious of their genealogy, certain divisions within which are highly important features in the construction of personal identity. These segmentary kinship units locate the Rajput in contexts of family history and locality. The largest kinship unit within the Rajput *jati* (caste; literally, type or genus) is the *vamsh* (very roughly translatable as family in its broadest sense). In Rajasthan there are three great *vamsh*: sun, moon, and fire.[5] Rajputs understand themselves to be descended from these sacred phenomena (figs. 8, 9, 10). The *vamsh* to which the ruling family of Mewar belongs is the solar family, this identification being succinctly made in the Udaipur coat of arms, in which appears a great sun with a stern mustached visage. It is prominently displayed above the great central entrance to the City Palace.

---

3. Ibid.

4. A member of the royal family of Mansa (a small Rajput state) recalls that among the values stressed were the ideas of "generosity in victory, keeping your standard flying even in defeat," and so forth (Charles Allen and Sharada Dwivedi, *Lives of the Indian Princes* [London: Century Publishing, 1984], 53).

5. Respectively, Suryavamsh, Candravamsh, and Agnivamsh. Elsewhere in India there are other lines, notably the sage (Rishivamsh) and snake (Nagvamsh), from which Rajasthanis sometimes take wives.

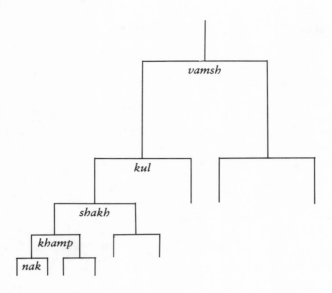

8. Rajput genealogical chart.

Encompassed by each individual *vamsh* are *kul*s, smaller kinship units.[6] Again, the closest English equivalent to *kul* is family, but in a more restrictive sense than the *vamsh*. The term is not, however, particularly narrow: *kul*s comprise many generations and link present to past over hundreds of years.[7] Examples of *kul*s belonging to the solar *vamsh* are the Rathaur *kul* of Marwar, whose capital was Jodhpur, and the Kachvaha *kul* of Jaipur—both prominent *kul*s in Rajasthani history.[8]

Each Rajput *kul* traces its origin to a heroic ancestor, who typically left a homeland ruled by an older male relative or conquered by a foreign invader. Udaipur's royalty belongs to the Guhil *kul*, which was established by a colorful character named Guha after his father's kingdom

6. Examples of other *kul*s include—the solar *vamsh*: Bumdela *kul*; the lunar *vamsh*: Jadav, Tumvar, and Gaur *kul*s; the fire *vamsh*: Cauhan, Solamki, Pamvar, and Pratihara *kul*s (Norman Ziegler, "Action, Power, and Service in Rajasthani Culture" [Ph.D. diss., University of Chicago, 1973], 39 and passim).

7. The Rajput *kul* in Rajasthan bears little resemblance to the shallow Nepali *kul* described by Bennett (*Dangerous Wives*, 18–21). In theory the Rajput *kul*s number thirty-six, all considered ancient (there is controversy about the constituents of this list; see Ziegler, "Action Power," 3). Whereas some of the myriad *kul*s in Nepal consist of only the members of one household, in Rajasthan fragmentation is assumed to occur at the level of kinship subgroups (*shakh*, *khamp*, etc.). Legitimacy as a Rajput is often considered questionable if identification with one of the thirty-six *kul*s cannot be established.

8. Like the Sisodiyas belonging to the solar *kul*, they claim to be descended from the great Ram, hero of the *Ramayan*, himself a scion of the sun.

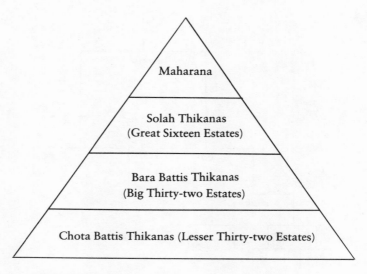

9. Chart of Mewar *thikana*s.

in what is now Gujarat was destroyed by enemies in the sixth century.[9]
According to legend, Guha was born after his father's death. His
mother, who had been on a religious pilgrimage, was informed of the
conquest as she was returning home. Shortly afterward, she took refuge
in a cave to deliver her son and, after entrusting him to a Brahman,
became a *sati*. Because of his unusual place of birth, the boy became
known as Guha (cave), from which the patronymic Guhil was derived.
Guha grew up in a forested area populated by members of the Bhil tribe.
Enormously popular, he was eventually elected king of the Bhils at Idar
(also in Gujarat). He was officially invested with royal authority when
a Bhil cut his own finger and with his blood applied to Guha's brow the
red mark (*tika*) of sovereignty.

Guha becomes the first sovereign of the line that is established in the
fortress of Chitor after ten generations, according to tradition. That feat
is performed by the legendary Bappa Rawal, whom contemporary Rajputs often name as the "founding father" of the kingdom of Mewar.[10]

9. Tod's dating (*Annals and Antiquities* 1:71) comports with the genealogical record
at the Udaipur City Palace. On the evidence for such a date, see Ram Vallabh Somani,
History of Mewar (Jaipur: C. L. Ranka, 1976), 33–34.

10. Bappa (child) is a nickname and Rawal (king) is his title. Tod and Ziegler date
Bappa's ascension to the mid-eighth century (Tod, *Annals and Antiquities* 1:71, 188;
Ziegler, "Action, Power," 115); the Udaipur City Palace record and Somani (*Mewar*, 43–
44) concur. At the top of the stairs Bappa Rawal's picture greets visitors as they enter the
Udaipur City Palace Museum.

a, Ad Mata (the Jhala *kuldevi*); *b*, *c*, kite forms of Naganecha Ji (the Rathaur *kuldevi*); *d*, *e*, suns indicating Suryavamsh descent.

10. State crests with *kuldevi* and *vamsh* insignias.

Like Guha, Bappa Rawal was born after his father was slain and raised in the hills by a Brahman.[11] He grew up to become a precocious young prince (tricking hundreds of naive maidens into marrying him) and eventually managed to ingratiate himself with the Mori ruler of Chitor, whom he later deposed in a coup. Hence whereas Guha is considered

11. This repetition of mythical detail tends to meld or conflate the personalities and histories of the two heroes in the minds of many Rajputs today.

the original patriarch, Bappa is credited with having given the *kul* its kingdom.

Progressing down toward smaller kinship units, the next unit after the *kul* is the *shakh* (branch) (see fig. 8). Rajput genealogies are given as family trees. Thus although *kul* does not literally mean "tree trunk," it stands as the trunk in relation to the largest unit it encompasses, the *shakh*. The *shakh* is often a very important unit; it is founded when a group breaks away from the *kul*, relocates, and then gains military or political power. The *shakh* to which the Udaipur royal family belongs is the Sisodiya, which takes its name from the small medieval state of Sisoda, ruled by Guhils.[12] Its scions inherited sovereignty of the Chitor branch of the Guhils in the early part of the fourteenth century, that is to say in the chaotic aftermath of the sack of Chitor by the Muslim conqueror Ala-ud-din.[13]

After the *shakh* come the *khamp* (twig) and the *nak* (twig tip).[14] These smaller kinship units, typically defined by and named after the places in which their earliest members lived, play a minimal role in the formation of Rajput identity today.[15] Many of the people I spoke with during interviews or other conversations could not even name their *khamp* or *nak*. There are exceptions. Virtually everyone knows that the

12. Tod gives alternate etymologies for the term Sisodiya. In one, the king accidentally swallowed a piece of meat in which there was a gadfly. To cure him a physician ordered that a cow's ear be cut off; disguising it in cloth, he attached a string to it and dangled it down the king's throat. It lured the gadfly from the king's stomach back out the king's mouth. When the king learned that cow flesh had passed his lips, he decided "to swallow boiling lead (seesa)" to purify himself (*Annals and Antiquities* 2:564). I heard this story from two Rajput men. In Tod's other version (1:176 n. 3), which I have not heard from informants, the king (whom Tod cites only as the expelled king of Chitor) founded a town "to commemorate the spot, where after an extraordinarily hard chase he killed a hare (sussoo)." The historical origins of the founding of this kingdom remain obscure.

13. On genealogy at Sisoda and Sisodiya ascendance see ibid. 1:216; and Dasaharatha Sharma, *Rajasthan through the Ages* (Bikaner: Rajasthan State Archives, 1966), 672–73. Rajputs often anachronistically name Bappa Rawal as the founder of the Sisodya dynasty because they see acquisition of Chitor as the start of the rule that the Sisodiyas have enforced for centuries. Ziegler also does this ("Action, Power," 115).

14. On Rajput kinship segmentation see Ziegler, "Action, Power," 36–58; and Brij Raj Chauhan, *A Rajasthan Village* (Delhi: Vir Publishing House, 1967), 50–56. Other descriptions are those of Richard Fox, *Kin, Clan, Raja, and Rule* (Berkeley: University of California Press, 1971); and Adrian Mayer, *Caste and Kinship in Central India* (Berkeley: University of California Press, 1970). But these do not accurately describe the system of kinship segmentation employed by Rajasthani Rajputs.

15. These lesser units were important in medieval times when they were smaller and had internal political solidarity (Ziegler defines the "middle period" as eighth through seventeenth centuries ["Action, Power," 47]). The lesser unit names often derive from their original locales: thus the Mertiya Rathaurs belong to the *khamp* (the twig from Merta), though many Mertiyas, including those of Ghanerao, a prominent Mewar *thikana*, have for centuries lived away from Merta.

khamp for the Udaipur royal family is the Ranavat, which is appropriately named for it is the *khamp* from which the future king (*rana*) is
chosen when the royal family fails to produce an heir and so must adopt.
This fact is significant because of the seven most recent Maharanas, only
the current one was not adopted.

Of all the units mentioned, those that play the largest role in defining
Rajput identity today are the *kul* and the *shakh*. Lesser units are too
narrowly fixed, and the *vamsh* is too inclusive and remote a category to
hold much meaning for individual members.[16] The *kul*'s importance is
linked to the fact that Rajputs generally regard it as the unit of exogamy.
This is interesting because reviewing the medieval archives, scholars
have found that intra-*kul* marriages were actually allowed if *kul* members belonged to different *gotra*s (the *gotra* is a rather hazily defined
group of people who claim spiritual descent from a common Vedic
sage). Norman Ziegler finds that in practice this problematic unit is generally identical to the *khamp*.[17] Rajputs today, however, both say that
one should not marry within one's *kul* and in fact practice *kul* exogamy.
Of the marriages I recorded (the marriages of respondents and those of
their parents), there was not a single instance of intra-*kul* alliance.

Apart from the practical matter of exogamy, the *kul* has importance
because theoretically at least it is the unit protected by the familial goddess, the *kuldevi*. I say theoretically because in certain instances a *kuldevi* protects not a *kul* but a *shakh*, a *shakh* that has become so independent and powerful that its members have come to think of it as a *kul*
except when specifically placing it in the context of other kinship units.
This confusion is vividly apparent in the case of the Sisodiyas.[18] When
asked what kind of Rajputs they are, Sisodiyas invariably answer "Sisodiya," just as Rathaurs answer "Rathaur." Sisodiyas never respond
"Guhil," that is, with their *kul* name. Sisodiyas and non-Sisodiyas alike
conceptualize Sisodiyas and Rathaurs as equivalent units. They speak of
this Rathaur girl marrying that Sisodiya boy and so forth.

When one points out to Sisodiyas that technically they are Guhils
first, they typically respond, "Yes, Guhil is our *jati*" (a word employed
to refer to the largest Rajput segmentation unit and also, as here, to refer

16. It seems likely that the Suryavamshi *kul*s practiced elaborate sun worship in ancient times (Tod, *Annals and Antiquities* 1:179), which would have sponsored greater
vamsh awareness and solidarity.
17. Ziegler thoroughly discusses the *gotra* issue ("Action, Power," 38), and Bennett
shows the *gotra* to be vague and indefinite in Nepal (*Dangerous Wives*, 16–17).
18. Tod also noted this conceptual confusion (*Annals and Antiquities* 1:71). A similar
confusion occurs in the case of the Bhattis, who belong to the Yadav *kul*.

generically to any segmentation unit), but they do not indicate awareness that the two groups, Sisodiya and Rathaur, are different segmentation units. Thus the Sisodiyas think of themselves as Sisodiyas in the
first instance and refer to their divine guardian, Ban Mata, as goddess
of the Sisodiya "kul."

Finally, the *kul* (or "kul," as in the case of the Sisodiya *shakh*) is
crucial to identity because it is the category that Rajputs understand as
primarily determining inherited traits. Character traits inherited
through the blood are thought to be illustrated, developed, and even
strengthened by the honorable action of *kul* members.[19] Therefore the
Sisodiyas, who refused to cooperate with Muslim conquerors and British reformers, have enjoyed throughout Rajasthan an unparalleled reputation for reckless courage and autonomy.[20] Sisodiyas believe that their
bloodline, like their glory, has been proven and nourished by their martial history. By contrast, the ruling *kul* of Jaipur, the Kachvaha *kul*,
bears another sort of reputation. Jaipur, located close to Delhi and
therefore vulnerable to Muslim attacks and British influence, has been
known for its flexibility and pragmatism.[21] One of its great heroes, Man
Sinh, was actually a general in the Moghal army. In sum, although both
Sisodiyas and Kachvahas are proud of their histories, the Sisodiyas have
enjoyed a superior prestige throughout Rajasthan because they were
able to maintain their independence longer.[22]

As these sentiments indicate, Rajputs have been keenly aware of their
family heritage and concerned with how it compares to other families'
heritages. The history of their family behavior, they say, reveals their
character, the innate "stuff" of which family members are made. Honorable action enhances character, which in turn makes more honorable
action possible. In this way status and prestige accumulate.

Despite the place that Rajputs give to the *kul* as the foremost source

19. On the transmutability of code and substance, see Ziegler, "Action, Power," 25; and
McKim Marriott and Ronald B. Inden, "Towards an Ethnosociology of South Asian Caste
Systems,"in *The New Wind,* ed. Kenneth David (The Hague: Mouton, 1977), 227–38.
20. Rudolph and Rudolph describe the martial ethic that Udaipur has come to repre-
sent as comprising heroism, valor, and imprudence ("The Political Modernization of an
Indian Feudal Order," in *Essays on Rajputana* [Delhi: Concept Publishing, 1984], 43–45).
On the warrior's duty never to shrink from a fight, see Pierre Filliozat, "The After-Death
Destiny of the Hero According to Mahābhārata," in *Memorial Stones,* ed. S. Settar and
Gunther D. Sontheimer (Dharwad: Institute of Indian Art History, Karnatak University,
and Heidelberg: South Asia Institute, University of Heidelberg, 1982), 4–7.
21. Rudolph and Rudolph, "Political Modernization," 43–45.
22. As one Jaipur nobleman noted, Tod's *Annals and Antiquities* bolstered Mewar's
prestige by concentrating heavily on its achievements and glories. Also see Rudolph and
Rudolph, "Political Modernization," 43.

of prestige and honor, except at its inception the *kul* has not functioned as a political institution. *Thakurs* (kings) from various *kuls* have owed primary political allegiance not to their *kul* but to the maharaja whom they have served. Thus although Rajputs understand *kul* or *shakh* blood as the source of their prestige, they also understand that the glory gained by their ancestors, the glory that both proved and strengthened their *kul* blood, has derived from service that is not necessarily direct service of the *kul*.[23]

Because the interrelated duties to preserve and strengthen the *kul* and to serve a king are basic to the Rajput system of values, it is essential to explore the basic political structure of Rajput hierarchy and obligation. I use the illustration of Mewar because much of the information in succeeding chapters comes from Mewar *thikana*s and because it clearly demonstrates the way in which traditional status and duty have spawned attitudes that continue to find expression within the modern Rajput community.

MEWAR'S POLITICAL STRUCTURE

At the top of Mewar's status pyramid is the Maharana, whose massive City Palace dominates the Udaipur horizon. Directly below him are the *thakur*s of the Solah Thikanas, the great "Sixteen Estates" constituting the innermost circle of authority and power. After the Solah Thikanas are the Bara Battis (Big Thirty-two) Thikanas, which are followed in turn by the Chota Battis (Lesser Thirty-two) Thikanas (see fig. 9).[24]

The families at each political level belong to different *kul*s and *shakh*s. The apex is always Sisodiya: as we have seen, the Maharana belongs to the Ranavat *khamp* of the Sisodiya *shakh*. Directly under him are the sixteen kings from the Solah Thikanas. Their families are sometimes listed as follows:

> Three Jhala, three Cauhan, and four Cumdavat has Mewar
> Two Saktavat, two Rathaur, a Sarangdevot, and a Pamvar[25]

Named in this poem (*doha*) are several Sisodiya *khamps*—the Cumdavat, the Saktavat, and the Sarangdevot. There are also families from the

---

23. The Mertiya Rathaurs of Ghanerao, for example, served the Udaipur Maharana and the Jodhpur Maharaja and received the support of both at different times.

24. Each level includes more estates than the name implies as the Maharanas made additional *thikana* grants at various levels of status. They occasionally demoted estates from one group to another.

25. N. T. Cauhan of Tamla House first recited this poem (*doha*) to me.

Jhala, Cauhan, Rathaur, and Pamvar *kuls*.[26] The noblemen from these estates served the Maharana as members of his advisory council. They gave advice when he solicited it and provided troops when needed. Today they continue to advise the Maharana when he summons them.

The members of the lesser estates, whose families represent a broad range of Rajput backgrounds, interact with these sixteen families socially but demonstrate a special reserve and respect when speaking of members of the Solah Thikana families. Like the Solah Thikana families, the two groups of Battis families attended the king and fought his wars.

One might suppose that these estate categories would be mere relics of the past, yet they continue to have symbolic and social importance. This was especially evident during my stay when a bitter succession dispute erupted within the royal household. The Maharana, who had been estranged from his elder son and had for many years relied on his younger son to assist him in managing his properties, died unexpectedly.[27] The younger son assumed, as many in Udaipur did, that he would inherit his father's position and title.[28] The Solah Thikana lords, however, refused to accept a breach of tradition. Having caucused, they voted their support to the elder son and encouraged him to move back to Udaipur from Bombay, where he had been in business. When the time came for the elder brother's installation, however, the lords had to perform the investiture rituals outside the palace because the younger brother had locked the palace gates.

The predominantly Brahmanical investiture ceremony, which was performed in front of a large crowd, had as its climax a traditional Rajput rite: the Lord of Salumbar, one of the foremost estates of Mewar, unsheathed his sword, sliced open his hand, and placed a drop of his blood on the elder brother's forehead. This ritual act clearly conveyed the idea that the Maharana can and must rely on the support of the lords whose estates were granted by his ancestors.[29] More generally, the participation of the lords in the investiture as a whole reaffirmed the traditional hierarchy of estate households. Seated after the Lord of Salumbar

26. The Solah Thikanas named in the poem are Jhala: Bari Sadri, Gogunda, Delwara; Cauhan: Bedla, Kothariya, Parsoli; Cumdavat: Salumbar, Devgarh, Amet, Begum; Saktavat: Bhindar, Bansi; Rathaur: Badnor, Ghanerao; Sarangdevot: Kanor; and Pamvar: Bijoliam. Other *thikanas* sometimes listed in this group include Bhainsrorgarh, Kurabar, Meja, and Sardargarh. On the history of these estates, see Gaurishankar Hirachand Ojha, *Rājpūtāne kā Itihās* (Ajmer: Vedic Yantralaya, 1932), 2:1181–1301; and Tod, *Annals and Antiquities* 1:401.

27. Among these are the Lake Palace and Shiv Niwas hotels.

28. Although titles are no longer legally recognized, local custom preserves their usage.

29. The act of solidarity recalls the election of Guha by the Bhils at Idar.

were the other Solah Thikana lords, each in his appointed place. Behind them sat the members of the lesser estates, also ranked. All the lords wore their traditional finery, replete with dress turban and polished sword, which emphasized the conviction that although Rajput legal authority has passed, the ceremonial and social structure of Rajput community has been and must continue to be preserved.[30]

This conviction is expressed in ceremonial displays such as the investiture and also in the way Rajputs bring up their children. Many men and women told me that they try to endow their children with pride in their Rajput legacy. Moreover, they hope to cultivate in their sons and daughters what they understand as the inherent Rajput character and demeanor. They emphasize that Rajput constitution, when properly cultivated, enables its possessors to suffer whatever hardships may come. Developing the Rajput traits of bravery, strength, and honor, they believe, will help their sons to realize modern ambitions.

Because the family fortunes of most Rajputs have diminished, if not disappeared, some Rajputs have of necessity taken up occupations. Some have joined the army, a respected profession that many Rajputs practiced during the days of the British. In joining either the army or the police, Rajputs have been able to perform tasks at least partially consistent with their traditional occupation. Other Rajputs have kept their palaces and, with varying degrees of success, turned them into hotels. Still others have tried their hands at farming or other businesses.[31] Almost all have recently realized the importance of giving their sons good educations, that they might take up professions enabling them to support their families after they marry.[32]

Although these Rajputs have lost power over their *thikanas*—they lost political authority to govern and the ability to collect taxes after Independence—they still receive public deference from villagers living in the towns in which their estate residences are located. One king whose estate I visited can barely drive his car around his capital because villag-

30. This ritual occasion fits under the rubric "cultural performance" as used by Milton Singer, "The Great Tradition in a Metropolitan Center: Madras," in *Traditional India*, ed. Milton Singer (Austin: University of Texas Press, 1959), 145–46. A number of inheritance issues are being litigated. At present, the younger brother continues to manage the hotel properties and the Maharana Mewar Trust; the older brother has been active in politics.

31. Popular options include managing tea plantations elsewhere in India and investing in mining operations in the marble-rich hills around Udaipur.

32. The new emphasis on education contrasts with the wisdom, which is expressed in the following proverb, "A Rajput who reads will never ride a horse." It expresses the vanishing Rajput conviction that modern education only erodes Rajput values and abilities (Rudolph and Rudolph, "Political Modernization," 41).

ers are constantly bowing to him with folded hands; they oblige him to return the gesture by nodding and folding his hands above his steering wheel. The lords are celebrities, whose actions villagers carefully scrutinize and discuss as items of local news. Thus those who used to be ruled still indirectly reinforce among their erstwhile rulers a disposition toward conserving Rajput style and attitude.

The basis of the deference given by many villagers and expected by many Rajputs is the notion that in the past Rajputs have been the protectors of kingdoms and *thikana*s, including the villages those realms comprise. As hereditary warriors, they were the source of internal security. Although these days all Rajputs, like members of other martial groups, add the word Sinh (lion) to their given names, family genealogies reveal that in times past Rajputs in some lineages attached *pal* (protector) to their names instead of or in addition to Sinh.

This notion of the Rajput as protector is broad, particularly when attached to members of the nobility or royalty. A good ruler is one whose virtue and strength infuse his realm with justice and vitality. By definition a good king, a protector, makes for a good (prosperous and righteous) kingdom whereas a bad king, not a protector, makes for a bad (indigent and immoral) kingdom. This notion, summed up in the proverb *Yatha Raja, tatha praja* (as the king is, so are his subjects), is an ancient pan-Indian idea elaborately expounded in classical Sanskrit and Tamil literatures.[33] Thus the Rajput rulers and their ranks were thought to safeguard the welfare of all. Many Rajput *thakur*s today continue to regard their ancestors and sometimes even themselves in this rather ideal way.[34]

A major component in the traditional Rajput role of protection is responsibility for guarding the safety and the virtue of women. All Rajputs can narrate episodes of Rajput chivalry. Favorites are those detailing the rescues of fair damsels from lustful marauders. Warriors riding off to battle are often said to have been inspired to great bravery by the knowledge that they were protecting their women back home. But protecting women includes more than guaranteeing them safety from assault; it also includes ensuring that women do not deviate from their proper roles back home. A wife who is allowed to become unchaste is

33. Well-known examples are the Sanskrit epics and *dharmashastra*s (legal codes) and the Tamil classics, the *Tirumulai* and the *Silappadikaram*.

34. I have met a number of Americans who respond negatively to this "patronizing" attitude. I think more young Indians in towns and even in villages may share this response than their elders, who grew up under Rajput rule.

understood to sap her husband's strength and so his ability to perform his protective role;[35] a breach in protection sets off something like a chain reaction. In brief, a woman's disloyalty is thought to cause severe injury to the strength and character of her husband and by extension to those of his family. Now as in the past, Rajput men are keen to preserve those aspects of their way of life that will protect women from the temptation to engage in behavior destructive of honor and family. Particularly in conservative Mewar, both men and women stress the importance of preserving as much as possible traditional, that is to say, domestic female roles and values.

WOMEN'S TRADITIONS AND LIFE STAGES

The most striking feature of a Rajput woman's home life is an observance of some form of *parda*. *Parda*, which literally means "curtain," refers to the seclusion of married women.[36] Rajput women refer to *parda* as the most characteristic aspect of a Rajput woman's identity. Their interpretation of the term, however, has proven fluid.

Traditionally *parda* referred to the division of a household into women's quarters (the *zanana*) and men's quarters (the *mardana*).[37] The men of the family (husbands and brothers, fathers and sons) entered the women's quarters for brief visits. Sometimes they ate there or slept there with their wives. When they came, they announced their presence in advance by coughing, shuffling, or some similar cues. Nonfamily men were excluded from entering the women's quarters and married women were barred from entering the men's quarters. One middle-aged member of a royal household told me that even as a child she was not allowed into the *mardana* of her father's household, so strict was her family.

Because of this strict *parda*, women generally did not worship in local

35. See David Dean Shulman, *The King and the Clown in South Indian Myth and Poetry* (Princeton: Princeton University Press, 1985), 102; and Wendy Doniger O'Flaherty, *Śiva* (Oxford: Oxford University Press, 1973), 178.

36. For an introduction to comparative conceptualizations and dimensions of *parda*, see Hanna Papanek and Gail Minault, eds., *Separate Worlds* (Delhi: Chanakya Publications, 1982); David G. Mandlebaum, *Women's Seclusion and Men's Honor* (Tucson: University of Arizona Press, 1988); Patricia Jeffery, *Frogs in a Well* (London: Zed Press, 1979); Lila Abu-Lughod, *Veiled Sentiments* (Berkeley: University of California Press, 1986).

37. Observed by various high castes throughout India, *parda* has meant different things in different areas and communities. As examples, see two essays in *Separate Worlds*, ed. Papanek and Minault (Mary Higdon Beech, "The Domestic Realm in the Lives of Hindu Women in Calcutta"; and Rama Mehta, "Purdah Among the Oswals of Mevar").

temples (though they might occasionally travel veiled and chaperoned to faraway pilgrimage places or go briefly to a nearby shrine and worship there with their faces hidden from public view). Nor did they participate in religious ceremonies such as festivals, unless these were celebrated in the zananas of royalty or the nobility. Moreover, they lacked easy access to temples located in the mardana. For their visits special arrangements were always made.

Today some households still maintain a rigid interpretation of parda. Others have only recently begun to relax it. Most women today practice some modified form of seclusion. Whatever form parda takes, it is often summed up by the statement, "We Rajput women do not mix." By this is meant that although most Rajput women move about freely within their households—there being no longer a formal division of mardana and zanana—they do not mix or mix only minimally with male guests and then only with those male guests who are old family friends. Therefore, every Rajput social event I attended was really two events: the men gathered in one part of a household to enjoy one another's company and the women gathered in another part to discuss things of interest to women.

In accordance with parda, most noblewomen avoid going out in public. They have themselves driven across the street rather than walk, for the street is the quintessentially public place.[38] A few women occasionally run errands in town, but when they do they take along a driver and perhaps a friend as chaperone. Servants and children do most of the grocery shopping. When necessary, Rajput women send servants to summon merchants and tailors to their homes.[39] Most women will still not go into local temples, though some will visit outdoor sati and kuldevi shrines when their privacy can be ensured. It remains the case that women prefer to worship these and other divinities at home.

While maintaining parda to this extent at home, many women have adapted it to suit the exigencies of travel. They more or less conform to the policy of "when in Rome. . . ." Thus one royal woman told me that although she would never think of appearing in public in her home town, she would freely shop in the city of Pune (in Maharashtra) because no one there would recognize her. Similarly, many noblewomen who do not go out in Udaipur will go out in large cities, especially cities

38. During my research stint, I knew only one woman in Udaipur who drove; she took up driving a jeep to help her husband in his political campaign. Two or three other women have taken up driving since 1985, and a few have appeared openly to campaign for Rajput candidates to national and state legislatures.

39. Many of these merchants and tailors belong to families who have served Rajput households for generations.

outside of Rajasthan. Still others from the Udaipur area will never show their faces in their *thikanas* but will run essential errands in Udaipur.[40]

Although *parda* is loosening, it remains an extremely cogent symbol. It summarizes what is deemed admirable in the character of Rajput women and serves as a standard for evaluating behavior.[41] Therefore Rajput women say that although their way of life is changing, they want to educate their daughters to show respect for the ideal of *parda* by acting with modesty (*sharam, laj*) and the honor and dignity that modesty confers on themselves, their husbands, and their families.[42] As Rajput men do they emphasize that the old customs and values (*riti-rivaj*) will help their children accommodate to change.

For women, the idea of preparing for change is nothing new. Rajput girls have always been told that they must learn modesty because when they marry they will have to live in a new family, accept its customs, and obey its elders. By teaching daughters modesty and the self-effacing sacrifice it presupposes, mothers prepare their daughters for the inevitable resocialization that they will undergo as brides.

Rajput mothers say they are strict with their daughters so they will be able to adjust to marriage,[43] yet these women allow their daughters far more freedom than they give their young daughters-in-law. Except for ceremonial occasions an unmarried daughter does not wear traditional Rajput dress (*kancli-kurti*), which consists of a long full skirt, a brief underblouse, a long vest, and a half-sari tucked in at the waist and pulled over the head and shoulders. While the daughter-in-law wears this traditional dress, or occasionally a modern sari, the unmarried daughter wears a western skirt and blouse to school and typically goes about her household in a three-piece Panjabi suit, which consists of cotton leggings, a *kurta* (a long shirt-like garment with slits up the sides), and a *dupatta* (a scarf draped over her breasts). She may even wear jeans or a dress. When the daughter marries, she may continue to wear such clothes on trips home but will change back to more traditional attire before returning to her husband's household (fig. 11).

40. *Parda* here contrasts with that of Rajput village women, who say they also keep *parda* but not as strictly as noblewomen do. Because the men leave the village for the fields or other jobs each day, women move about freely outdoors until evening. They remain strict about veiling and speak only in whispers in the presence of elder male relatives.

41. Such a symbol Sherry Ortner classifies as a key symbol ("On Key Symbols," *American Anthropologist* 75 [1973]).

42. The honor that *parda* brings to women, their husbands, and families is discussed by the works cited in note 36 and in chapters following.

43. Sudhir Kakar's work indicates that all girls learn this lesson (*The Inner World* [New York: Oxford University Press, 1981], 62). Rajputs feel that they are exceptionally strict with their daughters.

11. Rajput noblewomen and children.

Some of the older women think that these days daughters are over-indulged. These women recall their childhoods, when spontaneity was discouraged and courtly decorum was everything. In their time they were not to laugh or speak loudly on pain of receiving a sharp slap or some stronger punishment. Back then, they add, most families did not want their daughters educated because education would make them dissatisfied with their lives. One woman said that she was taught to read but that her parents prohibited her from reading newspapers because they felt that women should not concern themselves with events in the outside world. Women should focus their attention exclusively on the home.

Now most aristocratic Rajput families send their girls to school. The girls attend private schools, often Catholic girls' schools.[44] Recently many families have sent their daughters to college. They give two reasons for this. A college education prepares a girl for an occupation in case she becomes widowed and, by an even more unfortunate turn of luck, is left with no money to support herself and her children. Even more important, it helps a daughter's marriage chances. Families with educated sons want them to marry educated girls who will prove intelligent companions. Moreover, parents speak of the need for intellectually talented daughters-in-law who can bear and raise clever children. Even so, sometimes families who want an educated girl also fear that her education will make her too independent. I learned of several instances in which weddings were held just before a bride was to receive her diploma. Some of the timings may have been coincidental; auspicious marriage dates do often fall right before graduation. But others were certainly not coincidental. One young woman told me that her pregraduation marriage was a compromise demanded by her in-laws during engagement negotiations. She surmised this was fairly common. Other women I asked about this said they thought it happened only occasionally.

Despite the new (if qualified) emphasis on education for girls, the chief ambition that girls maintain is to be a good wife. Of course, this is easier if they acquire good husbands, and so many of them keep a weekly *vrat*, a religious fast, to please the god Shiv, whom they consider a model husband.[45] As to the choice of husband, girls leave that up to

44. Rajputs approve of the regimented education that such schools provide and appear unconcerned with the threat of conversion. I know of only one aristocratic Christian Rajput family in the Udaipur area.

45. For more information on *vrat*s, see the following section on protection.

their parents. Arranged marriages are an iron rule, a rule almost universally accepted as being in the interest of bride and groom. Young women and men are considered too inexperienced in the ways of life to be able to choose suitable marriage partners.

In Rajasthan, as in many other regions of India, families try to marry their daughters into families higher on the social scale than they are.[46] *Kul* membership and position within the noble hierarchy are crucial determinants of social position. To some extent wealth is also recognized as a determinant for it typically accompanies social position, but wealth without status is considered insufficient.[47] One young noblewoman explained the rationale behind this notion of hypergamy: "We always try to marry our daughters up. It's best for the families. We don't want to take a daughter-in-law from higher up because she'll be used to being treated highly and used to having lots of things; she just won't fit in." In other words, such a daughter-in-law will not be able to serve her in-laws well because she will feel superior to them.

Although "marrying up" is the norm, the contracting families' status difference is often small or even fictional. Families like to contract with families with similar backgrounds, standards, and ideas. When roughly equal families enter into marriage, it is the marriage ceremony itself that creates and states an inequality. This inequality is often temporary, for such families generally marry their own daughters into families with status similar to the status of those families from which its daughters-in-law come. It may even marry its daughters into the extended families of its daughters-in-law.

In times past, when marriages were polygamous, the same general notions applied to the first marriage a son made.[48] Often between near equals, a son's first marriage was intended to ensure that heirs would come from the best possible stock. Second, third, and other wives, however, could come from less illustrious backgrounds. Some could even come from lower castes.[49] When polygamy was practiced, hyper-

---

46. On hypergamy see Ziegler, "Action, Power," 51; David F. Pocock, *Kanbi and Patidar* (London: Oxford University Press, 1972), esp. 158; Ronald Inden, *Marriage and Rank in Bengali Culture* (Berkeley: University of California Press, 1976); Lina Fruzetti, *The Gift of a Virgin* (New Brunswick, N.J.: Rutgers University Press, 1982); Nur Yalman, *Under the Bo Tree* (Berkeley: University of California Press, 1967); and Mildred S. Luschinsky, "The Life of Women in a Village in North India" (Ph.D. diss., Cornell University, 1962).

47. Rajputs display a special disdain for what they refer to as "new money" people.

48. The Hindu Marriage and Divorce Act of 1955 disallowed Hindu polygamy.

49. See Ziegler, "Action, Power," 52–55; and more generally S. J. Tambiah, "From Varna to Caste through Mixed Unions," in *The Character of Kinship*, ed. Jack Goody (Cambridge: Cambridge University Press, 1973).

gamy was a more dynamic and influential principle of social organization.

The contemporary Rajput notion of hypergamy has one especially intriguing peculiarity: the principle of marrying west. Rajasthani Rajputs recognize that Rajputs living to the east of Rajasthan prefer to marry their daughters west toward Rajasthan, because that is where the most prestigious Rajput families live. Richard Fox notes that Rajputs in his area, eastern Uttar Pradesh, marry their daughters west.[50] Michael Mahar finds this to be true of "Khalapur," a Rajput-dominated village in northern Uttar Pradesh.[51] When at his invitation I visited this village, I was told by women in one Rajput family there that all Rajput families try to marry their daughters west toward Rajasthan. When I told her I was working in Udaipur, she also mentioned that Udaipur is the best place to be, for that is where the finest, bravest Rajputs are.

Sharing this belief, Rajasthani Rajputs try to marry their daughters within the state. As the young noblewoman I quoted above explained, "We don't want to give daughters outside Rajasthan because they won't fit in well and won't be happy. In Rajasthan we have high culture. Other places are usually less cultured." I found no convincing evidence, however, that noble marriages west are considered preferable within Rajasthan. One has to imagine that such a rule taken very seriously would drastically restrict marriage options in the western part of the state.[52]

Once a woman is married, she participates fully in all the traditions of her conjugal family and is expected to abandon traditions she has brought from her natal family that might conflict with those of her conjugal family. This is true even down to her style of dressing. Beginning with her marriage costume, she must accept dress styles and patterns typical of her husband's region. Most families, however, allow a wife some latitude. For ceremonial occasions such as weddings she must wear traditional local fashion, but at home she may wear dresses that please her, including clothes from home and even full saris, which are not traditionally worn by Rajputs.

In terms of behavior, a wife's all-encompassing responsibility is to

50. Fox, *Kin, Clan*, 38.

51. Michael Mahar, communication to author, July 1984. This village was studied by Leigh Minturn and John Hitchcock, *The Rājpūts of Khalapur, India* (New York: John Wiley and Sons, 1960); and Hitchcock, "Martial Rājpūt."

52. Rajput villages in the extreme western part of Rajasthan have a high incidence of female infanticide. A study of this practice would presumably produce a more complex explanation than this preferential marriage pattern.

protect the happiness and health of her husband.[53] She carries out this responsibility by attending to his needs, serving his family, and worshiping his gods. It is felt that if she performs these activities successfully and so fulfills the norm of protection, he will prosper; if not, he will suffer and perhaps even die. Being widowed is the worst fate a Rajput woman can imagine. She is meant for one man only, her husband. Remarriage is forbidden.[54] Thus becoming a widow is something that simply ought not to happen: a woman must do everything in her power to safeguard her husband's longevity.

In times past some women whose husbands died refused to become widows. Instead they burned themselves on their husbands' pyres. This practice was seen as a corrective for the fault of failing to protect a husband from premature death, of allowing his death to occur before hers. Those women who lacked the dedication necessary to die as *satis* were expected to lead a life of penance and privation. The general feeling was that a widow should want to live a hard life to make up for her failure as a husband-protector.

Today most women continue to feel that a widow should not greatly enjoy life. She should take pleasure in her children and family but should deprive her senses of physical enjoyment and lead a relatively stark existence. Widows should wear dull, simple clothing (though not necessarily the white clothing that is expected of widows in many parts of India) and no ornamentation. Moreover, they should no longer consume meat or wine, for they have no legitimate need for the passion such substances engender. In sum, the widow should shun merriment, devote herself to religious searching, and live out her life in anticipation of happier circumstances in her next life.

Although, as many Rajput women noted, there are cases in which widows are ill-treated, the general consensus is that in most noble families the widow continues to be loved. She is the mother of children, whose affection for her is undiminished. Society expects her to honor her husband's memory by living simply, but whatever harsh privations she endures should be self-imposed. The widow's life is not supposed to

---

53. The idea of women as husband-protectors occurs throughout India. For selected recent explorations of this theme see Susan Snow Wadley, ed., *The Powers of Tamil Women* (Syracuse: Syracuse University, 1980); Frédérique Apffel Marglin, *Wives of the God-King* (Delhi: Oxford University Press, 1985); R. S. Khare, "From Kanyā to Mātā: Aspects of the Cultural Language of Kinship in Northern India," in *Concepts of Person*, ed. Akos Ostör, Lina Fruzetti, and Steve Barnett (Cambridge, Mass.: Harvard University Press, 1982).

54. In most high castes throughout India only men customarily remarry.

be joyous, but most would condemn those who add to the widow's misery by scorning and abusing her.

RELIGION AND PROTECTION

Because a Rajput wife's ambition is to avoid becoming a widow, the religious practices a Rajput woman performs have everything to do with being a good wife, which is to say, a good husband-protector. The word women use to describe this ideal is *pativrata*, meaning "one who has taken a vow (*vrat*) to [protect] her husband (*pati*)." Sometimes they employ this word loosely to refer to any wife. But even in this generic sense it has an ideological nuance, for it implies a conception of how a wife should behave and of the consequences her behavior will bring.

A wife becomes a good wife, a true *pativrata*, by selflessly serving her husband and his family. This service includes attending to ritual and other religious responsibilities. Each household has its specific constellation of religious deities to whom household members, including women, owe devotion. They express this devotion in a number of ways.

Among these is the performance of *vrats*, the vows that entail fasting. Many unmarried girls keep a fast on Monday in order to please Shiv; many married women also keep this *vrat* in order to gain Shiv's protective blessing in their attempts to live as good wives. In addition to the Shiv *vrat* there are six other weekly vows, which makes one for every day of the week. Deciding which vow or vows to perform is generally a matter of personal preference. Except for the Monday *vrat*, Rajput women show little continuity in the weekly vows they keep. The same is true of fortnightly *vrats*, the vows coinciding with the full and new moons.

Besides weekly and fortnightly *vrats* there are annual vows, which accompany many major festivals. The two that have the largest following among women I interviewed are the Navratri vow and the Dashamata vow. Nearly all Rajput women perform Navratri Vrat. The reason they most often give is that Navratri is really *the* Rajput holiday—it commemorates a great military victory. Navratri celebrates the conquest by the warrior goddess Durga over an army of demons.[55] Thus a

55. The Navratri (Nine Nights) observance culminates in a celebration of Dashara (the Tenth), which commemorates Ram's victory over Ravana, the villain of the well-known epic, the *Ramayan*. On this day Rajputs worship their weapons and horses. Formerly (and in some places today) this veneration (*puja*) combined with a goat sacrifice.

Rajput woman performs the Navratri vow not simply because she is a woman but also because she is a Rajput.

The second vow, which a great many of the women in my survey mentioned, is predominantly practiced by women living in Mewar. This is Dashamata Vrat. Dashamata, whose name means "Mother of Fate," is worshiped by keeping a fast, by tying on a string necklace, and by reciting ten stories.[56] Rajput women do not conceive of Dashamata Vrat as an exclusively Rajput vow. Rather, they see it as a vow that Rajput women should perform because the Rajputs are a high caste and all high-caste women should perform it. Yet there is an implicit connection between Dashamata and the Rajput community: to the string necklaces that the vow requires women to wear, Rajput wives in this area affix their *kul* goddess pendants (*palas*). The avowed purpose of this *vrat* is to preserve a husband's health, which will be strong as long as his wife's necklace is unbroken. Each year after marriage, the wife replaces the string with a new one, thus renewing the strength of her commitment to the marriage. If the string breaks in midyear, she must replace it immediately in a special ritual.

These two *vrats* are characteristic of the vows women perform. They all stress the welfare of the husband, which must always rank first among a woman's concerns. A distinguished noblewoman most succinctly summed up this attitude: "One has many children but only one husband. My first allegiance must therefore be to him." I heard many variations on this theme. The point is not that children are not precious but rather that no other commitment rivals a woman's devotion to her husband.

Apart from *vrats*, Rajput women perform four major forms of regular religious devotion. The first is a regular honoring of the household deities, which is done both by women and by men. This is called *dhok dena*, the "giving (*dena*) of respect or prostration (*dhok*)." One shows respect by entering a temple or stopping at a shrine and then bowing to an image with palms joined. For the most part it is a voluntary and spontaneous matter. Some occasions, however, require a formal giving of respect. One must show respect to *kuldevis* and *satis* when one leaves for or returns from a major trip.[57] In this way one asks for protection during a journey and shows gratitude for a safe return. Second, one must show respect when one reaches the life thresholds represented by

56. Some connect Dashamata's name with the fact that ten (*das*) stories are recited.
57. Often women who are strict about *parda* will perform *dhok* from inside their automobile when there are nonfamily members at the shrine site.

rites of passage.[58] Families vary, however, in their determination of who must give *dhok* and when. All households require a groom to give this respect to his family's *sati*, *kuldevi*s, and perhaps other divine beings when he marries. The households also require a bride to do the same when she arrives at her new home. Some households require the bride to show respect before she leaves her natal home and its various protective deities. All households require an act of respect to their deities at the birth of a boy; some also require it at the birth of a girl. Finally, some families give *dhok* in conjunction with their children's first hair-cutting ceremonies.[59]

The next major form of religious ritual is the *ratijaga* (night wake). *Ratijaga*s are usually organized and performed by women, who are supposed to spend an entire night singing songs to honor the various deities and spirits dear to the household. Sometimes Rajput women actually do stay up all night singing, but often they delegate this task to servants and village women, whom they pay. Two figures who always appear in the lists of songs sung by families are the *kuldevi* and the *sati*. Others so honored may include various Bherus (local manifestations of the Sanskritic deity Bhairava; attendants of *kuldevi*s and other goddesses; see fig. 19), *pitr*s and *pitrani*s (male and female ancestors), and *jhumjhar*s (warriors who died violent deaths but continued fighting after death to exact revenge).[60] The *ratijaga* is performed in conjunction with the same ceremonies during which *dhok* is given, except the hair-cutting ceremony.[61]

Another shared form of religious observance is *puja*, a more elaborate and less spontaneous form of worship than *dhok*.[62] Performing

58. *Dhok* is not given in conjunction with funeral ceremonies, which are inauspicious occasions.

59. A child's first hair-cutting customarily occurs at a particular temple, often at a goddess temple. The University of Wisconsin film, *An Indian Pilgrimage: Ramdevra* (1977), has an excellent depiction of tonsure.

60. A queen (*thakurani*) from a Solah Thikana gave me a list of the songs that her family performs in the *ratijaga*s and names of those to whom they are dedicated: (1) Mata Ji; (2) Ekling Ji; (3) Kuldevi; (4) Bheru; (5) the *purvaj*s (ancestors); (6) Satimata; (7) the *jhumjhar*s (beheaded heroes); (8) memhdi (red clay with which women dye their hands and feet); (9) jhajham (the carpet ridden by gods and goddesses); (10) the *purvaj*s (again); (11) Satimata (again); (12) Kuldevi (again); (13) Bheru (again); (14) the *jhumjhar*s (again); (15) kukaro (the cock, who announces daybreak); (16) prabhat (dawn).

61. Komal Kothari identifies the *ratijaga* with the *jagran*, which, he says, is performed with birth and marriage celebrations as well as with ceremonies for death, house building, land purchasing, and well digging ("Epics of Rajasthan" [paper presented at the Conference on Oral Epics, the University of Wisconsin at Madison, July 1982], 5).

62. On *puja*, see Diana Eck, *Darśan* (Chambersburg, Pa.: Anima Books, 1981); and Norman Cutler and Joanne Punzo Waghorne, eds., *Gods of Flesh, Gods of Stone* (Chambersburg, Pa.: Anima Books, 1985).

puja, a devotee offers a divinity flowers, lamps, incense, or other pleasing substances, including food, and in return receives the divinity's blessing, which is represented by the *prasad* (leftovers) that the divinity gives back. On this basic level this *puja* resembles *puja* done in many other places in India, with perhaps one exception. As mentioned before, Rajput women tend to do almost all their *puja* at home. Because Rajput women maintain some form of *parda*, they do not like to enter local public temples. Sometimes they send servants to give offerings in such temples, but they tend to think it immodest and undignified to go themselves. Generally Rajput men also worship in their own homes. Their ancestors built temples within their estate palaces, so if men want to perform *puja*, they can do so there. These temples were mostly in the *mardana*, which meant that in former times women could not usually worship there. Today, however, because of the breakdown of intra-household *parda*, many women do worship in the *mardana*.

Members of the family perform *puja* for all the supernatural beings they worship. Among these are *kuldevi*s and *satimata*s as well as various *ishtadevta*s. Ishtadevta, a catchall term for divinities that do not easily fit into other categories, literally means "chosen (*ishta*) deity (*devta*)." The nomenclature can be misleading. Some *ishtadevta*s are selected by individuals who feel a rapport with them, and others are passed down through generations as deities requiring worship. They are thus "chosen" by the family, not by the individual.[63] In addition to worshiping such a family *ishtadevta*, however, the individual may worship other deities of his or her own pleasing.[64] A woman's options have an inherent limit: the deities she chooses must not draw her attention away from the deities worshiped by her conjugal family. Any natal deities she wishes to import may be thought competitive. If competition is perceived, a dutiful wife must abandon her personal *ishtadevta*s.

Finally there is the *bolma*, a vow that is usually connected with pilgrimage. Unlike the highly ritualized calendrical *vrat*s, *bolma*s are infor-

63. A good example is Ekling Ji (a form of Shiv), chosen by Mewar's legendary founder, Bappa Rawal. As the *ishtadevta* for the ruling family, Shiv may be referred to as a *kuldevta*. Here, *kuldevta* is synonymous with *ishtadevta*; Rajputs have no male deity to correspond to the female deity, *kuldevi*, which all Rajputs must have. When I first asked Rajputs about *kuldevta*s, the typical response was a look of incomprehension or condescension followed by a remark such as "You must mean our *kuldevi*" or "You must mean our *ishtadevta*." In other Indian communities the term *kuldevta* (or some linguistic variant of it) is used in quite different ways—and often, very loosely—to designate various relationships between deities and kinship groups. For examples, see Hiltebeitel, *Cult of Draupadī*; Tarabout, *Sacrifier*; Meyer, *Aṅkāḷaparmēcuvari*; Roghair, *Epic of Palnāḍu*; Bennett, *Dangerous Wives*; and Beck, *Three Twins*.

64. *Ishtadevta*s are often local forms of Shiv, Krishna, and Durga.

mal and personal promises made by individuals to deities. Besieged by problems, people resolve to do something that a deity desires, such as going on a pilgrimage to the deity's shrine and making certain offerings there.[65] They hope that in return the deity will assist them.[66]

Typically the *bolma* is made by a woman, who speaks on her own behalf or on behalf of her family, but a man can make a *bolma* if he wishes. The recipient of the *bolma* may be a deity whose image resides within the household or some other less familiar deity. In either case the *bolma* may require a pilgrimage to a special shrine dedicated to the deity. Among the women I interviewed in Mewar, I found some who had recently made *bolma*s to Avri Mata (whose temple is near Chitor, a former capital of Mewar), to Ram Dev (whose shrine is near Jaisalmer), and to Karni Mata (situated near Bikaner). They say that when the crises precipitating the *bolma* disappear, they will have to journey to these deities' primary temples. Whereas in some cases the pilgrimage itself will fulfill the *bolma*, in others the individuals have promised to perform special rituals.

Pilgrimage, as might be expected, is not something that noblewomen undertake freely. It means temporarily relaxing, if not abandoning, *parda*. When noblewomen do undertake pilgrimages to fulfill their *bolma*s, they adopt the kind of "when in Rome" posture already mentioned. They can be comfortable in public because they are far from home and their identities are unknown.

With this cursory sketch of religious tradition as background, it is possible to compare the separate modes of authority that inform men's and women's interpretations of their religiously articulated and sanctioned duties.

RELIGION AND AUTHORITY

The predominant authorities available to Rajput men for articulating their duty are two. First, there is Brahmanical authority. Rajput families formerly imported Brahmans from various parts of Rajasthan, particularly Gujarat. Some of these Brahmans were *pujari*s, temple officiants. Others were *purohit*s, advisors. The *purohit*s helped Rajputs to make

65. On Rajasthani pilgrimage (*jatra*) in general, consult Gold, *Fruitful Journeys*, 186–89.

66. Striking visual depictions of this type of vow, which is found throughout India under many different names, occur in the University of Wisconsin film *Ramdevra* and in *Sitala in Spring* (Calcutta: Shape Films, 1987).

proper decisions in administering their kingdoms or estates. They also taught Rajput boys lessons from Sanskrit texts, such as the legal codes (the *dharmashastras*) and the epics (the *Mahabharat* and *Ramayan*).

More important than this instruction was the education Rajput boys received by listening to the songs of the Carans, the second source of authority. The Carans' caste-associated duty was to keep Rajput genealogies. These genealogies were more than mere lists of names; they were repositories of glory and records of Rajput courage, conquest, and heroism. In reciting to Rajput men and boys the stories of their ancestors, the Carans related inspirational paradigms. By conforming to these paradigms, Rajputs knew that they were doing their duty—preserving and protecting society.[67]

Today Rajput noblemen no longer employ *purohit*s. And if they employ *pujari*s, they do so on a part-time or ad hoc basis. Moreover, they can no longer support Carans. Some Carans still keep the family records of Rajputs, but they also have full-time jobs performing other services in order to support their families. Even so, they continue to influence the Rajput conception of duty, for the stories that the bards once recited are now passed down by their former patrons.

Women have had neither source of authority. Carans used to record the genealogies of women in Rajput families, but those genealogies were little more than birth and marriage records.[68] They did not record the lives of women; they registered women's names. Furthermore, though Rajput women often had Brahman women perform *puja* for them, they did not have female Brahman advisors.[69] The Brahman women were not educated in Sanskrit. They simply knew certain rituals, the details of which they had probably learned from their husbands.

Lacking the two traditional authorities used by men, Rajput women have leaned heavily on the religious myths they have learned from one another for sources of religious and moral authority. The myths explain, exemplarize, and legitimate the explicit rules of behavior they have

---

67. Ziegler characterizes the Caran's function: "The Caran was the bard and poet of the Rajpūt. He possessed the *gīt* and the *dohā* (songs and poems of praise), the *vārttā* and the *bāt* (inspirational historical stories), and the *bhūmḍ* (a form of ridicule), the sounds which exemplarized the Rajpūt and his actions and in turn supported the order of society" ("Action, Power," 28–29).

68. These genealogists were called Ranimangas.

69. Rajput women sometimes refer to any female Brahman whom their families employed as "*purohitani*" and describe the *purohitani*'s functions as those of a *pujarani*. They use both words to refer to a woman hired to perform *puja*. A number of the Brahman women who performed rituals were impoverished widows who supported themselves by serving the ritual needs of Rajput women.

learned from their elders. In the various myths associated with the major Rajput devotional traditions women observe, especially *kuldevi* and *sati* traditions, and in the myths detailing the lives of beloved Rajput heroines, women find paradigms that help them construct personal interpretations of *pativrata* duty.

In short, in one way or another the myths from these traditions inform and explicate the *pativrata* ideal. As an ideal, as an image, as a symbol, the *pativrata* brings together two separate sets of norms: those related to Rajput caste and those related to female gender. At the same time, because both Rajput caste duty and female duty are in their own ways duties of protection, the ideal powerfully articulates for women a twofold protective ethic.

CHAPTER 2

Kuldevi Tradition

Myth, Story, and Context

The *kuldevi* has a crucial role in the religious lives of Rajput men and women: she is the foremost divine guardian of their fortune and honor. Many of the myths that recount the miraculous deeds she performs as guardian not only make wonderful reading—they abound in romance, intrigue, danger, and conquest—they also give access to the worldview of Rajput women.

A goddess begins her career as a *kuldevi* when she becomes incarnate at a critical point in time in order to rescue an endangered group of Rajputs whom she judges worthy of her protection. In most cases she reveals herself to their leader and inspires him to surmount whatever problems he and his followers face.[1] Afterward she helps him establish a kingdom, at which point he and his relatives become the founders of a kinship branch (*kul* or *shakh*) with a discrete political identity. Later the *kuldevi* intermittently manifests her presence by helping the group overcome other military and political crises. These manifestations are celebrated in myths chronicling the origins and early achievements of the Rajput groups that *kuldevi*s protect.[2]

Rajput women perceive themselves to be less familiar with such *kul-*

1. In this respect the *kuldevi*'s first appearance resembles the appearance in the *Mahabharata* of Krishna, who ultimately reveals himself as God to the troubled prince Arjuna and guides his performance of martial duty.
2. Recently some noblemen have written family histories based on such myths and other genealogical materials; they have incorporated elements from the narratives of Carans and local histories by Tod (*Annals and Antiquities*), Ojha (*Rājpūtāne*), and Kaviraj Shyamaldas (*Vīr Vinod*, 4 vols. [Udaipur: privately published by the Mewar darbar, ca. 1884 and reissued, Delhi: Motilal Banarsidass, 1986]).

devi myths than Rajput men are. They say that these myths belong to the realm of history (*itihas*), which they understand as a male domain. When asked about the "historical" myths—myths I call foundation myths to avoid the appearance of continually certifying their historicity—women typically claim that their husbands know history, but they do not: "What do I know of history? You ask my husband!" Because Rajputs no longer support Carans as bards, the traditional means of reciting Rajput genealogies and their related myths has been lost. It is perhaps for this reason that many Rajput husbands now believe that they know less than their wives about "such religious matters." In fact, women often do know more than their husbands about foundation myths, the details of which rarely find their way into modern written histories precisely because they are mythical, not strictly factual.

In addition to these foundation myths, Rajput women know stories relating to the services that the *kuldevi* has rendered to the particular household, often fairly recently. Generally referred to as "stories" (*kahaniyam*) rather than history and understood as the proper subjects of female expertise, they constitute the primary source for women's appropriations of *kuldevi* tradition. They may be myths handed down through generations of women living in a *zanana*, or they may be accounts of events witnessed by a living narrator. In either case, the stories have never been the responsibility of Carans.

In recounting a *kuldevi*'s aid to individual family members, the narrators commonly use a household setting and always emphasize the sacredness of domestic *pativrata* duties. Because the narrators are almost exclusively women, whose sphere of responsibility is the home, the accounts are more immediately relevant to women than foundation myths, which describe the establishment of kingdoms and/or dynasties in very remote times. Unlike the foundation myths, which can be located within a scheduled sequence corresponding to a genealogical sacred history, these stories—which I call "household stories"—detail incidents that are timeless: they take place in an indefinite past or they are contemporary. In both cases they relate standard variations of recurrent scenarios. It is precisely their timeless redundancy that keeps them meaningful to all times. Moreover, their recurrence does much to explain the shared conception of women as more personally involved in "such religious matters" than their husbands, because the stories women tell always seem relevant to their pressing concerns.[3]

3. This distinction between "itihasic" and domestic myths roughly corresponds to the South Indian distinction between *puram* (public) and *akam* (domestic) myths. A. K.

This chapter explores foundation myths and household stories to un-cover the ways in which the *kuldevi* serves women both as a protector and as a paradigm of protection. It sets forth connections between foun-dation myths and household stories and suggests that these connections reveal important relations between lineage and household on the one hand and caste and gender on the other.

THE FOUNDATION MYTHS

For the most part the narratives to be recounted are gleaned from my interviews with Rajput women.[4] A couple of narratives (Jamvai Mata variant two, and Naganecha Ji variant one), however, were recited by noblewomen's male relatives. I have chosen to include them not because women were unfamiliar with these variants—in fact, the wives knew these stories—but because the accounts given by the men in these two instances contain important elaborative detail scattered among numer-ous women's accounts.[5] The women who narrated the other accounts gave the most lucid and comprehensive versions of the myths that I dis-covered in the course of research. All accounts here are verbatim.[6]

I begin with the story of Ad Mata, the *kuldevi* of the Jhala *kul* (see fig. 10*a*).[7] The Jhalas presided over two of Mewar's foremost noble es-

---

Ramanujan carefully contrasts these story genres in "Two Realms of Kannada Folklore," in *Another Harmony*, ed. Stuart H. Blackburn and A. K. Ramanujan (Berkeley: University of California Press, 1986). He notes that *puram* stories, which bards traditionally recited in public, are longer and more detailed than the *akam* stories, or "granny's tales," which women traditionally recited in their households.

4. Unlike the stories of many popular deities, these Rajput goddess stories are not sold as pamphlets outside the gates of public temples or in urban bookstalls.

5. Although "itihasic" in substance, these accounts are so terse as to imply a stylistic "intertextuality," for such brevity is typically characteristic of *zanana*, or in South India, of *akam* tales. See Ramanujan, "Two Realms," 43, 51. The bardic versions of these tales would be filled with details and names.

6. Because each narrator did provide his or her own variation, I present here no "right" myth. Many narrators, particularly men, cautioned me not to heed others' ac-counts because they would doubtless be "wrong" in certain respects. Narrators believe they are relating essential truths. The idea that there are variations of a foundation nar-rative and that these are interesting in themselves—they reveal concerns of contemporary narrators—is one that occurs to Rajput narrators no more readily than it would to most nonacademic religious persons in other cultures. Incidentally, the idea of variations of *kuldevi* narrative seemed to cause much more anxiety than variations of *satimata* ac-counts. Because each family has several ancestors who became satis, a discordant variant would be about a different ancestor—such conclusions were often drawn when others commented on interviews being conducted. I have used such contextualizing accounts from these other sources where indicated.

7. In Gujarat she is referred to as Shakti Mata (personal communication from Jaya-sinh Jhala, 3 Oct. 1987).

tates, Bari Sadri and Delwara (see fig. 5), as well as over Jhalawar, an independent kingdom that split off from the Cauhan-ruled kingdom of Kota.

AD MATA

> Three little boys, princes of the royal family, were playing outside the palace when a mad elephant suddenly charged. Ad Mata, their spinster auntie, had been watching them from a second-story window. Just in time, she reached out for them with her arms, which grew and grew until they extended all the way down to the children. She snatched up the children and lifted them into her embrace. In this way Ad Mata saved the princes and so the royal lineage.

Another variant adds that because Ad Mata rescued the boys, the line descending from one of the princes came to be known as *Jhala*, meaning "snatched" or "grabbed."[8] This etymology is well known by Jhalas, who date the origin of their *kul* to this *kuldevi* miracle (*camatkar*).

Next is Jamvai Mata, the *kuldevi* of the Kachvaha Rajputs of Jaipur state (see fig. 20).

JAMVAI MATA

> The Kachvahas used to live in Navargarh in central India, the place where Nala and Damayanti used to live. They left that place in search of a kingdom and wandered toward Rajasthan. When they arrived, they met resistance from some tribals.[9] There was a big battle between the Kachvahas and the tribals where Rajgarh Dam is now [about forty minutes' drive from Jaipur].[10] The Kachvahas fared badly. They lay wounded and dying on the battlefield and there was no water for them to drink. They began to think of Parvati and she became a cow. She stood over the dying soldiers and poured out her milk, which revived them. They renewed their attack and achieved victory.

A variant of this myth provides more detail.

> The Kachvahas came from Navar near Gwalior in Madhya Pradesh. They fought their way to Dosa, which they won from the Gujar Rajputs. They took some lands from the Mina tribe by treachery. Finally, at . . . Rajgarh, they were defeated. Dularai, their leader, was badly injured. He lay unconscious and dying on the battlefield. Jamvai Mata appeared to him in a vision.

8. Jhaliyodau: caught, seized (Hindi: *parkada hua*); in Sitaram Lalas, *Rājasthānī Sabd Kos*, vol. 4, pt. 3 (Jodhpur: Caupasni Siksa Samiti, 1978), s.v.

9. Speaking English, the narrator used the term "tribal" nominally, as it often occurs in local Indian English.

10. Henceforth, all bracketed remarks are my own.

She said, "I am the *kuldevi* of the Minas, but I am angry with them. I am a vegetarian but they offer me meat and wine in my temple." Jamvai Mata then turned herself into a cow and sprayed milk on Dularai's face. She revived the rest of the Kachvahas in the same way. Meanwhile the Minas were rejoicing over their victory. They were drunk. The Kachvahas successfully attacked them. Since then Jamvai Mata has been our *kuldevi*.

A third *kuldevi* is Naganecha Ji, protector of the Rathaur *kul* (see fig. 10*b, c*). She oversees the state of Marwar as well as Ghanerao, a Solah Thikana.

NAGANECHA JI

Naganecha Ji came with our ancestors when they moved here [Jodhpur] from the south. When Sinha Ji [a Rathaur king] was carrying her around his neck, she demanded that he put her down at Nagana. She wanted to stay there. He slept and she became anchored in the ground, never to move. From that spot a snake slithered away.

This account, like the one that follows, yields a murky picture of the form in which Naganecha Ji arrives. The informant implies that the goddess was worn as a pendant, a *pala* (a form in which goddesses often travel; see fig. 18); other accounts have it that the king bore her temple icon on his shoulders or upper back. The nature of her original form does not appear to be critical. What should be noted is that this foundation myth assumes Naganecha Ji's association with the Rathaurs in their former home. In traveling from that home the goddess manifests two forms, which serve different purposes. Her first form, anchored at Nagana, establishes that as the new territory for her protégés.

Her second, which is a mobile form, shows that she is not confined to one place. As a serpent she accompanies her protégés when they engage in conquest. An alternate version of the myth makes this clear:

Naganecha Ji came with our ancestors when they journeyed from Idar [in Gujarat]. While they were fighting for Nagor, Naganecha Ji became their *kuldevi*. At Nagana they built a temple for her. She was called Naganecha Ji—Nagana plus *ish*, "deity." She appeared to Cumda Ji Rathaur, who had prayed to her because he was losing a battle. She manifested herself as a snake and from then on was always with him. Because of this the Rathaurs were able to conquer Marwar.

Fourth, there is Ashapura, protectress of the Cauhan *kul*, which ruled the states of Kota and Bundi as well as such Udaipur-linked *thikana*s as Bedla and Kothariya.

ASHAPURA

My forefathers used to wage many wars. One time my ancestor and his army had run out of rations on the battlefield. Annapurna [a Sanskritic goddess, whose name means "She Who Has (Gives) Food"] appeared to my ancestor in a dream and said, "I will become a green fly and sit on your arm while you fight. You will win many villages." [Having received food and the protection of Annapurna's avatar] he was able to conquer 1,444 villages in a single night. Since then we worship both Annapurna and Ashapura [Annapurna's avatar, "She Who Has (Grants) Wishes"].

The final *kuldevi* to be discussed is Ban Mata, guardian goddess of Mewar (fig. 12) and, inter alia, the Mewari *thikana*s of Bansi, Amet, Kurabar, Kanor, Begum, and Salumbar.[11]

BAN MATA

The *kuldevi* for the Sisodiyas used to be Amba Mata. Then, when the Sisodiyas were at Chitor, the *kuldevi* became Kalika Mata.[12] There is still a temple for her there now. Later, when the king conquered Gujarat, he demanded a Gujarati princess in marriage.[13] That princess had always wanted to marry the Sisodiya king. She had even sent him a letter telling him that. Her *kuldevi*, Ban Mata, had determined to help her accomplish this aim. After the conquest, the marriage occurred. When the princess left for her new home, Ban Mata came with her in the form of a pendant. That is how Ban Mata left Girnar (though there is still a temple for her there) and came here.

A second account is not so much a variation as another etymology, one that states a homology between the Sanskritic goddess Durga and the *kuldevi*.

The Sisodiyas used to worship Durga, Mata Ji. Banasur was a demon who fought with Mata Ji. She conquered him. From then on she was called Ban Mata.

11. The name Ban was pronounced and written in many different ways: Ban, Baen, Bayan, Byan, and Vyana. Written sources tend to prefer Bayan, but informants usually spelled out Ban when I asked them to spell their *kuldevi*'s name.
12. The antecedents of Ban Mata are vague. Amba and Kalika are Sanskritic epithets and so do not characterize these goddesses as discrete local incarnations. As we shall see, these stories refer to a *kuldevi* preceding the appearance of Ban Mata but give her no specific local name or identity. There is a Kalika Mandir at Chitor.
13. Tod identifies the king as Bappa Rawal and the bride as the daughter of Esupgole, prince of the island of Bunderdhiva (*Annals and Antiquities* 1:197). Another narrated variant identified Ban Mata as the daughter of a Caran in the village of Khod; Hamir, the great Sisodiya leader, heard of her powers, worshiped her, and asked her blessing in his attempt to reclaim Chitor from the Moghals. She aided him and he installed her as Sisodiya deity. This variant places the adoption of Ban Mata just after the Sisodiya line of Guhils came to the throne rather than after the Guhils first won Chitor, as Tod's variant has it.

12. Ban Mata image, Chitor.

These myths conjointly illustrate a number of fundamental points. First, every *kul* explicitly associates the appearance of its *kuldevi* with a critical act of divine guardianship. The goddess utilizes her power (*shakti*) to rescue royal heirs, revive dying soldiers, and establish Rajput kingdoms.

Second, the *kuldevi*'s power of protection is directed toward the king and his family. The goddess appears to the king (or prince) and either with him or through him protects the *kul* and hence the realm. Thus, Jamvai Mata protects Dularai, Naganecha Ji guards Cumda Ji, Ad Mata saves the little princes, and so forth.[14] Afterward the *kuldevi*'s primary relationship remains with the king, who tends to her needs just as his own servants tend to his. This close mythical association between king and goddess means that the *kuldevi* is identified with the royal family and conceptualized with reference to the protective functions it performs. Her temple is patronized by the royal family and is located in or near its palace.

Because of this close relationship between king and *kuldevi*, worship of the *kuldevi* and service of the king are intertwined. The king attends the *kuldevi* through personal acts of devotion and through public ceremonies, such as buffalo sacrifices, which are held in conjunction with the biannual festival of Navratri.[15] The *kuldevi* protects him and through him the kingdom. Historically, members of the *kul* have served the king, whose authority has been legitimated by *kuldevi* worship on the part of both king and *kul* members.

Another thing clear from the myths is that the *kuldevi*'s foremost arena of protection is the battlefield. Kings and other *kul* members are warriors. They guard and increase not only the territory of the realm but also its glory. From the beginning, a kingdom attempts to expand through battle, which is the caste duty of all Rajput men and the principal measure of their personal worth. Because battle is the route to glory and prosperity, the great king is a conqueror.[16] As the Rajput king and his army fight to subjugate new land, the *kuldevi* accompanies the

14. This shared scenario varies markedly from others elsewhere in India. For example, one South Indian lineage deity (*kulateyvam*) is venerated after being sacrificially beheaded (Hiltebeitel, *Cult of Draupadī*, 336, citing Reinich). It is evidently not unusual in South India for such a deity, especially a goddess, to be venerated as a *kul* deity after she punishes the king or threatens to kill him for inappropriate behavior (Meyer, *Aṅkāḷaparmēcuvari*, 187, 253; and Tarabout, *Sacrifier*, 132).

15. Details of this festival are given below.

16. See, for example, *Agni Purāṇaṃ*, trans. Manmatha Nath Dutt Shastri, 2 vols. (Varanasi: Chowkhamba Sanskrit Studies Office, 1967), 778. On the expansion of South India kingdoms, see Shulman, *King and Clown*, 35–36.

king as a snake, sits on his shoulder as a green fly, or, in still another tale, flies above him as a kite (an eagle-like bird of prey).[17] Thus in her mobile animal form the *kuldevi* is identified with the growing might, resources, and renown of the *kul* or *shakh* she protects.

The last crucial point about these tales is that a *kuldevi* is homologous with the great Sanskritic Goddess, particularly in her warrior aspect, Durga.[18] In the myth of Jamvai Mata, the first narrator states that the warriors "began to think of Parvati and she became a cow." Thus the *kuldevi* is conceived of as an incarnation (avatar) of Parvati, herself one of the best known forms of the Goddess. Ashapura is understood as an emanation of the Goddess, Annapurna, whose power to provide food is the basis for the *kul*'s triumph. Ban Mata is understood to replace Kalika Mata, whose name is another epithet of the Goddess. She, in turn, is understood to have taken over from Amba Mata, who bears yet another Sanskrit epithet. These sequential substitutions symbolically connect the local goddess with the great Sanskritic Goddess.

The etymology of Ban Mata provided by one woman confirms the general identification of the local goddess with the great Goddess. She says that the local *kuldevi* is so named because, as the Goddess, she defeated the demon Banasur. The woman does not know any details of this story. I do not know whether she encountered the Sanskritic story of Banasur[19] or simply assumes that the *kuldevi* received her name because she defeated a demon who must have had that name.[20] Both pos-

17. Goddesses are associated with bird and snake imagery elsewhere in India; see examples in Beck, *Three Twins*, 155–56; and Meyer, *Aṅkālaparmēcuvari*, 194. Several men told me that in pre-British days kings often began campaigns just after Navratri-Dashara celebrations.

18. Sanskrit literature often treats various goddesses as phenomenal manifestations of a single female goddess, the Devi, who embodies motivational power or *shakti* (also a name for the Devi), which is conceived as female. Through the process of Sanskritization, by which local deities are identified with Sanskritic or "Great Tradition" deities, *kuldevis* are sometimes generally associated with the Devi and sometimes specifically associated with individual Sanskritic goddesses (especially Parvati, the wife of Shiva [Hindi: Shiv]). See further discussion in Wendy Doniger O'Flaherty, *Women, Androgynes, and Other Mythical Beasts* (Chicago: University of Chicago Press, 1980), 71, 82 ff.

19. This is Asura Bana; in "Aniruddha's Hymn" from the *Harivamsha*, he imprisoned Aniruddha because Aniruddha was infatuated with Bana's daughter, Usha (Thomas B. Coburn, *Devī Māhātmya* [Columbia, Mo.: South Asia Books, 1985], 284–85). In a story of Banasur from the *Kanyaksetramahatmya*, Bana demands a share of Markandeya's sacrifice and is cursed by the sage to be killed by a virgin, who turns out to be Parvati (David Dean Shulman, *Tamil Temple Myths* [Princeton: Princeton University Press, 1980], 145). The name Ban Mata may also suggest an association between the *kuldevi* and Shiv, known by the epithet Baneshwara in some shrines in the Udaipur area. No informants made this association in their comments or used the epithet for the Mewari *ishtadevta* Ekling Ji.

20. A man from the Hara *shakh* of the Cauhan *kul* linked another *kuldevi* and a demon in a distinctive Ashapura narrative. He told me that Ashapura, who used to live

sibilities point to a Sanskritic homology. Moreover, even if the story of Banasur is only a local or unique version, it employs the popular Sanskritic convention of referring to deities by the names of demons they have killed. The most famous epithet, of course, is that of the Goddess as Mahishasuramardini, "Slayer of the Buffalo Demon."[21]

This speculative homology joins an omnipresent homology between all *kuldevi*s and the Goddess expressed during Navratri, the festival celebrating her conquest over her buffalo demon foe (see fig. 16). On this day the *kuldevi* is worshiped as Durga. The *Devimahatmya* or *Durga Path*, a Hindi translation, is recited in great Goddess temples and *kuldevi* temples alike. Moreover, *kuldevi*s are as often referred to as Durga, Devi, Kali, Camunda, and Shakti, all Sanskritic-tradition epithets, as they are by their individual local names. The import of this equation of the local *kuldevi* with the Sanskritic Goddess is an implicit identification of *kul*, or in this case *shakh*, history with cosmic history. The *shakh*'s victories coincide with the Goddess's divine victory over the demon army led by Mahish.

The homology between Durga and *kuldevi* in the contexts of the Navratri ritual and the Mahishasur (Sanskrit: Mahishasura) myth brings to light some important assumptions about kingship. In Navratri buffalo sacrifice, which ritually reenacts Durga's conquest over Mahish, the king stands in the role of primary sacrificer.[22] Like the goddess Mahishasuramardini, the king is the slayer of the buffalo, who is the (demonic) enemy. Like the goddess, the king severs the buffalo's head, blood from which he then offers to the goddess. At the same time the king is identified with the victim, Mahish, who is king of the demons.[23]

---

in an ashapala tree—from which she got her name—revived his ancestor, killed by a *rakshasa* (demon) who had eaten all but his bones; the ancestor was called Asthipal (*asthi* [bones] and *pal* [protector]).

21. A similar epithet is Vritraghni, "killer of Vritra," who is Sarasvati (Alf Hiltebeitel, *The Ritual of Battle* [Ithaca: Cornell University Press, 1976], 153). There is also the example of Madhusudhana, "Slayer of Madhu," a title for Krishna used throughout the *Bhagavad Gita*. See, for example, J. A. B. van Buitenen's translation, *The Bhagavadgītā in the Mahābhārata* (Chicago: University of Chicago Press, 1981), 71, 73.

22. Where buffalo sacrifices are performed by Rajputs ("sons of kings") who are not in fact kings, the sacrificers stand in the position of the king relative to the sacrificial victim, the buffalo. As elsewhere in India, the Rajput does what the Brahman priests cannot, i.e., he spills blood. Priests direct the sacrifice and read from the *Devimahatmya*, but only the warrior can decapitate the victim.

23. See Madeleine Biardeau and Charles Malamoud, *Le sacrifice dans l'Inde ancienne* (Paris: Presses universitaires de France, 1976), 146. Also see the discussion of Mahish as Potu Raja in ibid., 150; in Hiltebeitel, *Cult of Draupadī*, 37 n. 8 and passim; and in Gunther D. Sontheimer, *Pastoral Deities in Western India* (Oxford: Oxford University Press, 1989), 56–57.

Thus the blood he offers is also his own.[24] The demon Mahish, liberated by death from his demonic buffalo form, becomes the Goddess's foremost devotee. The king, also represented as the *kuldevi*'s foremost devotee, offers her his death to assure her victory over the enemies of his kingdom.[25] Thus Ban Mata bears the epithet Bukh Mata, "Hungry Mother," for she needs blood from her royal protégés to protect them.[26] Such an identification of king as sacrificer and sacrificed is widely documented by scholars treating Vedic and popular sacrifice.[27]

This same double identification is seen in the traditional construction of warfare. The king, who is protected by the Goddess (as *kuldevi*) and who acts as she does when he kills his enemies, also gives his life in battle. Thus again, the king is not only conqueror of Mahish but also Mahish, the king-victim. To sacrifice one's life in battle, also called *balidan*, is the warrior's desired destiny.[28] As foremost and quintessential warrior, the king gives his blood on the battlefield, which nourishes the *kuldevi* who protects the *kul* and kingdom.[29] At times Bukh Mata has needed the blood of many kings and soldiers to make battle successful. Hence the *kuldevi* helps the king protect and strengthen his kingdom but, like Durga "liberating" Mahish, she also leads him and his soldiers toward glorious death in battle.

One myth, which was told to me by the brother of an informant, makes the identification of the king as sacrificer and sacrificed particularly vivid. He said that the Muslims had killed all his ancestors in their erstwhile home at Narola. Only the pregnant queen escaped and managed to deliver the heir. When the boy, Vijay Raj, was old enough, he was married to a daughter of the Jaisalmer king. The Muslims were keen

24. In a Madhya Pradesh estate where one noblewoman grew up, male family members cut their arms to offer their *kuldevi* their own blood on Navratri. On buffalo sacrifice as symbolic enactment of human sacrifice, see Biardeau and Malamoud, *Le sacrifice*, 148; Herrenschmidt, "Le sacrifice," 150; and Hiltebeitel, *Cult of Draupadī*, 63. I shall discuss animal and human sacrifice in greater detail in my study of hero worship in Rajasthan.

25. For a more detailed sketch of this myth see David Kinsley, *Hindu Goddesses* (Berkeley: University of California Press, 1986), 96–99.

26. See chapter 3 for details of the story by which Bukh Mata gained her epithet.

27. On the king's roles as sacrificer and sacrificed see Jan Heesterman, *The Inner Conflict of Tradition* (Chicago: University of Chicago Press, 1985), 110; Hiltebeitel, *Cult of Draupadī*, 63, 77; Filliozat, "After-Death Destiny," 4; Shulman, *King and Clown*, 36, 286–87; and Beck, *Three Twins*, 53.

28. For exploration of this widely recognized theme, see Hiltebeitel, *Ritual of Battle*; Heesterman, *Inner Conflict* (particularly his chapter, "The Case of the Severed Head"); and Beck, *Three Twins*, 51–52.

29. On the notion that eating flesh "makes" a goddess protect her wards, see Meyer, *Aṅkāḷaparmēcuvari*, 168.

to kill him; they pursued him wherever he went. Just after the marriage
his *kuldevi*, Ashapura, appeared to him and said:

> I am your family goddess and I want to see you settled down. Tomorrow you
> go to a particular lake and you'll see a herd of buffalo bathing. In the herd
> will be a big male much bigger than normal. He'll have a gold ring in his
> nose. You kill him. Inside his stomach you'll find a big sword, which will stay
> with the ruling head of state in times to come. You will be a ruler now. That
> sword should be handed down from generation to generation.

> After that Vijay Raj was successful against the Muslims.

The narrator then noted that "the sword has remained with the family but the golden bracelet, which is supposed to be worn by the ruler—
you remember, the bracelet that was worn by the buffalo in his nose—
is not with us any more. Maybe it got worn out or lost."

This account succinctly links buffalo sacrifice with success in war. It
also identifies the king who kills the buffalo both as sacrificer—from the
sacrifice he performs he gets a sword for battle and for more sacrifices—
and as victim—because he is to wear as a bracelet the gold ring that the
buffalo (the leader of the herd) once wore in its nose. The *kuldevi* gives
the king the implements he needs for his success and her satisfaction.

The foundation myths presented above articulate an understanding
of royal and *kul* or *shakh* power as divinely legitimated. The king and
his warriors are guided by a *kuldevi*, whose duty as a war goddess is to
facilitate their performance of military duties. What, then, can be the
relevance of the *kuldevi* to the lives of women? To answer this question
we must further ponder the connection between the concepts of caste
and gender. The way that men and women understand the powers of
the *kuldevi* reflects their suppositions about the norms Rajputs espouse
and the roles women have. For women, these suppositions sometimes
prove troublesome.

The most important supposition shared by men and women is that
caste rules or norms relate closely to the caste duties performed by men.
Rajputs, we have seen, have been rulers and warriors. That these duties
are construed as male duties is seen most clearly in the ideal of the Rajput as a protector of women. Rajput men are to administer and defend
their realms in such a way that women need never fight in defense of
personal honor and family reputation.[30]

30. Tod attributes the Rajput protectiveness of women to the Rajput susceptibility to
women: "If devotion to the fair sex be admitted as a criterion of civilization, the Rajpoot
must rank high. His susceptibility is extreme, and fires at the slightest offense to female
delicacy, which he never forgives" (*Annals and Antiquities* 1:223).

Ideally then, women do not perform these caste duties; they perform female duties, such as housekeeping and child rearing. Caste-related norms, however, apply to women as they do to men. Honor, courage, dignity, generosity, and *kul* loyalty are the virtues expected of a Rajput, male or female. Here trouble surfaces. For men, norms and duties are closely associated. For women, however, norms that derive from men's caste duties must be applied to duties understood as gender-affiliated. Furthermore, because gender-affiliated duties have their own normative ideals, there is always potential for friction between duty-alienated caste norms and duty-related gender norms.

The traditional norms of womanhood are subsumed within the central ideal of the *pativrata*, whose duties are those essential to being a good wife to her husband, a good mother to her children, and a good daughter-in-law to her husband's parents. All female duties derive from the *pativrata* ideal. If a woman is devoted to her husband, exemplary performance of all secondary duties will naturally follow.

Rajput women's conception of their *kuldevi*s clearly reflects this *pativrata* ideal. Like the men in their families, Rajput women understand *kuldevi*s as protectors but relate to them primarily as protectors of the household rather than as protectors of an extended kinship group. The *kul* (or *shakh*) is not a group with which women identify or interact in any concrete way. It is relevant to them only insofar as it impinges upon the home. Thus women tend to tell stories in which their *kuldevi*s render aid to household members.

THE HOUSEHOLD STORIES

The following story, related by a prominent Udaipur noblewoman about her conjugal family's *kuldevi*, illustrates the type of aid *kuldevi*s give within the context of the family.

> Kuldevi [Ban Mata] appeared to me once. She had a *lota* (vessel) of water, which she gave to me. It was during the war (1965)[31] and my husband was in the army. He had been shot. The doctors operated on him. I was there. Kuldevi came to me in order to give me the *lota* of water for my husband to drink. She also gave me a rose and told me to put one of its petals in my husband's mouth. At first I thought that Kuldevi was just my sister, but then I realized who she was.
>
> I knew that the doctor had said that my husband should not drink water, so I was afraid to give him any. Then the nurse—she was a Catholic sister—

31. The 1965 war involved India and Pakistan.

saw Kuldevi (just as I saw her). Kuldevi was wearing a beautiful red Rajput dress with find gold beadwork. After a time Kuldevi walked away. I asked the nurse where she had gone. The nurse said, "Maybe she's in the waiting room." I went to look for Kuldevi but she had disappeared. I went downstairs and asked the sentry if he had seen a woman leave. He said, "It's 1:00 A.M. and visiting hours ended at 11:00 P.M. Of course nobody came out the door." She had vanished.

As I said, I was afraid to give my husband the water. I thought the doctor would be angry because he had said that my husband should not drink or eat anything. So I didn't give my husband the water and the rose. Instead, I fell asleep. Kuldevi came to me in a dream—this time she came in a dream and not before my eyes—and she said, "You must give him the water and rose petals." So I awoke and gave them to him.

The next morning the doctor came to me and said, "Congratulations, your husband will recover." He recuperated right away.

Women say that *kuldevi*s appear in dreams and visions in order to help women avert family misfortune. Many examples of this could be cited. The most common cases of catastrophe aversion involve ailing husbands or, less frequently, children. Women also say that often a *kuldevi* appears not to avert misfortune but to help a protégée prepare for misfortune by warning her of its approach. One women states:

Whenever trouble is going to happen she comes to help us by warning us. She has more than one form (*rup*) but she is always very beautiful. She looks like a *suhagin* [an auspicious married woman]. Our *kuldevi* came to my mother to tell her my grandfather was going to die. Two days later he passed away.

This account specifically names the form in which *kuldevi*s inevitably appear in the household stories. Whereas the foundation myths generally depict her in an animal form (a snake, a kite, etc.), the household stories describe a particularly lovely *suhagin* (*pativrata*). In another such account a woman reports that her family's *kuldevi*, who appeared to her in a dream, looked like a *suhagin*. The *suhagin* then became a flame that grew into a large fire. Not long after this dream, its recipient suffered the loss of a relative. The woman said that the dream fire foreshadowed the lighting of her relative's funeral pyre. She understood the dream not as a bad omen, even though it predicted the death of a family member, but as a helpful summons that enabled her to ready herself and her household for an approaching crisis.

Thus the two basic services *kuldevi*s perform are rendering aid in times of desperation and giving warnings when trouble is imminent. The goddesses use the media of dreams and visions. Interestingly enough, not a single woman I interviewed, or for that matter any Rajput woman or man I met during my stay in Rajasthan, mentioned possession in discussing *kuldevis* and their deeds. Because this seems unusual—village and lineage deities in many communities throughout India do possess their devotees—I asked a few women about *kuldevi* possession. They responded that *kuldevis*, and *satimatas* for that matter, do not possess Rajput women. To find out whether their answers were representative, I undertook a separate survey of fifty women (nobles and villagers) with explicit questions about possession. Over and over I heard the same response: such possession does not occur.[32] Moreover, women tended to treat this whole line of questioning about possession as silly and irrelevant.[33] Some found it insulting, either to Rajput women or to *kuldevis*.

As everyone made perfectly clear, possession is not a dignified sort of thing. Rajput women, being very protective of their composure (what we might call "self-possession"), do not like the idea of rolling about on the floor, letting their hair fly loose, neglecting their head coverings, and so forth. Not only is such behavior immodest, it has sexual overtones. As one woman explained about possession, "We don't like the idea of something coming into our bodies . . . that's why we keep *parda*."

Although it might at first seem surprising that a goddess's possession of a woman would have such overtones, it is less so when one learns that the primary deity of which women think when they think of "possession" (*bhav ana*) is Bheru Ji (Sanskrit: Bhairava).[34] Bheru Ji is an attendant of various goddesses (including *kuldevis*) as well as a deity in his own right. An insatiably lusty bachelor, Bheru Ji delights in seducing women, especially young virgins. In Rajasthan as elsewhere, Bheru Ji's

32. Although thorough speculation on why possession does not occur would be a digression, I address possession because one might expect to find it associated with goddess tradition. It is hard to discover why people lack a certain belief. To ask them why they lack the belief—i.e., to ask them why they do not think as outsiders expect—is, of course, to invite artificial responses. Answers to such questions can be gleaned only through inference, except perhaps in instances where a belief was previously held and then consciously abandoned.

33. The questions treated both *kuldevi* and *sati* possession. The responses were identical: it does not happen. Of fifty women interviewed, forty-nine said they knew of no *kuldevi* possession (one was unsure); all said they knew of no *sati* possession. The one informant who mentioned an incidence of *kuldevi* possession—involving a female relative who was possibly possessed while my informant was a little girl—was not sure whether the possessing deity was a *kuldevi* or another goddess or whether the relative was sober or tipsy as she was at least occasionally known to be. A number of witnesses drew the latter conclusion.

34. As one woman explained to me, "I have never heard of a *kuldevi* who possesses people. They just don't do that. *Kuldevis* are not like Bherus!"

possession is associated with sexual penetration.[35] Thus while acknowledging that Bheru Ji can possess (Rajput women and women of other
castes venerate Bheru just before marriage so that he will not violate
their virginity as they prepare to become sexually active), Rajput women
deny that he possesses *them*.[36] Rather he possesses low-caste people,
both men and women. In particular, he possesses *bhopa*s, mediums,
who become possessed while performing Bheru Ji veneration. In trance,
the *bhopa*s are clairvoyant and will answer questions put to them. Although *bhopa*s are good at helping people identify and interpret dreams
sent by *kuldevi*s and *satimata*s, they are not primarily associated with
these family guardians.[37] In the village in which I worked, Bheru possession occurs not at the *kuldevi* temples or any other goddess temples but
in the Bheru Ji temple, which is situated on the village boundary and far
from other temples and shrines.[38]

Thus the low-caste associations of Bheru possession seem to combine
with the sexual associations to make possession unappealing to Rajput
women. Perhaps the low-caste associations also help explain the absence of possession among Rajput males.[39] Neither Rajput women I interviewed formally nor Rajput men I interviewed informally knew of
any *kuldevi* or *satimata* possession of Rajput men. Being less concerned
with chastity than women are, Rajput men might be less daunted by the
sexual aspects of possession (or at least possibly, possession by women)
but equally uneasy about its associations with status.[40]

There is a notable exception to this discomfort with possession. Rajput men and women say that sometimes ancestors (*purvaj*s) do possess
family members. *Purvaj* possession may manage to escape the low-caste
and sexual connotations of Bheru possession because ancestors share
the same caste and blood as their possessed descendants and because
familial closeness tends not to be construed as sexual. Even cross-gender
possession seems to raise no concern about incest, for there are instances

35. Gold, *Fruitful Journeys*, 257–58.
36. See ibid., 95, 197 n. 8.
37. They also grant various blessings, such as fertility.
38. The primary *bhopa* at this temple is a Raika, a member of a caste of goat and
sheep herders.
39. In the 1950s G. Morris Carstairs noted a tendency among high castes to perceive
possession as generally associated with low castes in his village (less than a half-hour's
drive from the village where I worked) (*The Twice-Born* [Bloomington: Indiana University
Press, 1967], 26, 92–93).
40. Rajputs and others tend to understand Rajput men in general as rather virile, lusty
sorts. Thus there are many stories about the size of ancestors' extensive harems and the
lasciviousness of their dancing girls.

of women being possessed by deceased brothers and sons. One commonly mentioned instance of ancestral possession among women, however, was the possession of a bride by the deceased wife of her husband.[41] Either envious of the living or feeling neglected by the living, ancestral spirits must be venerated to keep them from making mischief in the household.[42]

In brief, *kuldevi*s and *satimata*s like to keep their distance even from those whom they protect. Rather than possess, they prefer to send instructive visions and give warnings. The *kuldevi* stories often combine these two services. They tell of times in which a *kuldevi* appears in order to warn but also to help avert an impending crisis. These stories invariably involve a situation where a *kuldevi* becomes manifest because her worship has been neglected in some essential way. She warns that unless her worship is performed properly, various undesirable consequences will ensue. A warning appearance is typically accompanied by bad omens: cows' udders wither, children come down with fever, money problems arise or intensify.

Despite the unpleasant or even frightening character of these appearances and omens, the warnings *kuldevi*s provide are considered blessings. The *kuldevi* is not understood as malevolent toward her protégés. Some say she only warns of bad consequences; she does not cause them. Those who believe that she does cause harm say that she is right to do so because she has been insulted by ritual neglect. One woman explained that a *kuldevi* must be respected because she is like one's mother. If she causes harm in the short run, it is for the best in the long run. As another woman put it: "How will our *kuldevi* cause us harm?

41. A detailed account of a Jaipur noblewoman's possession by a female ancestor (*pitrani*) several generations ago occurs in the "Amar Sinh Diary" (its abridged version will be published by Mohan Sinh of Kanota and Susanne Rudolph and Lloyd I. Rudolph). Ann Gold describes the possession of village brides by their husbands' deceased wives in *Fruitful Journeys*, 67–68. I have wondered whether Rajputs who have been exposed to western education might not have gradually come to perceive *kuldevi* and *satimata* possession as superstitious (see Brij Raj Chauhan, *A Rajasthani Village* [Delhi: Vir Publishing House, 1967], 206–7) but then also wondered why in that case, they continue to believe in ancestor possession and Bheru Ji possession now. Interestingly, although all village women did not believe in *kuldevi* and *satimata* possession, a few did believe that on rare occasions local Rajput women and men have been possessed by a village goddess. Perhaps villagers have absorbed the nobility's opinions about Rajput traditions but kept other local ones. I hope to investigate such matters in my work on hero worship.

42. Rajputs' ancestor worship is similar to that of other castes in Rajasthan. Ancestors are installed in small shrines, often in pleasant places away from the household such as shady patches under trees and along the edges of wells. Sometimes the ancestors prefer a more intimate location in pendants (*putlis*), which people have made by local metalsmiths (Sonis) and which they hang around their necks. For more on ancestor veneration, see Gold, *Fruitful Journeys*.

She sits on our shoulders." Here referring to the kite (*cil*) form (*rup*) of her *kuldevi*, this woman expresses the sentiment that whatever the *kuldevi* does, she intends to protect the line that belongs to her. If neglected, she instructs devotees so that they will mend their ways and once again deserve her protection.

When the *kuldevi* decides to teach her devotees a lesson, that is, to punish them for their own good, she often does so by withdrawing a bodily fluid, as the omens listed above indicate. She evaporates the milk of cows, which is associated with the nurture of children in two senses: it is given by mothers to children for their nourishment and it is homologous with mother's milk, the cow being the quintessential symbol of motherhood. Furthermore, she causes fever: she dries up the water in the body. The victims here are generally children, but sometimes husbands.

Another way she tends to punish, destroying financial security, is not literally a mode of dehydration. Nevertheless, in describing situations in which *kuldevi*s have hurt family resources, two women resorted to the same hyperbolic expression, "There wasn't even enough money to buy milk for the children!" The ease with which these women associated impoverishment with fluid deprivation strikes me as suggesting that women do perceive a connection between the two.

The dehydration type of warning, so appropriate to the Rajputs' desert environment, correlates with the way a *kuldevi* renders direct aid. When the soldier is dying in the hospital, his *kuldevi* delivers to his wife life-saving water. When the Rathaurs are critically wounded on the battlefield, she appears as a cow to splash life-renewing milk on their faces and into their mouths. Hence when rescuing and reviving her male protégés and their children, the *kuldevi* functions in her domestic aspect. Even though in the household she makes her will known by afflicting children and husbands with various kinds of dehydration, she is not to be blamed or resented for these afflictions.[43] She withdraws by implication; she gives outright. Thus when women restore their proper ritual practices, the *kuldevi* resumes her active role as the giver of fluids.

Here it is clear that while the *kuldevi* appears wholly in her *pativrata* aspect in the context of her role as family protector, she also demonstrates *pativrata* behavior in serving her role as *kul* protector. Thus there

---

43. In allowing or even in causing dehydration, the *kuldevi* seems to deny her children her maternal breast rather than protect them. But this act does not transform her conceptually into a hostile goddess as described, for example, by O'Flaherty, *Women, Androgynes*, 90–91.

is an undeniable crossover of imagery between the domains of women's and men's worship. Before I can discuss this crossover with greater specificity, I must say something more about the household-linked contrasts between the *kuldevi*'s relationships with women on the one hand and with men and children on the other.

Whereas the *kuldevi* serves as the dispenser of fluids to men and children, she does not serve in this capacity relative to women. Rather, she coerces women (sometimes gently, sometimes not so gently) to better serve an analogous role. She nurtures and protects men and children as every *pativrata* should. Moreover, her purpose of afflicting the family in the first place is to ensure that the woman whose task as a *pativrata* is to protect her husband and his family will perform the ritual duties that guarantee family welfare and prosperity.

The giving of fluids is to be understood as the quintessential mode of protection rendered by *kuldevi*s and *pativrata*s alike. The fluids revive and strengthen blood, the loss of which means death. Just as the *kuldevi* conserves and invigorates the blood of the *kul*, a woman, through her rituals, by her daily household duties, and with her chastity, protects the blood of her family. The *pativrata*'s rituals promote the longevity of family members. Her dutiful performance of household responsibilities increases her reservoir of virtue (*sat*), which rituals fortify and conserve. Finally, her chastity preserves her sexuality for the purposes of procreation within the family. It protects the purity and strength of the family's bloodline. By these means, the *pativrata* serves her household as the agent of the *kuldevi* she venerates.

In short, although as *kul* protector the *kuldevi* has intervened in events on the battlefield, it is as a household protector that she has most actively regulated her protégés' lives. Wars are occasional occurrences; family mishaps are endless recurrences. Hence, although the *kuldevi* is a warrior goddess, she has always been busiest as the day-to-day guarantor and delegator of protective *pativrata* responsibility.

If we consider this often overlooked domestic dimension of *kuldevi* tradition, we can see that the limited conception of the *kuldevi* as a warrior goddess is insufficient. True, men and women share this *mardana*-derived conception. As the core of *kuldevi* worship, it provides the foundation myth that serves as a basis for the *kul*'s subsequent sacred genealogy. As we have seen, however, women utilize far more than this common core. Accounts such as the hospital story and the dream stories show that women accept the common tradition but enrich it by imposing on it their domestic (*zanana*-linked) goddess. The iconography of the goddess metamorphoses in the process. The snake or kite becomes a richly adorned *pativrata*.

This expansion engenders a formal paradox: the *kuldevi* is a virgin and a *pativrata*. As a warrior goddess, she is not the mere consort of a male deity; she appears unattached and unconstrained. In temples her icon stands alone or surrounded by attendant goddesses. Many myths refer specifically to her virginity. The story of Ad Mata, for example, presents the *kuldevi* as a spinster. Karni Mata, a Caran *kuldevi* who is claimed by some Rajputs as well,[44] also remains a maiden. She changes herself into a lion to frighten away her groom for his own good and then, having thus revealed her divine nature, arranges for the betrothal of the amazed young man to her younger sister, who is a more suitable bride. Other *kuldevi* myths simply imply a *kuldevi*'s unmarried status by making no mention of a consort. Finally, as noted, the *kuldevi* is directly identified with Durga, whose very power derives from her status as a virgin unrestrained by male control.

Yet as the household stories illustrate, through the female appropriation of the *kuldevi* the goddess is transformed into a lovely bride whose guardianship and implicit instruction help her protégées to be virtuous and dutiful wives. Thus although based on the image of the warrior goddess, the unmarried and fierce virgin who protects the *kul*, the female conception of the *kuldevi* entails a predominant notion of the goddess as wife and mother. It is this *suhagin* image that shapes the foremost experience and expectations of the women who perform domestic *kuldevi* rituals. The images, then, are fluid: although an ordinary woman cannot be virginal and married according to context, a goddess can be.[45]

Although the domestic or *zanana*-linked conception of the *kuldevi* has more impact on the lives of Rajput women, the warrior conception that underlies it is never wholly absent. For one thing, Rajput women are aware of their female ancestors who were forced by disaster to fight in battle. Those ancestors are heroines of whom Rajput women speak readily and exuberantly. Highly revered, such women are few because *parda* prohibited public appearances under all but the most desperate

44. Some Rathaur women claim Karni Mata as their *kuldevi*. As we shall see, Rajput women have sometimes adopted alien *kuldevi*s, who attend or eventually supplant their *kul* or *shakh kuldevi*s. Like Naganecha Ji, Karni is often depicted as a kite on the battlefield, which makes the association between them especially easy.

45. On paradox and divinity, see O'Flaherty, *Śiva*, 4 ff.

circumstances: a proper woman would not leave the domain of the household unless faced with the death or the imminent death of her husband. Thus female performance of caste military duty has been permissible only when the female duties of *pativratas* are terminated or severely threatened.

Even today Rajput women maintain that instilling the discipline required to meet a military emergency remains essential to the proper raising of daughters, though their expectation that women will ever have to participate in battle is minimal. A number of women made this point about the socialization of their daughters. One young *thakurani* (noblewoman), who is from one of the foremost Mewari households, went into this matter in great detail. She explained that even though these days a Rajput woman might never face the prospect of battle, the socialization that prepares a Rajput woman for battle is essential as it reinforces the vow of self-sacrifice that all women must make as *pativratas*.[46]

Moreover, the lore of the militant Rajputni (female Rajput) comes down to children as part of their Rajput heritage.[47] The image of the Rajput woman with sword in one hand and shield in the other remains an important element of the mythic consciousness of Rajputs—especially of Rajput women—today (figs. 13, 14). It is painted on palace entryways and printed on the covers of children's story books.[48] Iconographically, it is an image of Rajput woman in the role of *kuldevi*: it is the lone protectress who fights among men on the battlefield (fig. 15).

That the warrior aspect of the goddess underlies the domestic aspect and is contextualized as a contingency does not mean, once again, that these aspects are perceived as opposed. Often secondary literature on the Sanskritic Goddess draws a rather rigid dichotomy between the

46. In the same vein, another woman said, "I want to bring up my children to know tradition—discipline is necessary for them, otherwise there can be no strength (*bala*) in one's life." The ethos of sacrifice and the stern tone that women often adopted when explaining the necessity for its preservation often brought to my mind television recruitment commercials for the Marine Corps. The women's serious tone no doubt reflected both conviction and fear of impending lapse given the changing social climate.

47. There are various stories of Rajput heroines. The most popular of these among Rajput women are recounted in chapters 5 and 6.

48. A militant Rajput woman is strikingly depicted on a second-story balcony wall in the Udaipur City Palace Museum. This figure is typical of the painting style found, particularly on entryway walls, throughout Rajasthan. Crude life-sized paintings of Rajput women also appear as "doorkeepers" at the entryway to the Kota City Palace Museum. Other good examples illustrate the covers of children's pamphlets like *Rājpūt Nāriyāṃ* by Acarya Catursen (Delhi: Prabhat Prakashan, 1984) and *Rājasthān ke Durg* by Rajkumar Anil (Delhi: Sahitya Prakashan, 1984) (see figs. 14, 15).

13. Relief image of a Rajput woman bearing a shield (by permission of the Udai-pur City Palace Museum).

आचार्य चतुरसेन

राजपूत नारियाँ

14. Rajput woman gives her son a sword to encourage him to be a brave soldier (from a local pamphlet entitled *Rajput Women*).

15. Rajput woman leading a charge (from a local pamphlet entitled *Forts of Rajasthan*).

militant aspect of the Goddess—the dark, furious, awful, and uncontrolled side of her nature—and the wifely aspect. It conceives the Goddess in her dark aspect as threatening and understands the Goddess in her light aspect as nurturing.[49] Left uncontextualized, however, this stark characterization may be inadequate, not least of all because it ignores the question of focus. It fails to ask, threatening to whom? Protective of whom?[50] To be sure, in Sanskrit literature a militant goddess is potentially dangerous to all: wrath once engendered is hard to repress, even when it has achieved vengeance. This is the message conveyed by the Puranic myth of Kali in which she defeats a demon army to preserve cosmic order and then herself poses a threat to the cosmos. Still, the message of Kali's overflow of energy is arguably not of malevolence toward her allies but of power; she does not have to stop destroying when she has finished destroying enemies (she can be maleficent) if she is intoxicated by demon blood. On the more immediate, mundane level—and in terms of this study a more important level—the Goddess's anger, however destructive, is triggered by and directed toward her enemies, which means the enemies of those she protects (gods), enemies whose defeat finally reestablishes order in the world.[51]

In a similar way the Rajput *kuldevi* is understood as originally and ultimately protective. Even in her warrior mode, when she demands the blood of *kul* members, she is thought vicious not to the *kul* but to the forces opposing it. Moreover in Rajput mythology, the question of nonspecific or spillover aggression does not even arise. The blood of protégés is necessary to defeat enemies (all wars have casualties), but the goddess is satisfied with triumph. She does not run amok and violate her role as guardian.

49. For superb discussions of these aspects in various contexts, see O'Flaherty, *Women, Androgynes*, 91–92; and Kakar, *Inner World*, 79–112.

50. Because a virgin goddess is unrestrained, she is sometimes characterized as sexually aggressive and therefore dangerous, desiring to consume her victim literally or sexually, the two being identified with each other and with death. Classed as malevolent, she is contrasted with the sexually controlled goddess, the married one, who is deemed creative. Some studies on goddesses artificially separate and polarize these aspects. As the stories in this chapter show, aggression is not necessarily or logically antithetical to the function of protection. The stories do not always consider an aggressive goddess as malevolent even to enemies: she may kill enemies (demons) for benevolent purposes (to preserve world order or liberate *bhakt*s from demonic existences. Nor do they necessarily perceive the sexuality of the goddess (tied either to virginal or conjugal lust) as dangerous—it is essential to procreation. In no mythology does a *kuldevi* jeopardize her virginity on the battlefield or elsewhere. For an exemplary discussion of the fluidity of aspects generally polarized, see Ann Grodzins Gold, "Cow Worship, Goat Talk" (paper presented at the American Anthropological Association Meeting, Denver, November 1984).

51. Having praised her *kuldevi*, one woman remarked, "She gives trouble to others, but she only does good for us [Sisodiyas]."

Hence the difference between *kul* goddess and family goddess cannot be easily formulated in terms of hostility and control.[52] No general contradiction is perceived between the role of warrior guardian and *pativrata* guardian. Rather, the relation between the goddess's two aspects remains fluid. The form of the goddess changes: on the battlefield she is the fierce virgin, and in the household she is the prototypical *pativrata*. Nevertheless, the nature of her protective purpose does not change. She is a *kul* guardian who also protects the family. Her modes of protection may clash in actual situations, for the interests of the *kul* and family are not always synonymous. This fact does not, however, alter the ideal conceptualization of her protective roles as complementary.

To recapitulate, the *kuldevi* as *kul* guardian is for women the basis of the *kuldevi* mythology they know and the potential source of inspiration in the unlikely event that they should ever have to participate in warfare. This means that the *kuldevi* as warrior goddess constitutes a relatively diminished presence in the religious lives of most women. On a regular basis Rajput women worship the *kuldevi* as a *pativrata* and hope through their worship to perfect their roles as *pativratas*. The consciousness of the *kuldevi* as a domestic being is not, however, a correspondingly diminished presence in the minds of Rajput men. At times it seems to overwhelm the conception of the *kuldevi* as a warrior goddess.

This is the case with Jamvai Mata, who appears on the battlefield not as a wild belligerent animal but as a cow, a domestic animal and India's ultimate symbol of motherhood. Shortly we will see that this reversal tends to undermine her status. Here it provides the sharpest image of the transfer of the maternal conception of the goddess to the male domain. Other examples are not wanting.

One involves a goddess not always explicitly identified as Ban Mata but who appears to Bappa Rawal, the illustrious forefather of the Sisodiyas, in order to instruct him in the use of weapons. In so doing she performs what is assuredly a *kuldevi* function. Mounted on a lion at a site consecrated to Shiv, she is clearly homologous with the Sanskritic warrior Goddess (see fig. 16). She appears to Bappa Rawal during the final stage of a tripartite scenario in which he learns of his destiny. The first stage is defined by an episode in which Bappa discovers that one of

52. My persistent questions on the malevolence of *kuldevis* seemed to provoke only disagreement or ridicule. The goddess's violence does, of course, provide cause for ample pyschoanalytic interpretation, but here I am attending to the narrative level and conscious motivation, which analyses of goddess texts often treat lightly (presumably because abundant exegetical commentary is unavailable). Such analyses often assume a radical conceptual polarization of the goddess's characteristics.

the cows he is tending is not producing milk and determines to resolve this mystery. He follows her as she wanders off across some fields, then discovers her discharging all her milk on a stone *ling* (literally the "mark" or "sign" of Shiv—an erect phallus) hidden by some grass in the midst of a grove.[53] Here the cow suggests Bappa's destiny, for Bappa will become the first among devotees to Ekling Ji (One *Ling*), a form of Shiv, as well as the ruler of Mewar (fig. 17).[54]

During the second stage Bappa receives instruction from the sage Harit, who has been performing *tapasya* (ascetic penances) at this spot to venerate Shiv. Harit initiates Bappa into the mysteries of devotion to Shiv and, before departing for heaven in his chariot, informs Bappa that Shiv intends him to be the founder of a ruling dynasty. Finally, during the third stage Mata Ji appears in order to give Bappa practical advice along with some of the weapons he will need to establish his kingdom.

This story relating the three stages of Bappa Rawal's supernatural instruction directly corresponds to the three stages of learning that any male child undergoes. In the beginning Bappa's guide is a cow, a maternal figure. She directs him to the point where he is ready to undergo religious education. At this time, he leaves his "mother" to receive instruction from a guru. This period effectively constitutes his *upanayan*, his initiatory rebirth, which the male who is his spiritual teacher must supervise and during which Bappa Rawal progresses from boy to man and from cowherd to king. In the third stage the Rajput, now aware of his caste duty and destiny, accepts his relationship with his protectress.

This scenario also clearly demonstrates a transformation of the strictly maternal into a predominantly military type of female guardianship. The cow represents Bappa's mother, who is not included directly in this mythical journey to Bappa's destiny.[55] The guru is a spiritual father figure.[56] It is during the initiatory period spent with Harit that the transformation of guardianship from maternal to martial occurs. After a spiritual introduction to manhood and cultus, Bappa takes on this new

53. The *ling* form of Shiv represents the coincidence of Shiv's antithetical traits, asceticism and eroticism. His phallus is erect because he is an ascetic (he stores his semen rather than spilling it) and because, associated with fertility, he is also a woman-chaser. On Shiv as celibate and seducer, see O'Flaherty, *Śiva*.

54. Because Bappa is the first among devotees, each of his ruling descendants has borne the title of *divan* (chief minister) of the Ekling Ji temple. These descendants have had an important ritual role in the life of the temple.

55. On the cow as a conventional mother substitute in Indian stories, see Shulman, *Tamil Temple Myths*; O'Flaherty, *Women, Androgynes*.

56. See Robert Goldman, "Fathers, Sons, and Gurus," *Journal of Indian Philosophy* 6 (1978): 325–92; and Carstairs, *Twice-Born*, 71–72.

relationship with the feminine, which is essential to the performance of caste duty. His prior relationship with the maternal, be it mother or cow, does not disappear. It becomes imposed on the relationship with the goddess who will from then on be his primary guide, his *kul* guardian.

Another example is that of Ad Mata, who, we recall, rescues three little princes from a charging elephant. She extends her arms, which are at once symbols of military might and maternal affection. The boys (it is significant that they are boys, not men) are delivered from danger into the loving embrace of their aunt. That she is an aunt is also important as it underscores the ambiguity of her nature. She is a maternal figure—she is a beautiful woman and she performs a maternal act of protection by clutching the two boys to her breast. In addition, she is a warrior *kuldevi*—she is unmarried and she rescues the royal heir from certain death. Her maternal embrace represents her acceptance of the royal heirs as protégés in the *kul*.

Rather than cite further instances of the insinuation of maternal into warrior imagery, it seems more productive to investigate the important characteristics of insinuation shared by all *kuldevis*. First, all *kuldevis*, like all goddesses, are called Mata Ji (mother). The importance of this epithet can be overstressed; the Mata Ji epithet is doubtless conventional. But no epithet of the Goddess can simply be dismissed.[57] The name (used perhaps more than any other to refer to the Goddess or to a *kuldevi*) underscores the point that all warrior goddesses, unmarried though they be, are potential wives and mothers and brings to light the assumption that all goddesses, married or not, are mothers to their protégés.[58] The *kuldevi* is perceived as a loving mother to all *kul* members, whose personal health she nourishes in the household and whose social welfare she supports on the battlefield.

Second, *kul* members inevitably understand their *kuldevis* as belonging to a group of seven goddesses. They conceive each *kuldevi* as the central figure in the heptad.[59] The identity of the other goddesses changes from *kul* to *kul*, but the convention of a group of seven remains constant. The idea of a goddess heptad is by no means a Rajasthani convention. The notion of seven related goddesses is found in myriad

57. Coburn, *Devī Māhātmya*, 75–78.
58. Thus, in the *Teviparakkiramam* 9 (quoted in Shulman, *Tamil Temple Myths*, 310), Shakti (the Goddess) is Bhavani (the great genetrix) and also Durga (the female warrior).
59. This centrality is also demonstrated in one family's *kuldevi* image, which, family members say, is made of seven metals.

16. The warrior goddess Durga slays Mahish, the buffalo demon (image from an icon shop near the Ekling Ji temple).

17. Ekling Ji, Mewari incarnation of Shiv (devotional image from an icon shop by the gates of the Ekling Ji temple).

Indian traditions, both Sanskritic and regional.[60] In fact in Rajasthan as elsewhere the seven local goddesses are often equated with the Sapta-matrikas, the "Seven Mothers" who are found in Sanskritic tradition from Vedic through Puranic times.[61] Sculpted images of the Saptamatri-kas are found throughout Rajasthan.[62] As in Sanskritic literature, many of these goddesses are portrayed as *shaktis* (consorts, embodiments of female force) of various pan-Indian deities. They are joined by a male figure, one of various Shaiva deities.[63]

In Mewar, many married Rajput women wear gold pendants en-graved with the seven *kuldevi-matrikas*, who are rendered as small stick figures accompanied by their even smaller companion Bheru Ji, the Shaiva guardian figure associated with the Goddess in local mythology (figs. 18, 19).[64] Whereas the sculptures in most cases make clear icono-graphic associations between the goddesses and the gods for whom they are *shaktis*, the stick figures are devoid of iconographic detail and ap-pear to be autonomous.[65] These associations facilitate the assigning of various identities to the goddesses. Thus when listing the seven mothers, a woman typically includes the name of her *kuldevi* and other *kuldevi*s with whom she is familiar but then fills out her list with epithets of the Sanskritic Goddess. These are not the names found in traditional San-skritic lists of the Saptamatrikas. The Sanskritic lists name such god-desses as Aindri, Brahmani, and Vaishnavi (whose names reveal their husbands' identities); Rajput women invoke such random epithets as Kali, Kalika, Camunda, and Candi, who are all ultimately and often vaguely associated with Shiv but who are also independent of him in

60. A good example of a regional heptad is mentioned by Meyer, who says Ankalam-man and Mariyamman are often thought to be two of seven goddesses, the other five of which are identified variously by different informants (*Aṅkāḷaparmēcuvari*, 52; also Shul-man, *Tamil Temple Myths*, 153).

61. Coburn, *Devī Māhātmya*, 313–30; Kinsley, *Hindu Goddesses*, 151–60; and Mi-chael Meister, "Regional Variations in Mātṛkā Conventions," *Artibus Asia* 47, nos. 3–4 (1986): 233–46.

62. Examples are the Saptamatrika sculptures in Mandor (near the railway station) and in the Jhalawar Museum; the Varahi from Kejda in the Udaipur Museum; and the Maheshwari from Mandarra in the Mt. Abu Museum (personal communication to author from Cynthia Packart; see Cynthia Packart Stangroom, "The Development of the Medi-eval Style in Rajasthan" [Ph.D. diss., Harvard University, 1988]). For detailed analysis of Saptamatrika sculpture see Meister, "Regional Variations."

63. For sculptural variations on the identity of this male figure, see Meister, "Regional Variations."

64. Women wear these along with a tiny pendant of Chink Mata (Sneeze Mother), who nullifies the inauspicious effects of sneezes.

65. The sculpted Aindri has an elephant, Varahi has a boar's face, etc.

18. *Pala* (*putli*): embossed pendant with images of the seven *kuldevi*s and Bheru Ji.

action and have full-fledged mythical personalities and cult followings of their own.[66] Thus the Rajput *kuldevi*s included in such a list clearly have Shaiva associations (through the names that fill out the list and the presence of Bheru) but in local mythology are not really represented as married to Shiv.[67]

Rajput women think of their *kuldevi-matrika*s as largely independent of male association on the battlefield. Yet within the household context the *kuldevi*s are clearly understood as domestic. Worshiped by women as *pativrata*s, they nurture the family in various ways, not least by pro-

66. Camunda appears with the other goddesses more closely tied to their consorts in post-Gupta sculpture, which Meister takes to be an index of Shaiva dominance. Eventually Saptamatrika tradition breaks from Shaiva dominance (Meister, "Regional Variations," 240–43).

67. Logically and formally, the *kuldevi* is married to Shiv when she is homologized to his Sanskritic companion, but Rajput women do not expressly draw this conclusion.

19. Local wall painting of Devi attended by light and dark Bheru Jis.

moting female fertility.[68] *Kuldevi*s facilitate the production of sons who will continue the lineage.[69]

Although the *kuldevi*'s function as a promoter of female fertility is a crucial one, I have delayed its treatment until now for two reasons. In the first place, I consider it particularly appropriate to a summary discussion of the complementarity between *kuldevi* aspects. In promoting fertility, the *kuldevi* protects both the family and the *kul* to which it belongs. By their birth, sons extend the *kul*; as soldiers they protect it. In the second, I think the association of *kuldevi* with fertility should not receive undue emphasis. Certainly, the *kuldevi* helps women to conceive sons, who will expand the family and hence strengthen the *kul*. But she should not be reduced and squeezed under the rubric of "fertility god-

68. The dual nature of these *kuldevi*s compares to the dual nature of Shiv as an erotic ascetic (O'Flaherty, *Śiva*). Shulman discusses the virgin and married characteristics of goddesses in a Tamil heptad (*Tamil Temple Myths*, 153).

69. Sanskritic Saptamatrika tradition also identifies the *kuldevi*s as independent warriors and as mothers. Even where the Matrikas bear their consorts' names, they fight independently on the battlefield; in the *Devimahatmya*, male wrath produces the goddesses, who are thus aspects of their partners but fight alone against marauding demons (Coburn, *Devī Māhātmya*, 314–16). Some mythic traditions associate these goddesses with the Krittikas, the mothers of Skanda (ibid., 317 ff.; Meister, "Regional Variations," 242 ff.). My informants never referred to the Krittikas (Pleiades), but note that the martial-maternal role fusion revealed in *kuldevi* veneration is exhibited also in Matrika-Krittika mythic tradition.

dess." In the *kuldevi* stories, the goddess's promotion of fertility appears less as a primary, and more as a support, function. It goes almost without saying that in protecting the family and *kul* a *kuldevi* must ensure offspring, upon whom the survival of both depends. Thus in many households women wishing to have children worship their female ancestors' *kuldevi* pendants, which are kept in a special basket in the *zanana* shrine.

A good illustration of the *kuldevi*'s role in fostering fertility is provided by the following story:

> My grandmother was a great devotee of Camunda. When she had just given birth and was in a state of impurity, Devi [Kuldevi] appeared to her. Devi was wearing orange and was accompanied by a man in a white dhoti. People say this man was Bheru Ji, though others say maybe it was Shiv. If it was Bheru, then it was Gora Bheru Ji [Bheru in his light, benign aspect]. In this vision Devi gave my grandmother seven gold *madaliyau*s [upper-arm bracelets consisting of linked rings] and promised her that the family would prosper for seven generations. Before leaving, Devi told her not to reveal this to anyone.
>
> The next morning my grandmother thought that this had all been a dream, but later she found the *madaliyau*s under her pillow. Then my grandmother's elder sister-in-law arrived at the doorstep. While she stood at the threshold [not coming inside because of the ritual impurity associated with birth], my grandmother told her what had happened despite Mata Ji's warning. Her *bhabhi sa* (elder sister-in-law) then said, "You are mistaken. I gave these to you last night. Now you must give them back." You see, she wanted the *madaliyau*s for herself.
>
> The next night my grandmother had the same vision, but this time Mata Ji said, "I'll give you one more chance. I'll give you only three *madaliyau*s and this time just silver ones, not gold ones. Because of this the family will not be as prosperous as it would have been and the duration of the boon will be only three generations." This time my grandmother kept the secret of the *madaliyau*s and after that did regular *puja* to Mata Ji.

In this story told by a distinguished Mewari *thakurani*, the *kuldevi*'s domestic associations are unmistakable. The goddess arrives on the occasion of childbirth. Moreover, the token of good fortune she delivers is the bracelets worn by married women in that family. Finally, the boon that she gives is prosperity for the family line: for seven, then three, generations the family will succeed. Generations mean progeny, the sine qua non of prosperity.

Hence the *kuldevi* protects and increases the blood of warriors on the battlefield, as symbolized for example by Jamvai Mata's mass revival of fallen soldiers. She also protects and increases the blood of the families constituting the *kul* both by rescuing individual men, as in the case of the nobleman wounded in the war, and, more commonly but less dramatically, by promoting fertility upon which family and *kul* depend. Men and women alike worship her as the *kul* military goddess, but women give primary importance to her *pativrata* aspect. And so the dominating aspect of the *kuldevi*'s character correlates with caste duty in the case of men and with gender norms in the case of women. Nevertheless, the male and female orientations toward the *kuldevi* are in the first instance complementary. Ideally, *kul* protection and family protection are compatible, just as in principle *kul* and family are mutually reinforcing social units.

KULDEVI VENERATION: *MARDANA* AND *ZANANA*

Because the *kuldevi*'s aspects ordinarily relate as complements it is possible to delineate their separate devotional contexts: *mardana* and *zanana*. Although the specifics of *kuldevi* worship vary from household to household, it is striking how *kuldevi* veneration within each household differs in its two contexts. Despite the recent deterioration of physical *mardana-zanana* segregation, the principle of segregation continues to have a significant impact on the interpretation and performance of *kuldevi* tradition.

For example, in many of the *thikana*s I visited the *kuldevi* temple is located either inside the *mardana* or completely outside the household. Both the *mardana* and the outdoors were, and in some cases still are, out-of-bounds to women. Past practice varied as to whether women were allowed to visit these temples under circumstances assuring their modesty. In one *thikana* where *parda* still remains in effect the *kuldevi* temple, which is located in the *mardana*, has a back entrance. Women use this entrance at times appointed for their worship. Clearly, however, this temple and other temples similarly situated have been chiefly identified with and attended to by male family members and Brahman officiants. Today many women still do not know much about what goes on in exterior temples. One woman told me that she had never even visited the main *kuldevi* temple of the *thikana* into which she was married. It is located just outside the main entrance to the household. Another said that she had been inside her in-laws' main temple once, when she gave *dhok* before entering her new home as a bride; she did not know much about the temple because while visiting it she observed *ghunghat* (she covered her face) and could see almost nothing at all. Since then *parda* has prevented her from returning.

At least partly because of the location of *kuldevi* temples within male quarters or outside the home, women's worship of the *kuldevi* has evolved along its own lines. Physical segregation has emphasized the distinctions between the roles that *kuldevis* have in the lives of men and women. Even where *kuldevi* temples were found in the *zanana* (my preliminary evidence suggests that this was fairly rare) or where temples were found in both *zanana* and *mardana* (also atypical as a *kuldevi* is generally understood to have one central presence within a *thikana* or a state), distinct liturgical traditions would have tended to evolve. In the former instance, the times for men's and women's worship would be different. This temporal separation would reinforce the thematic or role-related segregation in the same way as the location-related segregation would.

Furthermore, men's worship of the *kuldevi* would inevitably be understood in terms of state: ritual would emphasize the unique relationship between the king or *thakur* and the *kuldevi*. Women's worship, however, would stress not the relationship of women as queens with *kuldevis* but that of women as wives with *kuldevis*. The domestic motifs that interested *pativratas* would predominate.

Where two temples have existed, one temple—most probably the *zanana* temple—would have been derivative of and subordinate to the other. The elaborate Brahmanical ritual (*puja*) would have been performed in the dominant temple, which held the household's finest icons and received the household's richest offerings. Thus worship in the two temples would have differed qualitatively as well as thematically.

Now as in the past, in most *zananas* what is to be found in women's quarters is not properly speaking a temple (*mandir*) at all but a crudely designated "place," *thapana* (Hindi: *sthapana*), where the goddess has been located. This place may simply be an area of a courtyard wall. Or it may be a spot in a room specially set aside for this purpose. A goddess's place is designated by drawing a trident (*trishul*) in vermilion (*sindur*) and perhaps decorating it with strips of shiny colored foil called *malipanau*. Worship is simple, ranging from the occasional giving of respect (*dhok*) to daily or special *pujas*. A Brahman priest or priestess may perform the rituals, help perform the rituals, or have nothing at all to do with a particular *thapana*.

The difference between the relatively formal worship of the *kuldevi* in the *mardana* and informal worship of the *kuldevi* in the *zanana* is seen most vividly during the celebration of Navratri. Although celebrations of Navratri in *kuldevi* temples are no longer the grand affairs they were until quite recently, where the traditional rituals are performed even in attenuated fashion, they are performed in *kuldevi* temples by men. The buffalo sacrifice is directed by a Brahman officiant and performed by a male Rajput family member. In days past, the killing of a buffalo or goat (a buffalo substitute) with one slash of the sword was incorporated into the ceremony as a ritual test of young warriors' mettle. It was considered an initiation into manhood.

Women have had no direct role in the blood sacrifice.[70] Rather, they have participated in the Navratri observance by fasting. For the nine days of the festival some women abstain from consuming wine and meat because these are sacred to the *kuldevi*. Others eat one meal a day but make a point of consuming wine and meat for the exact same reason. The most zealous maintain a complete fast throughout.

Because the purpose of the Navratri *vrat* (vow to fast) performed by women is to preserve their husbands' welfare, its focus is predominantly domestic. Nevertheless, a few men fast along with their wives; presumably their motives are linked to the aspirations of Rajput men. Although nowadays these motives may relate to earning a living unrelated to warfare, their expression through this traditional martial means may well reflect a man's concern to conduct his affairs in a way commensurate with Rajput dignity, privilege, and, above all, duty. If so, his *vrat*, performed on the quintessentially Rajput festival, is tied thematically to the formal ritual and blood sacrifice performed at the temple, activities in which he, unlike his wife, participates directly.[71]

One nobleman whose family I came to know well during my stay spoke of Navratri and the fast he observed during it as a revification of the past. He credited his ritual observances with linking him to his ruling forefathers who had upheld Navratri and other Rajput traditions. Clearly, his participation was permeated with nostalgia about the vanished past in which Rajputs were kings and warriors and was geared toward preserving that martial legacy. The protection sought by men and women appears to remain oriented toward, though not encompassed by, concerns of caste duty on the one hand and gender norms on the other.

In general, during Navratri and at other times, the conceptualization of women as family-protectors has resulted in a reliance on women to organize and supervise household rituals, even those in which they do

70. Traditional households performed the *balidan* in the *kuldevi* temple compound—typically outside the women's quarters and often out of view from *zanana* windows.
71. This analysis comes from a Rajput nobleman from a large Mewar *thikana*; he keeps a Navratri *vrat*.

not participate directly. While women engage in types of veneration in various ways distinct from those of men, responsibility for the proper performance of ritual cuts across this distinction. This fact is nowhere so evident as in the appearances by *kuldevi*s in the dreams of women to motivate them to rectify all sorts of ritual mistakes.[72] As one woman commented, "It's a good thing when Kuldevi comes in our dreams. She comes when she is happy with us but she also comes when there is a mistake in the *puja*. Then she gives us trouble (*taqlif*) until the mistake is cleared up." Even where the *kuldevi* gives trouble in conjunction with a dream warning and the one who suffers directly is a husband—indeed, he may well be the ritual offender—the problem is considered to belong to the woman in whose dream the *kuldevi* appears. It is her responsibility to right the situation that offends the *kuldevi*.

In sum, the separation of women's quarters from men's quarters has allowed distinctively domestic religious traditions to develop. The impact of these traditions has not, however, remained in seclusion along with the women who have promulgated and practiced them. Wives have been responsible for the fortunes of the *mardana*, as *kuldevi* dreams and visitations clearly illustrate. This responsibility has accorded women an authority in religious matters that extends past *parda*. As will soon become more vividly apparent, the responsibility of *pativrata*s to protect men has made women's worship of *kuldevi*s a source of influence over the religious life of men.

I have delineated a theoretical complementarity between the *mardana*-linked conception of the *kuldevi* as *kul* protector and the *zanana*-linked conception of the *kuldevi* as family protector. Symbolically, the *kuldevi* brings together these functions, which may be opposed logically.[73] In certain contexts, however, a *kuldevi* represents not unity but conflict.[74] During times of adjustment and change, the *kuldevi* may symbolize not the coalescence but the disharmony of the duties she performs. This is indeed the case when women devotees experience disso-

72. I did not formally interview men about *kuldevi* dreams but did meet many husbands, brothers, and sons of noble and royal women; a good number listened in on part of the interviews. Only once did I hear of a *kuldevi* appearing in a man's dreams, but even in that case the man was unsure whether he saw his *kuldevi* or another superhuman being. No dream or vision stories told by women involve men's dreams. It seems that like fasts and other domestic rituals, dreams and visions are phenomena primarily associated with women, perhaps increasingly so because men have been involved in fewer public religious performances since 1947.

73. See O'Flaherty's discussion of Shiv as the "erotic ascetic" in *Śiva*.

74. On symbol and conflict see Suzanne Hanchett, "Ritual Symbols—Unifying or Divisive," in *Religion in Modern India*, ed. Giri Raj Gupta (Delhi: Vikas, 1983), 134.

nance with regard to their own competing norms of caste and family protection.

The next chapter focuses on dissonance in order to address the intentional or motivational dimension of *kuldevi* veneration and discern presuppositions about the caste-linked and gender-derived aspects of religious socialization. Moreover, it argues that examining the role of personal choice in religious socialization reveals the substantial impact the *zanana* has had in shaping and revising the *kuldevi* traditions of both families and *kuls*.

CHAPTER 3

Kuldevi Tradition

Interpretation and Intention

A Rajput wedding is a grand affair. Out on a lawn and under a colorful tent men enjoy one another's company while sampling liquors and traditional spicy edibles. Most sport elegant turbans and long dark high-collared coats with light-colored breeches. Elsewhere, in the household apartments or perhaps in a courtyard, women also enjoy themselves. Wearing their finest Rajasthani dress, satin or chiffon heavily embroidered with gold threads, and their heirloom jewelry studded with gems and seed pearls, they exchange stories and repeatedly compliment their hostess. In time word passes from the men's celebration to the women's that the groom's procession has arrived. The women rush to a balcony or roof to see the groom; riding high atop a much decorated elephant he approaches with his entourage of male relatives.[1] If the sun has set, the procession is guided by kerosene lamps, which enhance the drama of the spectacle. Everyone seems happy and even thrilled—everyone but the bride.

During the first Rajput wedding I attended I was invited back into a bedroom to meet the bride, who was not participating in the festivities taking place in the outer parlor. When I entered the bedroom I found her quietly weeping amid several young friends and relatives, who alternated between sharing her grief and trying to cheer her up. I was surprised and said so. In my country, I explained, brides and their brides-

---

1. As with many high-caste communities, Rajputs include no women in the groom's procession; his female relatives are expected to stay home.

maids spend the minutes before the wedding ceremonies giggling, preening, and teasing. My audience was incredulous. One asked, "You mean in the States girls aren't sad to leave their families?"

For Rajput girls, getting married not only means leaving the family; it also means leaving the familiar. In most cases both the people and the ways of the conjugal family are unknown. Thus a bride faces learning to love and respect a groom whom she has never met (her parents having chosen him for her) and, in so doing, learning to accept his familial customs, traditions, and gods. To a bride on her wedding day, this may be overwhelming.

Sad to leave her family, the bride is of course excited about the step she is taking. This is the biggest day of her life, the day she accepts the role of *pativrata*. Thus, while brides may be teary-eyed or withdrawn, in most cases they are not wholly negative about the idea of marriage; usually one can catch on their faces the occasional hint of a smile.[2] The night before they danced with their girlfriends to Rajasthani folk music and cheerfully, if anxiously, discussed the next day's events. On the whole, brides are not simply miserable; they are ambivalent.[3]

The dissonance a bride feels during her marriage ceremony is just the beginning. As the bride adjusts, she finds herself facing new conflicts, conflicts inherent in her role as Rajput *pativrata*. One place this is particularly apparent is in the bride's assumption of devotional responsibility for her conjugal family's *kuldevi*.

KULDEVIS AND DISSONANCE

Because when a woman marries she loses membership in her father's *kul* and becomes a member of her husband's *kul*, she is expected to worship the *kuldevi* who protects its members. Thus, the very first thing a bride must do when she enters her husband's household is to give respect (*dhok*) to her new *kuldevi*.[4] This is a caste norm; every Rajput must loyally propitiate the *kuldevi* who has accompanied the family's *kul* into battle.

2. No doubt women who are mature at the time of their marriage are less sad and frightened by the prospect of marriage than younger girls. Because members of the nobility now consider a college education desirable for daughters, girls' marriage age is now fairly high (late teens, early twenties). It is not so for village girls, who marry at an earlier age. Throughout India girls' age at marriage has gradually been rising (Doranne Jacobson and Susan Snow Wadley, *Women in India: Two Perspectives* [Delhi: Manohar, 1977], 43).

3. For an account of this ambivalence among Bengali brides, see Manisha Roy, *Bengali Women* (Chicago: University of Chicago Press, 1975), 83–86.

4. Cf. Bennett's discussion of Nepali women's veneration of lineage deities in *Dangerous Wives*, 133.

Tension arises when a bride feels she cannot immediately, or sometimes even eventually, abandon her loyalty to the *kuldevi* associated with her parents' *kul*.[5] Having worshiped the *kuldevi* of her natal family throughout childhood, she may well find it hard to trade devotion to a beloved deity with proven powers for devotion to an unknown deity with unproven powers.[6] She may continue to venerate her natal family's goddess and perhaps feel entirely justified in doing so. She understands that the natal *kuldevi* will protect her in her new home by helping her to do her duty as a wife, which means protecting the welfare of her husband. Here arises a disjunction between the wife's Rajput caste-derived norm of worshiping the conjugal *kuldevi* and her gender-associated duty of protecting her husband to the best of her abilities.

The retention of primary loyalty to the old *kuldevi* is a potential source of friction between the bride and her husband's family. The reason is easily surmised. Like members of other Hindu castes, Rajputs generally live in extended families. More than members of other castes, Rajputs take brides from distant locations.[7] The explanation they usually offer is that this practice is a holdover from the times when Rajputs sought to make political alliances with many different states through the marriages of their daughters.[8]

Thus in a Rajput home with five sons there could well be five daughters-in-law hailing from diverse and distant locations. Each bride might be tempted to retain loyalty to her natal family's *kuldevi*. Under these circumstances it is difficult to see how the conjugal family's *kuldevi* could long continue to reflect *kul* unity and inspire solidarity. If daughters-in-law, the primary socializers of children, retain their old allegiances, the family's *kuldevi* tradition will disintegrate.

It is therefore far from surprising that mothers-in-law have pressed their daughters-in-law to express foremost loyalty to the conjugal

5. On the similar attachment between Himalayan village daughters-in-law (of various caste backgrounds) and their natal goddesses, see Sax, *Mountain Goddess* (Oxford University Press, forthcoming), 95–103.

6. A few women said that in their natal families daughters did not witness *kuldevi* formal ritual worship but could view the *kuldevi* image when ritual was not being performed. In general families allow daughters to participate in household ritual, including *kuldevi* worship. In many families before her marriage the daughter must first visit her natal *kuldevi* to pay respect (*dhok*) and seek her blessing for the marriage.

7. This practice is as true of villagers as of the nobility; see Janice S. Hyde, "Women's Village Networks" (paper presented at the Conference on Preservation of the Environment and Culture in Rajasthan, Rajasthan University, Jaipur, India, December 1987).

8. The other standard reasons Rajputs give is that distance (1) ensures an absence of previous contact and avoids suspicions of a so-called love marriage, non-arranged and therefore scandalous; (2) makes it difficult for brides to run home to mother if they are upset; and (3) brings in outside blood to invigorate a family's bloodline.

family's *kuldevi*. As many women remarked, "A bride has no choice in the matter. She must worship her husband's *kuldevi*." One might speculate that responding to such pressure a daughter-in-law would seek to find some way of worshiping the *kuldevi* of her conjugal family, thus demonstrating loyalty to husband and caste, while continuing to worship the *kuldevi* of her natal family, thus demonstrating faith in the old *kuldevi*'s capacity to protect her and in so doing help her protect her husband and family.

As it turns out, women have indeed approached and reconciled their conjugal and natal *kul* goddesses, and they have done so in various ways. Viewing these options will throw light on the subtler motivational indications of the *kuldevi* myths and stories with which we have already become familiar.

The first solution was revealed to me by an older noblewoman known throughout Udaipur's Rajput community for her piety. During her interview and in several subsequent conversations, she explained that it is possible and legitimate to reconceive one's natal *kuldevi* as an *ishtadevta*, a deity of choice. In her household temple she not only worships her husband's *kuldevi* (Ban Mata), she worships her father's *kuldevi* (Naganecha Ji), whose image is also present. She said that her father's *kuldevi* had become her *ishtadevta* and that as an *ishtadevta* the goddess protects not the *kul* but the family.[9] Thus by reclassification the woman has taken her natal *kuldevi* out of direct competition with her conjugal *kuldevi*.[10]

I find it particularly significant that this woman, considered a very traditional and venerable older lady by the community, offers a division-of-labor compromise unapologetically. At the very least it illustrates the same flexibility of interpretation apparent in the solutions utilized by other women.[11] Here as elsewhere the functions that two *kuldevis* perform are no more theoretically antagonistic than when one *kuldevi* performs them. What is important is that whereas the conjugal *devi* has

9. The idea that women import deities, especially goddesses, to their in-laws' households exists in many parts of India; see Herrenschmidt, "Le sacrifice," 141; Vidal, "Le puits," 38; and Berreman, *Hindus of the Himalayas*, 97. In Hiltebeitel's *Cult of Draupadī* (264–65), the in-marrying bride is herself a goddess.

10. Asked to name their *ishtadevta*s in formal interviews, women did not list their natal *kuldevi*s. Yet when I asked those women whose household temples contained natal *kuldevi*s what status the *kuldevi*s had, they either claimed them as *ishtadevta*s (most people believe that one can have as many *ishtadevta*s as one wishes) or invoked one of the solutions listed below.

11. Because this woman's daughters married into her father's *kul*, her *ishtadevta* became their *kuldevi*, which made their transition particularly easy.

two potentially conflicting loyalties, *kul* and family, the natal *devi*, brought in as a household goddess, has only one loyalty: the family, whose preservation is the foremost concern of her *pativrata* devotee. The *kul*, as I have said, is to a wife largely an abstraction, its operation being for the most part peripheral to her household-delimited life. She relegates the unknown conjugal *kuldevi* to the unfamiliar domain of *kul*, while the known *kuldevi* settles into the home that has replaced the natal household.

A second way women rationalize their retention of allegiance to the natal *kuldevi* is to identify both *kuldevis* with the Sanskritic Goddess (Devi, Shakti, Durga), of whom all other goddesses, they say, are forms or emanations. Just as all official *kuldevis* are homologized to the great Goddess on Navratri, the competing *kuldevis* are now both homologized to the Goddess, so that the tension between them is reduced. In interviews women frequently spoke of both goddesses as Shakti or Devi (Sanskritic names) and, if pressed about this, pointed out that ultimately the new *kuldevi* is the old *kuldevi*. Aptly summarizing this shared understanding, one noblewoman said that "all Rajputs worship Devi" and another that *kuldevi* forms differ, but their essence is one (*kai rup hoti haim; sacmuc ek hi haim*).[12]

Thus a woman may call the new *devi* "kuldevi" but identify her with the old *kuldevi*, whose function in the new *kul* is family protection. This accommodation is facilitated by the fact that women typically worship the *kuldevi* in the form of her symbol, the *trishul* (trident). Because of this, they need little or no visual accommodation. Very few women have pictures of anthropomorphic *kuldevi* icons to ornament the goddess's *zanana* shrine. Such lithographs of *devis* as are commonly available for popular goddesses (such as that in fig. 16 or even those of local goddesses) in the bazaar are not, or perhaps not yet, commonly available for most *kuldevis*. Even in cases where they are available, the focus of veneration remains the *trishul*, the prominent representation of the goddess in most *thapanas* or household temples.[13] Hence, the Sanskritic transference remains particularly easy.

In short, the identification of both goddesses with the Sanskritic Goddess allows the identities of the two goddesses to merge one into the other; both may be subsumed within the identity of the Goddess, or one may subsume the identity of the other. Because the imagery of the fa-

12. Hindu tradition often identifies local deities with one great deity; see examples in Beck (*Three Twins*, 27) and Bennett (*Dangerous Wives*, 48).
13. I have seen only two lithographs in use, one in each of two households.

miliar tends to dominate the imagery of the unfamiliar, it is likely that
in the short run the goddess homologized to Devi will be the old *kuldevi*
functioning primarily as a household deity, even where the goddess's
name remains that of the new *kuldevi*. In the long run, however, the
bride's participation in the rituals for the new *kuldevi* and her absorption of the mythology belonging to the new *kuldevi* will allow for a
gradual transformation.

A third situation is that in which the old *kuldevi* is retained as a *kuldevi* but given less observable status than the new *kuldevi* in terms of
image (generally *trishul*) location and ritual performance. When I visited
the family shrines and temples of women whom I interviewed, quite often I found a *kuldevi* image flanked by images of other *sakhi* (companion) images. Sometimes these were *kuldevi*s; sometimes they were other
local goddesses. In both cases the cohorts were worshiped but given less
attention than the main *kuldevi*.[14]

In some of the *kuldevi* temples one can find a basket containing gold
kuldevi pendants worn by now deceased members of the *zanana* (see fig.
18). As noted earlier, each pendant depicts a *kuldevi* in the company of
six other, identical, *kuldevi*s. Each *kul* gives its own *kuldevi* precedence
but recognizes the importance of subordinate sister goddesses. The six
sisters of the conjugal family's *kuldevi* take on aspects attributed them
by the women wearing their images as pendants. Because the images are
iconographically indistinguishable—all the *devi*s are identical stick figures while Bheru, their male escort, is a diminutive stick figure at the end
of the line—women can and usually do identify one of the companion
figures with her natal family's *kuldevi*, then identify as many of the others as they can as *kuldevi*s with whom they are familiar, their father's
kuldevi often being first among these. The *kuldevi* forms, like their functions, are, quite simply, substitutable.

In sum, women have much opportunity to accommodate their old
kuldevi tradition to the demands of the conjugal family.[15] Paradoxically, the flexibility that can soften the mandate that the new *kuldevi*
replace the old also contributes to gradual religious accommodation.
Eventually, modes of rebellion or even subconscious reconceptualiza-
tion transmute at least partially into avenues of acceptance. It makes

14. Many *kuldevi* temples contain only the *kuldevi* and attendant goddesses; others,
relatively multipurpose, also contain various *ishtadevta*s.
15. Margaret Trawick notes that the influence daughters-in-law tacitly wield instan-
tiates the creativity of various often unrecognized subalterns. Another example is the co-
vert power slave women exercise in raising their masters' children (personal communication to author).

sense that over time, as the new daughter-in-law becomes better integrated into the household and learns about the domestic history of its *kuldevi* (such as the time the *kuldevi* cured an ailing husband or saved the family from financial ruin) she will become increasingly able to attribute to the new *kuldevi* a complete character. The conjugal *kuldevi* comes to protect not only the *kul* but also family, the bride's consuming concern. The family rituals in which the bride participates gradually take on more meaning, and hence inspire her faith, at the same time that her faith in the old *kuldevi*, who is now removed from the context of her family ritual, is weakening.

Up to this point I have not mentioned the woman who consciously tries to suppress any desire to worship her paternal *kuldevi* and other natal family gods. This omission may seem strange in view of the fact that most women vehemently express their desire to fulfill the expectations of their husbands' households (*sasurals*), but even those women who wholeheartedly commit themselves to accommodation must go through a time of adjustment. It is inconceivable that their resocialization can be instantaneous. Some women speak openly of the difficulty they had adapting to their new family traditions. At the very least, every woman brings into her marriage preconceptions that affect the way she understands and worships her conjugal family's gods. Without consciously attempting to alter interpretation of the traditions she will do so; she imports ways of seeing, understanding, and contextualizing from her experience in her natal family. Only time and experience can bring her interpretation more or less in line with the traditions shared by the family as a part of the *kul*.

The question remains whether all importation ultimately fades into accommodation. Clearly not. There are many conditions under which young wives' resistance frustrates their accommodation to an appreciable extent. For example, if there are several daughters-in-law in a family, the bulk of the responsibility for carrying out religious observances tends to fall disproportionately on the shoulders of the senior daughters-in-law. The younger ones, busy with caring for the youngest children in the extended family and perhaps engaged in performing chores less desirable (heavier and more time-consuming) than those performed by senior daughters-in-law, are farther from the context of religious tradition and at greater liberty to improvise. Mothers-in-law often complained to me that although their older daughters-in-law have followed the traditions, the younger ones are just not interested in learning. They sometimes attribute this to the changing times, in which the young are less interested in learning the proper ways of doing things than they used to be. The same lament, however, is heard about women of very different ages, young brides and women with grown children. The younger daughters-in-law, it appears, have always had greater freedom of interpretation than have their elders, on whom the preservation of family tradition most depends.

Another common condition in which resistance persists is when a mother-in-law dies before or not long after the marriage of her eldest son. In this case the senior daughter(s)-in-law has no time to learn the traditions of worship by women of the family. This possibility was pointed out to me by a Mewari noblewoman who said that her mother-in-law died at a relatively young age. When her mother-in-law's health first began to fail, she found to her surprise that she suddenly felt a strong sense of responsibility for learning all the tradition she could while her teacher was still alive. She noted with regret that people she knew of in similar situations did not necessarily feel this responsibility or did not feel it before it was too late.

As my informant's comment suggests, even if a relatively young bride has the opportunity to learn the proper traditions from servants or daughters of the household, she does not always do so. Lacking incentives, a bride may retain many of the ideas she brought from her natal family. The segregation of religious ritual means that she will have latitude in performing female rituals. Whether she intends to deviate from the traditional patterns of her in-laws or not, she has more opportunity to incorporate her own interpretations than would otherwise be the case.

A third context in which variation is likely to occur is that of the small family unit. If an extended family happens to be small or has splintered into separate households, the possibilities for conscious resistance or unconscious deviation are great because there are few elderly women around to instruct and guide in the ways of devotion.[16]

The presence in a family of a daugher-in-law with unusual will power, charisma, or storytelling ability creates one more situation for variation. If she holds fast to the traditions of her natal family, she will disproportionately influence the religious ideas of other women in the family. The stories she tells may quickly merge with the religious lore of the family.[17]

16. This has been the case with small modern urban households.
17. When I was interviewing one woman, a more assertive woman in the same household often stepped in to give her version of a story. At times a woman being interviewed

Thus the extent to which a young bride accommodates over time depends on her character, disposition, and circumstances. I treated these conditions separately and sequentially. A typical family, however, contains several or even many daughters-in-law, perhaps representing two or more generations; each daughter-in-law influences the tradition even as she accommodates to it. This reciprocity dilutes the influence any individual wields on a household's tradition yet also shows that tradition does subtly evolve, even in a large family whose current daughters-in-law consciously lean toward accommodation.

At the same time, we need not assume that in-marrying women bring an infinite store of traditions. Families prefer to intermarry with certain *kul*s they feel have sufficient status and prestige. Therefore, the *kul*-related legends and the family-related ritual variations that arrive with daughters-in-law may be repeatedly reintroduced. Various daughters-in-law in a family may share a single *kul*; *kul*s may trade daughters back and forth over generations.[18] Such reinforcement surely increases the chances for the gradual and subtle incorporation of exotic traditions.

Moreover, the evolution of all *kuldevi* mythology, particularly family *kuldevi* mythology, is facilitated by the way women transmit myth. One woman hears a myth from a second woman and then later recalls the story line but not necessarily its identification with a particular *kuldevi*. Still later, when she recounts the myth to her children, grandchildren, sisters-in-law, or daughters-in-law, she may end up telling it in association with the conjugal *kuldevi*. In this way myths are continuously introduced from the outside. There is no other likely means to account for the striking similarity of family-related *kuldevi* narratives. Furthermore, this process affects *kul*-related mythology. It undoubtedly accounts for some changes within the mythic traditions of *kul* and state. To test this hypothesis, let us examine the evidence within the foundation myths.

---

deferred even when she had officially superior status to the relative interrupting her simply because that relative was better at storytelling, religious matters, etc.

18. For example, a standard marriage combination is Rathaur-Sisodiya. I charted 160 royal and noble marriages—eighty-eight married respondents and one unmarried respondent reported on their marriages (except in the case noted) and on their mothers' marriages (when they could remember their mothers' *kul*s). Roughly a quarter of the women interviewed claimed Sisodiya as their conjugal *kul* or their natal *kul* or their mothers' natal *kul*. Roughly a quarter claimed Rathaur as conjugal, natal, or maternal *kul*. A quarter of the Sisodiya women from these alliances had married Rathaurs and a quarter of the Rathaur women had married Sisodiyas. One-fourth (3) of the Sisodiya respondents married to Rathaurs said Rathaur was their maternal *kul*; one-fourth (3) of the Rathaur respondents married to Sisodiyas said Sisodiya was their maternal *kul*. The remainder (9) of these "repetition marriages" (15) included such patterns as Rathaur-Cauhan-Rathaur.

One of the most striking aspects of *kul*-related tales is their tendency to incorporate alternative themes—either in twin variants or within the same variant. We have already considered the first theme: the founding of a dynasty in association with the granting of victory by a *kuldevi* to a king and his *kul*. But the myths also speak of a *kuldevi* as coming to her new kingdom because she wishes to escort a bride marrying into the royal family.

Both themes occur in the story of the Sisodiya conquest of Girnar. Recall that the victorious Maharana weds a Gujarati princess who has fallen in love with him. The princess's *kuldevi* is Ban Mata. After the wedding, Ban Mata accompanies the princess to the Sisodiya capital. The myth gives Ban Mata's relationship with the princess as the reason for her decision to become the protector of Mewar. The bridal theme conveys the conflicting loyalties that a girl feels when leaving her home after marriage. The notion that the princess cannot bear to leave her protectress behind is conveyed by the *kuldevi*'s refusal to leave her. Having arranged for the victory of the Maharana in order to precipitate his marriage to the princess, the *kuldevi* has no intention of abandoning her. Hence Mewar receives a windfall profit: the guardianship of Ban Mata (see fig. 12).

This account comfortably accepts the idea that a *kuldevi* can come to a kingdom through marriage and even goes so far as to say that Ban Mata usurps the position of the former *kuldevi*, Kalika Mata, who is still actively worshiped as a Sisodiya guardian by visitors to Chitor.[19] In fact, located where it is, in the center of the group of monuments to which Chitor visitors flock, Kalika Mata's temple is much better attended than the small temple to Ban Mata, situated in the midst of the still inhabited part of Chitor where visitors rarely come.[20]

This bridal motif recurs throughout *kuldevi* mythology. Not every recurrence, however, includes the complete usurpation of a conjugal *kuldevi*'s position. As we saw in the discussion of brides' accommodation to the traditions of their *sasural*s, a *kuldevi* can fit into the *sasural*'s tradition without divesting the conjugal *kuldevi* of her title. There is the well-known story of a Marwari princess who marries the Maharana of

19. Because Kalika Mata is a Sanskritic goddess, many of the visitors who come to Chitor know and worship her. Her relationship with the Sisodiyas is affirmed by the framed lithographs of the hero Rana Pratap that grace her temple.

20. The Kalika temple has a full-time *pujari* (priest), but the Ban Mata temple, at least whenever I have visited it, is unattended except at morning and evening services. During my most recent visits, services were performed by a teenage boy, accompanied by many little neighborhood children playing drums and symbols.

Mewar. After the ceremonies have been completed and the princess is preparing to leave her parents' home, the Rathaur *kuldevi*, Naganecha Ji, hops into one of the baskets containing items for the dowry and remains hidden there until the long journey to Mewar is over. When the basket is unpacked, the stowaway *kuldevi* is discovered and dispatched back to Marwar. Later, however, Naganecha Ji again makes her way to Mewar and her beloved princess. Again she is sent home. Every time she travels back to Mewar she is discovered and returned. Eventually the *sasural* becomes resigned to her presence and begins to venerate her but continues to reserve its chief place of honor for Ban Mata.

This myth asks, may the *kuldevi* come along or must she stay home? Convention requires renunciation, but the princess and Naganecha Ji are inseparable. In the end, rebellion is defused and institutionalized. The *kuldevi* is relegated to an honorable but subordinate position. Today in the Ban Mata Temple of the Udaipur City Palace one can still see something of the mythic accommodation made.[21] Ban Mata retains her superiority. She is surrounded by an elaborate pantheon of attendant deities. The image of Naganecha Ji, however, is nowhere to be seen. When I inquired about Naganecha Ji in Ban Mata's temple, an elderly priest (*pujari*) explained to me that she is now kept in a closed chest (*tijori*). She is taken out for public viewing (*darshan*) only on designated holidays.[22] The priest said that she is to be venerated along with the great saints (*pirs*) who are connected with snakes and snakebite.[23] Because Naganecha Ji's animal form (*rup*) is a snake, she is venerated by some devotees as a goddess who can prevent and cure snakebite. Hence her services as a *kuldevi* have been specified and delimited; to the Sisodiyas she is not a full-fledged *kuldevi*, as she is to the Rathaurs. The worship of Naganecha Ji in Mewar has become calendrically contextualized and minimally important in the daily routine of temple ritual. It is possible that Naganecha Ji's stature has gradually diminished. In any case, the myth of Naganecha Ji suggests that her intrusion has been understood as significant and at least partially successful.[24]

21. This *kuldevi* temple is located within the *zanana*, which is unusual. The placement perhaps enhanced the household's readiness to accept the invading goddess since women often import their traditions.

22. Bhadva Sudi Satam and Magh Sudi Satam. On these days many women in North India keep *vrats* to protect family health and welfare (Mary McGee, personal communication to author). Rajput women mentioned neither date as a significant *vrat* in my survey, however. The nobility does not participate in these minor temple observances.

23. The *pujari* included in his list of *pirs* Teja Ji, Goga Ji, and Takha Ji.

24. When I read this account at a conference in Jaipur in 1987, a Sisodiya audience member denied that Naganecha Ji was sent back or that she is kept in a *tijori*. After the

To whatever extent the veneration of Naganecha Ji has infiltrated palace ritual, her myth demonstrates both the dissonance an in-marrying bride experiences and the challenge this dissonance may present to the ritual and mythic traditions of the husband's *sasural*. More important, it affirms the proposition that a bride's *kuldevi* may subtly or even drastically alter the devotional life of the *sasural*. The myth about Naganecha Ji and Ban Mata presents this alteration as partial; the myth about Ban Mata and Kalika Mata presents it as complete. These myths suggest specific historical changes in *kuldevi* tradition. But even if the myths do not show specific historical changes, they reflect a general consensus that although a *kuldevi* comes to a *kul* by presenting herself to the king at a time of crisis and then receives reverence from the families in the king's *kul*, a *kuldevi* may also come to the *kul* via the *zanana*, where she may partly or wholly supplant a preexisting *kuldevi*.

Standing in between the position of Ban Mata when she supplants Kalika Mata and that of Naganecha Ji when she joins Ban Mata as a clandestine attendant is Shila Mata, who could loosely be called the unofficial *kuldevi* of the Kachvahas of Jaipur. As we have seen, the official Kachvaha *kuldevi* is Jamvai Mata who first appears to the Kachvahas as a life-granting cow. Many of the Kachvaha women I interviewed, however, listed Shila Mata as their *kuldevi*.

The myth of Shila Mata, which is well known in Jaipur (much better known, even to the Kachvahas, than the myth of Jamvai Mata) is inscribed on a plaque outside her temple in the pre-Jaipur Kachvaha capital, Amber. The plaque gives two accounts of Shila Mata's appearance to the Kachvahas. The first is detailed; the second seems something of an afterthought.

The detailed account states that during the last quarter of the sixteenth century the great Man Sinh, Maharaja of the Kachvahas, unsuccessfully fought King Kedar in East Bengal. Frustrated, Man Sinh prayed to Kali, who granted him a vision, promised him victory, and exacted from him a promise that he would retrieve a stone image of her from the bottom of the sea. After his victory, Man Sinh fetched this image and

---

conference I questioned the chief *pujari* at the Ban Mata temple in Udaipur about the details of the story and viewed Naganecha Ji's image with him. He said that Naganecha Ji had always been welcome in the household—the Sisodiyas would not be inhospitable—but confirmed that she is kept in a *tijori*. His explanation was that the image is made of solid silver and kept hidden to preclude theft. I saw the image, a small one in a slightly larger box, but noted the presence of other expensive images displayed in the temple. The explanation I presented was reiterated by several prominent Sisodiya noblemen during that same return trip to Udaipur.

brought it back with him to Amber, where it became known as Shila Mata, the "Stone Goddess."

This account accords with the pattern described early in this chapter: a king is in trouble, a goddess appears to him in a vision, the king is victorious, and he adopts the goddess. The second account, however, conforms to the alternate pattern that has evolved: the *kuldevi* accompanies a young bride to her new home at the time of marriage and then wins acceptance there. This explanation of the arrival of Shila Mata holds that when King Kedar conceded defeat, he bestowed his daughter upon Man Sinh. At the marriage ceremonies he presented to Man Sinh the image of the goddess Jessoresvari, who came to be known as Shila Devi. Thus, like Ban Mata and Naganecha Ji, Shila Mata does not abandon her protection of the princess but rather establishes herself in the princess's *sasural*.

Shila Devi has been a formidable rival to Jamvai Mata. She has occupied an important place in the realms of state ritual and family worship. It would now be unlikely for her to usurp the status of Jamvai Mata. Modern records and communications being what they are, it is difficult to imagine a complete displacement of one *kuldevi* by another. Furthermore, because the institution of kingship has ended, it is doubtful that there could be an official (ceremonial or informal and gradual) *kuldevi* adoption that would be binding on a *kul* or *kul* subdivision. Nevertheless, in the minds of some individual Kachvaha women (whom other Kachvahas may think of as "misinformed"), Shila Mata has either taken over or encroached on the position of Jamvai Mata as *kuldevi* of the Kachvahas. In addition, the prominence of Shila Mata in the consciousness of both male Kachvahas and non-Rajput residents of Jaipur alike suggests that the general public believes she has appropriated a *kuldevi*-like status for herself, even though it technically or ultimately reserves for Jamvai Mata the appellation "kuldevi."

One reason that Shila Mata possesses such popularity is that she fits far better than Jamvai Mata the mold of *kul* goddess. Jamvai Mata, the myth goes, is a vegetarian teetotaler. One variant concludes that she is a Brahman—and this despite the fact that she was previously the *kuldevi* of a carnivorous tribe. Shila Mata, however, is a meat-eating, wine-drinking goddess like other Rajput *kuldevi*s. Consumption of meat and alcohol by Rajputs is traditionally justified (even though they have high-caste status) by the notion that both foods stimulate strength and passion, which are essential for battle. A goddess who abstains from, and even disapproves of, meat and wine is an odd war goddess indeed. Moreover, because Jamvai Mata abstains, Kachvahas give to Shila Mata the sacrificial (blood) offerings of Navratri. While they also celebrate the festival at Jamvai Mata's temple, they do so without the traditional offerings. Thus although both goddesses are homologized to the bellicose Durga, whose main text, the *Devimahatmya*, is read in almost all goddess temples on Navratri, it is Shila Mata who accepts the actual blood offerings that Durga requires in her temples and that Rajput *kuldevi*s receive elsewhere in theirs.[25] The Shila-Durga homology is simply more direct and explicit than the Jamvai-Durga one—Shila replaces the official *kuldevi* during the most important Rajput holiday.

What may give Shila Mata additional appeal to Kachvahas, and especially to Kachvaha women, is that the mythology of Shila Mata amply expresses the complexity and fluidity of *kuldevi* character. She is a full-fledged *kul*-protecting warrior goddess as well as a protector of brides as they assume their roles as *pativrata*s. Although the myth of Jamvai Mata incorporates both martial motifs and maternal iconography, it does so without explicit reference to her entry into the *zanana* (fig. 20). It may be that there was such a myth in the past but it is also likely that no such version existed, not least because the tribal origins of the goddess would make a marriage scenario significantly less plausible.[26] In short, the Jamvai Mata myth seems incomplete.

A final element of the Shila Mata myth bears contemplating. The first version of the myth explicitly identifies Shila Mata with Kali. This Sanskritic homology facilitates the introduction of the alien goddess into the palace. That Shila Mata is understood as Kali as well as Kedar's *kuldevi* is clear when we view the two Shila myths together. Because Jamvai Mata is similarly, though less fully, homologized to the Goddess, the possibility of competition between the goddesses can be dismissed

25. The distinction between meat-eating and vegetarian goddesses (or gods) is not absolute in India. Just as the virginal and married goddesses are ideal types that easily blur in myth and ritual, so the carnivorous and herbivorous forms often merge. Vegetarian offerings are often seen as symbolic substitutes for animal sacrifice. In goddess worship the coconut replaces the head offered in an animal (or human) *balidan*. In some places in India, vegetable or grain offerings are shaped into animals. On the identification of carnivorous and herbivorous forms of deities, see Biardeau and Malamoud, *Le sacrifice*, 139 ff.; Meyer, *Aṅkālaparmēcuvari*, 35–39; Roghair, *Epic of Palnāḍu*, 195–97; Tarabout, *Sacrifier*, 145; Galey, "Totalité," 80; Vidal, "Le puits," 50–51; and C. J. Fuller, "The Hindu Pantheon and the Legitimation of Hierarchy," in *Man*, n.s., 23, no. 1 (March 1988): 21–23.

26. An attendant at the Jamvai Mata temple at Rajgarh related to me the tradition that Dularai's wife had convinced him to build the *kuldevi* temple after his success in battle. None of my informants nor my Kachvaha taxi driver, who regularly escorts his mother to the temple, knew this tradition. The story intrigues me because it suggests the *zanana*'s perceived influence in the adoption of a *kuldevi* and hints at a special tie between bride and *kuldevi*.

20. Jamvai Mata, the Kachvaha *kuldevi* (oil painting from the home of Mohan Sinh of Kanota).

as illusory on the ideological level while being actualized on the socio-logical level.

Thus we can at the very minimum surmise that *kuldevi* worship is closely tied to both the *kul* experience of conquering a new land and the female experience of entering a new family. It is pointless to debate the "true" origins of particular *kuldevi*s. Whether the goddesses actually appear in conjunction with the conquest of new peoples, marriages, or combinations of both, the myths reveal an understanding of the *zanana* as a locus of religious change.

Hence, in sociological and mythic terms Rajput marriage entails var-ious arbitrations between competing female roles, be they those of women or of *kuldevi*s. Whatever the nature of the adjustment women make, we should not mistake it for something permanent. The tension in evidence at the time of marriage resurfaces during other specific in-stances when women encounter important social changes. We can best understand this by placing the twofold conception of *kuldevi* duty against the backdrop of male ideals, for when men actively pursue ulti-mate Rajput aims, the complementarity of female roles (both women's and *kuldevi*s') may quickly dissolve. Investigating the connection be-tween traditional male and female motivations will help us understand the way in which women interpret their continually evolving *pativrata* duty. Moreover, it will allow us to trace the conceptual means by which the traditional understanding of *kuldevi* protection has adapted to the contemporary context of Rajput society.

TRADITIONAL MALE AND FEMALE MOTIVATIONS

The traditional goals of a Rajput man are two: conquest and death on the battlefield. The relation between these two roughly reflects that be-tween the social and the individual. As a Rajput, a man works for the glorification of the king and the vitality of the kingdom he serves. He also strives for personal salvation, a place in warrior heaven (*virgati*) guaranteed by death in battle. These goals, formulated during a bygone era but still espoused and acknowledged by Rajput nobility, mutually reinforce each other. Victory is the social goal of the hero (*vir*) seeking personal salvation in death.[27]

A Rajput woman, as we have seen, aspires to preserve her husband's life. At the same time, she understands that her *pativrata* duty requires

27. On the antiquity of the hero's aspiration, see Filliozat, "After-Death Destiny," 4. *Vir*, incidentally, is cognate with the English "virility."

her not only to preserve her husband but also to serve him and be obe-
dient to him. She must sacrifice her personal desires to fulfill the desires
of her husband. Thus, if her husband wishes to die a glorious death on
the battlefield, she again experiences dissonance. As her husband's protector, she cannot logically support her husband's desire to attain
death—she hopes for victory and life. Whereas in the abstract she can
support the notion that Rajput soldiers should sacrifice their lives on the
battlefield so that families might be protected and can understand that
such sacrifice is his duty, she cannot wholeheartedly will that her husband sacrifice his life, for it is her duty to preserve him and his family.
Thus the prospect of a difficult battle has always carried with it the dilemma of conflicting loyalties.

The warrior-*pativrata* character of *kuldevi*s reflects this dilemma. In
the foundation myths presented above, however, the bellicose aspect of
the *kuldevi*, which is suggested by her wild animal form, is softened by
domestic maternal motifs. We must not mistake the presence of these
motifs for any compromise in the *kuldevi*'s belligerence. The martial and
the marital aspects coexist in the goddess who serves as guardian. To
protect, she requires both loving devotion and bloody sacrifice.[28]

This twofold demand emerges in the Bukh Mata (Hungry Mother)
narrative recorded by Colonel Tod.[29] The account is a vignette from his
story of the Sisodiyas' second battle against the Muslim conqueror Ala-
ud-din, who was determined to conquer Chitor, the capital city. As the
tale goes, one night the Sisodiya king was resting from a discouraging
day on the battlefield when he heard a voice that came from thin air. It
groaned, "I'm hungry." Just then his *kuldevi* appeared. The king asked
her why she was not satisfied with the eight thousand Rajputs who had
already sacrificed their lives to her in battle. She replied that she wanted
kings: "I must have regal victims; and if twelve who wear the diadem
bleed not for Cheetore, the land will pass from the line." The next night
she again appeared to the king, who was then in the company of his
council. She said she would remain as their protector only on the condition that the king crown each of his sons and then send them out alone
to die in battle. The king carried out her orders until only one of his
twelve sons remained alive. At that point he himself rode out into battle
to die, so that his son would live to preserve the royal line.

28. Cf. Meyer, *Aṅkāḷaparmēcuvari*, 168.
29. *Annals and Antiquities* 1:214–15; Tod dates this event as S. 1346 (A.D. 1290) or
perhaps thirteen years later. The Sisodiya king was actually the ruler not of Chitor, but of
Sisoda. His Sisodiya *shakh* later assumed the throne of Chitor from the (other) Guhils
ruling there.

This Bukh Mata story portrays the *kuldevi* as a devourer of her devotees.[30] That her consumption of them is understood as acceptance of
human sacrifice is even clearer in the story of a human sacrifice at the
later Sisodiya capital of Kumbhalgarh (see figs. 2, 3). While visiting the
ruins of Kumbhalgarh, I came across a small stone shrine honoring a
soldier who had volunteered to be killed as a sacrifice (*balidan*) to
Durga.[31] The sacrifice was necessary to ensure that the battle walls being
constructed by Maharana Kumbha would be strong enough to withstand sieges. The soldier was ritually decapitated, and his head rolled
down from the high ground upon which the sacrifice took place to a low
spot, where the shrine was constructed. His Rajput blood gave the fortress its strength.[32]

By taking Rajput lives, the warrior *kuldevi* frustrates the *pativrata*
purpose of husband-protection and so contradicts the domestic *kuldevi*
function. Thus, the prospect of a husband's death in battle emphasizes
the formal disjunction between the *kuldevi*'s protective purposes. Par-
alleling this disjunction is the dissonance of the wife who, in wishing to
obey her husband and to help him perform his duty, must support him
in his decision to fight yet do her best to save his life. As chapter 6 will
demonstrate, Rajput lore is full of ever-popular examples of women
who even made their husbands fight when the husbands were less than
enthusiastic. It has always been the duty of Rajput women to help their
husbands be not only as they are but as they should be, which is to say,
as men bent on performing Rajput duty.

Nevertheless, should the dutiful husband die, his death would stand
as an indictment of his wife's character. The wife would have failed to
protect his life as a *pativrata* should. Traditionally, the only way she
could prove her character was to sacrifice her life. By dying as a *sati*, she
shared the fate that her husband earned. This symbolic action is a solution, not a motivation, and it is a solution that attaches only after the
fact. As I learned from women during my stay, a good wife can never

30. There is also a story about the *kuldevi* Ad Mata, who devours in order to protect.
According to the version known to the Dhrangadra branch of the Jhala line, she ate
the leg of Harpal, the Jhala founder. He had offered it to her in a feast he had prepared
for her at a Solamki Rajput cremation ground. After consuming his flesh, she restored him
to health and enabled him to found a dynasty (M. N. M. [author], *The Hind Rajasthan*
[privately published as a tribute to H. H. Maha Raol Shri Pratapsingh Gulabsinghji,
Bansda, 1896], 511–13). Jayasinh Jhala also narrated this myth to me.

31. This shrine is still active; at the time of my visit incense was burning there. Two
guards told me its history, which a *thakur* acquaintance corroborated.

32. On similar construction sacrifices by women in Banaras, see Diane Marjorie Coccari, "The Bir Babas of Banaras" (Ph.D. diss., University of Wisconsin, Madison, 1986),
120.

vow or even intend to die a *sati* before her husband's death, for this would be to will his death and would contravene her foremost purpose as a *pativrata*. Women want to die before their husbands. Thus ultimate motivations cannot be logically harmonized while both husband and wife live. To this enigma we will return again and again in the chapters following.

In sum, battle has disrupted the traditional symbolic harmony between *kuldevi* functions. Because a *kuldevi* may allow a soldier to die, she cannot be said to protect his family always. Even though the hero's death glorifies his family, it causes misery and may also leave the family heirless. Ideally, the ethos of battle harmonizes with the welfare of the family, but in the actual circumstance of war, death becomes a threat to the household and the family line.

Given this traditional conflict between *kuldevi* functions in the context of actual or impending battle, we might wonder how the *kuldevi* functions in contemporary Rajput society. Nowadays Rajputs no longer have kings and armies. Thus battle is not the regular occupation of most Rajputs. Even when it is, which is to say for men who have joined the Indian army, the protection a *kuldevi* provides is to an individual who is a member of a *kul* but not to the *kul* and its sociopolitical subdivisions. Members of *kul*s and sub-*kul*s no longer fight together in battle. Moreover, death in battle is not what it was, a sacrifice for the *kuldevi* protecting the *kul* or a *kul*-unit as an entity.

As a result, the erstwhile military relationship between *kuldevi* and *kul* member has changed. It has become largely metaphorical: it applies the imagery of battle to economic and social endeavors aimed at benefiting the household.[33] In so doing, it has come to mirror the relationship between individuals and domestic *kuldevi*s. Hence, as we observed, men now concede that their wives know more than they about "such religious matters." The end of the Rajput states has meant the ascendancy of domestic *kuldevi* motifs, although, as the foundation myths demonstrate, the domestic and maternal aspects of the *kuldevi* have undoubtedly been an integral part of *kuldevi* tradition since its inception.

May we assume that this ascendance of household motifs means that the *kuldevi* has begun to lose her duality of character? Yes and no. The assertion by Rajput women that the *kuldevi* is benevolent—she does

33. See Harlan, "Social Change." This application of battle motifs to economic and political endeavors seems intensified after many recent successful Rajput electoral campaigns. The Maharana of Udaipur was elected to Parliament, and many Rajputs have taken seats in national and state legislatures.

what she does for the good of the group she guards—combined with the household iconography of the *kuldevi* as a *pativrata*, lend support to the idea that as the *kuldevi* becomes less tied to the context of *kul* and *kul* history and more fully located within the home, the domestic associations of the goddess will become increasingly dominant. Germane here is the apparent escalation among women of the practice of religious vows. This is undoubtedly associated with the increasing circulation of vernacular *vrat* pamphlets, which contain stories connected to the vows (*vrat kathas*) as well as instructions for their performance.[34] Many of the *vrat kathas* present characters who are paradigmatic *pativratas*; others provide no such succinct instruction. Most, however, relate to rituals intended to strengthen a woman's power to preserve her husband's life through dutiful wifely behavior and ritual devotion. Thus in one way or another women's rituals reflect an increasing reinforcement of the *pativrata* motif. In its light we must interpret the evolution of women's *kuldevi* worship.

And yet we must acknowledge that the military imagery of the *kul* goddess is unlikely to vanish altogether. Diminution of the *kul* context of *kuldevi* activity has reduced the potential antagonism between *kul* goals and female aspirations and individualized the *kuldevi*'s care. The *kuldevi* does not protect the *kul* as much as she does *kul* members. Nevertheless, the fluid duality of the *kuldevi*'s character, we recall, transcends its purely parochial expression. The *kul* goddess retains a strong Sanskritic valence. She has both her belligerent (dark, Kali-type) and the gentle (light, Gauri-type) associations. Thus amidst the host of *vrat* celebrations populating Hindu calendars, Navratri remains by far the most important celebration for Rajputs, male and female. Here the identification of the *kuldevi* with the Goddess preserves the complex character presented in the *puranas*. The performance of Navratri rituals gives full expression to conceptualization of the Goddess as warrior and renews the protection that the *kuldevi* extends to individuals as they fight the battles of everyday life. Just as domestic *kuldevi* imagery colored *kul* foundation myths, so now military *kuldevi* imagery colors the household-affiliated functions that the goddess performs for *kul* members.

In sum, the *kuldevi* retains her status as the chief divine protector of Rajputs in present-day Rajasthan. Moreover, she remains a symbol of

---

34. On *vrat kathas*, see Susan Snow Wadley, *Shakti* (Chicago: University of Chicago Press, 1975); Susan Snow Wadley, "Power in Hindu Ideology and Practice," in *The New Wind*, ed. Kenneth David (The Hague: Mouton, 1977); and more recently Mary McGee, "Feasting and Fasting" (Ph.D. diss., Harvard Divinity School, 1987).

the traditional Rajput way of life. As *kul*-protector, she belongs to the domain of history, the record of military achievements by Rajput males. As family protector, she is associated with the continuing welfare of individual family members. She reflects the dislocation experienced by women who marry from one *kul* into another and the dissonance shared by women who wish to support their husbands' careers while preserving their husbands' well-being. She is a complex deity, whose wisdom is assumed to transcend that of her devotees.

At the same time, the *kuldevi* continues to function as a paradigm. She is a home protector, as women should be home protectors, and she is a husband defender, as women should be husband defenders. Even when she harms family members to punish them for oversights, she serves as an exemplar, for women must also make decisions that disturb yet benefit the household. Paradoxically, the first such disturbance a woman causes may well be her importation of her natal *kuldevi*.

In worshiping the *kuldevi*, then, Rajput women seek to maximize their performance of the *pativrata* role that she embodies as a *pativrata* goddess and yet transcends both as household and as martial protectress alike. Nevertheless, the worship women render is not a passive response to the *kuldevi* but a continually transformative interpretation of *kuldevi* will and *kuldevi* tradition. Because for women the *kuldevi* is predominantly a household deity, she is interpreted and evaluated, reinterpreted and reevaluated, according to the changing perceptions women hold of domestic space, household duties, and *pativrata* devotion.

The next chapter addresses the question of how women interpret and emulate another sort of protectress—the *sati*. Unlike the dual-natured *kuldevi*, the *sati* has only one form, the form of the *pativrata*, and only one purpose, the protection of the household. Today as in the past, the *sati* unequivocally unifies the aspects of identity that, as we have seen, are not always compatible: being a good Rajput and being a good woman.

CHAPTER 4

Satimata Tradition

The Transformative Process

On the outskirts of Udaipur is Ahar, the dusty one-lane town that is the site of Udaipur's royal cremation compound. Entering the compound, a walled area of perhaps ten acres or so, the visitor passes constellations of large stone monuments (*chatri*s) in memory of Mewar's deceased monarchs. Further on are older cenotaphs, most of which have started to crumble. Field grass has sprung up between the stones in their long staircases; weeds and vines attack their bases. At the top of each staircase is a large covered platform in the middle of which is set a carved stone depicting a monarch and the women who shared his funeral pyre. Below the monuments are small platforms (*cabutra*s) supporting more such memorial stones—some of them comparatively crude—dedicated to less illustrious ancestors (figs. 21, 22).

Although commemorating the deaths of male ancestors and of their queens, they are often referred to simply as *sati* stones.[1] They celebrate the loyalty women have shown in abandoning life to join their husbands in the afterworld.[2] Thus each is marked at its apex with a relief carving

1. This is particularly true when they are referred to in English, whether by foreigners or by Indian historians and journalists. On these stones and their significance in Maharashtra, see Gunther D. Sontheimer, "Hero and Satī-stones in Maharashtra," in *Memorial Stones*, ed. S. Settar and Gunther D. Sontheimer (Dharwad: Institute of Art History, Karnatak University and Heidelberg: South Asia Institute, University of Heidelberg, 1982); on Karnataka and Maharashtra, see Romila Thapar, "Death and the Hero," in *Mortality and Immortality*, ed. S. C. Humphries and Helen King (London: Academic Press, 1982).

2. What percentage of Rajput women have died as *sati*s is unknown. Informed estimates, based on extant *sati* monuments, range between 1 and 2 percent, but no one really knows about medieval times.

of a woman's hand, the general representation of auspiciousness and in this narrow context the symbol for a *sati*. To one side of the hand is the sun, to the other the moon, which together are taken to mean, "So long as there shall be a sun and a moon, let this event be remembered." The *sati*s' stylized faces and postures are serene. They look peaceful. In fact, with their palms joined in an *anjali* (a prayer gesture with palms open and fingertips touching), the *sati*s seem lost in meditation.

The inner peacefulness of their expression mirrors the tranquility of the surroundings. Whenever I have visited Ahar, and I have done so often, I have shared only the company of furtive chipmunks in the underbrush and yawning buffalo off in the muddy stream bordering the cremation platform. True, I have seen at Ahar evidence of active veneration of the *sati* stones, many of which are adorned with vermilion and silver foil, but because most worship of *sati*s is done by women, who venerate *sati*s at simpler shrines in their households, such stones are left unattended most of the time. They may only be worshiped, in fact, when there is a marriage or a birth in the family, in which case they are given special tribute (*dhok*).

The composure of the *sati* images and the calm of their surroundings always strike me as oddly disquieting.[3] The serenity stands in ironic contrast to the violent way in which these women died. Sometimes as I have contemplated these stones I have imagined the scene that each commemorates. I have thought of a woman stepping out from the security of *parda* into a once somber, now expectant crowd of spectators, jostling one another to catch a glimpse of her mounting the pyre and becoming a *sati*. I have wondered: how could she stand the pain? Death by fire is unthinkable.

Be that as it may, my purpose in this chapter is to construct how it is that a *sati*'s death is "thinkable." I do not propose to assess the phenomenon historically:[4] I leave to others the task of addressing the political, economic, and social implications of *sati* immolations and assessing the extent to which such immolations were voluntary.[5] Rather, I intend to

3. In the village where I worked, the *sati* stones (one for each of the Rajput *kuls*, Jhala and Rathaur) were also situated in sedate surroundings. They sat on a *cabutra* under a tall shade tree on the village outskirts near the communal well.
4. For historical information, see Datta, *Sati*; Meena Gaur, *Sati and Social Reforms* (Jaipur: Publication Scheme, 1989); Romila Thapar, "In History," *Seminar* 342 (February 1988); Arvind Sharma, *Sati* (Delhi: Motilal Banarsidass, 1988); Veena Das, "Gender Studies," *Berkshire Review* (1986); and Courtright, *Dreadful Practice*.
5. See Veena Das, "Strange Response," *Illustrated Weekly of India*, 28 Feb. 1988; Thapar, "In History"; and other articles in *Seminar* 342 and *Manushi*, nos. 42–43. These are only a few of the many articles analyzing the controversy erupting from the Rup Kan-

21. *Sati* monuments at Ahar.

22. Detail from a *sati* stone, Ahar.

explain the ways in which Rajputs have understood *sati* immolation and analyze specifically what the *sati* has represented, what she has *meant*, to the women I came to know in Rajasthan during my time there (figs. 23, 24).[6]

In the minds of Rajputs the transformation of a woman into a *sati* does not, as is often assumed, result from the act of self-immolation. The word *sati* means "a good woman" and not, as English speakers tend to think, an act.[7] We may speak of *sati* as something one commits, but Hindi speakers define *sati* as that which one becomes (*sati ho jana*). This usage reflects the understanding all Rajput women have of the *sati*: becoming a *sati* is a process, a process instigated at the moment of marriage or occasionally even at the moment of betrothal. As we shall see, because there is parallel fire symbolism in the marriage ritual and *sati* cremation, circumambulating a funeral pyre transforms a fiancée into a

---

war case mentioned in the introduction. For further theoretical perspectives, see Lata Mani, "Multiple Mediations," *Inscriptions* (Santa Cruz: University of California, 1989); and Rajeshwari Sundar Rajan, "The Subject of Sati," *Yale Journal of Criticism*, vol. 3, no. 2, Spring 1990.

6. No study of *sati* tradition takes into account the testimony of living devotees and the community context; see remarks in the introduction.

7. English generally spells the word it uses to describe immolation "suttee."

23. *Sati* image from Ahar.

24. Popular depiction of a *sati* (from an icon shop at the gates of the Ekling Ji temple).

wife, who can then become a *sati*. Thus the transcendent powers that a *sati* wields are thought not merely the consequence of the act of dying; they are the result of her successful development of *pativrata* character as a married woman or even as a fiancée. In short, the *sati* serves women as an accessible ideal, for she has become a *sati* by fulfilling the role that they aspire to fulfill, that of the *pativrata*.

Before investigating the standard scenario that is thought to transform a woman into a *sati*, let me reiterate that today the practice of dying as a *sati* is largely extinct.[8] It is also illegal. On those rare occasions when it does occur, both the government and the press vigorously condemn it.[9] The near elimination of the custom, however, has not caused the worship of *sati*s to diminish. On the contrary. Rajput women continue to revere past *sati*s and admire their spirit as *pativrata*s, but most women now reject self-immolation as an option for themselves— not least of all, they readily say, because their relatives could be tried as accomplices. Becoming a *sati* would harm rather than help the family. The women in one *thikana* told me that not long ago a *sati* simultaneously appeared in all the dreams of the women in their household and ordered the family to allow no more *sati*s.

Nevertheless, Rajput women remain visibly proud of the courage and conviction that *sati*s have shown in dying and remain steadfast in their *sati* veneration. Because of this continuing reverence (and because self-immolation of this type still occasionally occurs), I use the present tense in describing *sati* tradition. When speaking of self-immolation, however, I intend the present largely in its historical sense.

STAGES OF *SATI* TRANSFORMATION

The transformation of a woman into a *sati* comprises three stages. The first of these is the *pativrata* stage. A woman becomes a *pativrata* when she marries. Thus the word *pativrata* sometimes simply refers to a wife. But as we have seen, even when used in this basic way it bears an ideological nuance, for it literally means someone who has made a vow, a *vrat*, to a husband, a *pati*. The substance of this vow is devotion, which is understood primarily as protection. If a wife is devoted to her hus-

8. Comparative work on contemporary instances of *sati* immolation includes Courtright, *Dreadful Practice*; and K. Sangari and S. Vaid, "Sati in Modern India," *Economic and Political Weekly*, 1 Aug. 1981, 1285–88.

9. Examples of condemnation include "Sati: A Pagan Sacrifice," *India Today* 15 Oct. 1987; and Bakshi, "Shame," *The Illustrated Weekly of India* 4 Aug. 1987, 20–23.

band and so protects him, he will prosper. If not, he will suffer and perhaps even die, which will bring misfortune to his family as well.

As a *pativrata*, a woman protects her husband in two basic ways. She
serves him: she sees to it that her husband's meals are hot and his clothes
are cleaned, obeys the commands of her senior in-laws, and tends to her
children. Second, she performs religious rituals, such as fasts. By doing
so she pleases various deities, who compensate her by protecting her
husband and helping her to be a better *pativrata*, thus increasing her
personal capacity to protect her husband.

If despite her devotion her husband dies before she does, she can escape culpability by following his body onto his cremation pyre. She
makes a *vrat*, a vow, to burn her body along with his.[10] By this vow she
is transformed from a *pativrata* into a *sativrata*, one who, as a good
woman (*sati*), has made a *vrat* to die with her husband.[11] In formulating
an intention to die she enters into the second stage of the *satimata* transformation process.[12]

When the *sativrata* perishes in her husband's cremation fire, she becomes a *satimata*. In this last stage, she joins other family *satimata*s in
protecting the welfare of the family she has left behind. Her protective
services are basically those performed by the *kuldevi* in her maternal
aspect. Yet the *kuldevi* is a bilocal, bifunctional being; the *satimata* stays
in one place and performs what is fundamentally one function. The
kuldevi serves on the battlefield as a *kul* protector and within the household as a family protector; the *satimata* devotes her undivided attention
to family protection.

Whereas the *kuldevi* is a goddess, the status of the *satimata* is far less
clear. Women I interviewed generally explained her status as lower than
that of a goddess (*devi*) but higher than that of an ancestor (*pitrani*).[13]
In some communities in Rajasthan people of various backgrounds may

10. In conversation women occasionally substituted the term *sankalp* for *vrat*.
11. As chapter 3 notes, a *pativrata* cannot intend, much less vow, to be a *satimata*
while her husband is alive: to do so would be to will his death before hers and to betray
her prior vow to protect him.
12. The terms *pativrata* and *satimata* are common but *sativrata* is not, though its
meaning is clear to all. It seems analogous to such "high Hindi" terms as *sakahari* (vegetarian) and *viseshkar* (especially); everyone knows these but few employ them in everyday
speech. People usually speak of the *pativrata* or *satimata*, not the *sativrata*, as deciding to
die. It is not especially significant that "sativrata" is seldom used colloquially; what is
important is that the *sativrata* period, the time between the *sati*'s vow and her death, is a
discrete period of transition. As this chapter shows, during this time a woman displays
supernatural powers and lays down rules for her future veneration. For convenience, I
employ *sativrata* when discussing this interim stage.
13. As I learned by blundering, it is rather insulting to refer to a *satimata* as a *pitrani*.

understand *sati*s to be goddesses or at least associate them with divine (goddess-like) power.[14] In either case a *satimata* seems not to have the range of character that goddesses generally have. Lacking the fierce animalian iconography of the battlefield *kuldevi*, she is ever the lovely and devoted wife, the embodiment of the *pativrata* ideal. In this form she protects *pativrata*s and encourages them, and sometimes coerces them, to perform their duties of protecting and increasing the family. Moreover, she functions as paradigm; she represents utter perfection of the *pativrata* role.

THE *SATIMATA* AS IDEAL

In the *satimata* is found the *pativrata* so perfected in *pativrata* virtue that she has transcended *pativrata* status. She stands for all that is appropriate in a married woman's behavior, all that is admirable in a married woman's character. Rajput women explain that she is the ideal woman and as such, the ideal Rajput woman.

What this boils down to is that Rajput women identify the perfection of the *pativrata* role as a Rajput capacity or talent. They feel that as Rajputs, they are endowed with the raw fiber that inclines them to become *satimata*s and that valid *sati* transformations are overwhelmingly Rajput.[15]

Because Rajputs associate *satimata* status with Rajput caste, they have often been leery of non-Rajput *sati*s. Their suspiciousness stems from the belief that inasmuch as non-Rajput women lack the innate

14. This conclusion I draw from conversations with Paul Courtright about shrines (mostly new ones) in eastern Rajasthan. In Mewar as elsewhere, some *sati* memorials depict *sati*s and their spouses as Shaiva devotees: they face Shaiva *ling*s. This context could be interpreted as identifying husband and wife with Shiv and his wife rather than as portraying devotion, but there is little evidence that women see it this way, especially as they identify the *sati* not as a *devi* but simply as a *sati*, a distinctive sort of being. Whereas women often homologized *kuldevi*s to the Goddess, they never did so for *satimata*s in interviews or informal conversations. Just as they corrected my insult of referring to *sati*s as *pitrani*s, they corrected my reductionism toward higher divinity. The spectrum of Hindu divinity is simply richer than that of many other, especially western, traditions. Incidentally, not once during my stay was a *sati* story placed in the context of the Sanskritic story of Shiv and Sati, who killed herself when her father, Daksha, insulted Shiv.

15. One woman summed up the situation: "Rajput women have the most of the qualities that an Indian woman should have." Still, Rajasthanis understand *sati* immolations as originally and predominantly a Rajput practice and disagree only on whether non-Rajput women can become legitimate *sati*s. The *sati* monuments in cremation grounds would indicate that *sati* immolations were most common among Rajputs, but there is no way of verifying this fact from physical evidence as not all *sati*s are represented by *sati* monuments. On the spread of *sati* tradition, see Thapar, "In History."

character with which Rajput women are endowed, they must find it difficult to formulate the heartfelt conviction essential to becoming a *sati-vrata*. Many Rajputs said to me that many non-Rajputs want to die as *sati*s only because they hope to improve their personal or caste status. By emulating this and other Rajput customs such as wearing Rajput dress, eating meat, and drinking wine, low-caste groups try to prove their claims that they are actually Rajput or at least Rajput-like.[16]

Rajput women eagerly condemn this imputed motive not only because they disapprove of caste mobility but also because they feel it makes a travesty of the *sati* transformation, the only legitimate motivation for which is unadulterated devotion to a husband. Since *sati* transformation represents self-sacrifice, to be valid it must result from pure selflessness, a condition realized only through sincere and skillful *pati-vrata* devotion.

The often voiced Rajput conviction that Rajput women are predisposed toward selflessness is predicated at least in part on the assumption that Rajputs are naturally inclined and bound by duty to sacrifice and give. As soldiers, Rajputs have had to sacrifice their lives, and as kings, they have had to provide for their subjects. Rajput women explain that just as sacrificing and giving have characterized the history of Rajput men, so they have characterized the history of Rajput *pativrata*s. Stipulating the meaning of these activities vis-à-vis caste duty will reveal more specifically the rationale of identifying true *sati*s as Rajput. Because, as we have seen, Rajputs think of caste duty, which is both martial and administrative, as primarily male, we should begin this endeavor by looking at the way in which the code of sacrificing and giving is thought to have directed the behavior of Rajput men.

Once again, to the Rajput, battle means sacrifice. It also means giving, for the ultimate gift a Rajput could give was his life. As Ziegler points out, death in battle has always constituted the fulfillment of duty and guaranteed personal salvation:

> Another term which was used to describe the great warrior, the *vaḍo* Rājpūt, was *dātār* (literally "the giver"), for the Rajput was seen as being the giver of gifts (*dāṃn, dat*) to the Brāhmaṇ, Cāraṇ, and Bhāṭ, the giver of grain and sustenance (*annandātā*) to those who served him, and the giver of protection

16. Throughout the Rajput community there is a particularly strong fear that daughters will unknowingly marry Darogas, persons descended from liaisons between Rajput men and non-Rajput consorts. Many Darogas have assumed Rajput manners, styles, and customs.

to all. He was also the giver of his life in the preservation of the moral order of society. This particular act of sacrifice was exemplified most clearly in the *sākā*, the great battle, to the death, in preparation for which the Rajput adopted the saffron turban and the saffron robes of the *sannyāsī* in order to show his unreserved commitment to battle and death in battle. Death in battle was itself seen as salvation, the fulfillment of the appointed task, and is expressed in the following terms—*vaḍo Rājpūt to kāṃn āyo*: "the great warrior fought and died in battle," that is, fulfilled his appointed duty and task (*kāṃn āyo*).[17]

Although this characterization is based on a study of Rajput history only through the midseventeenth century, the ideals described remain meaningful today. Rajputs no longer fight in Rajput armies but understand the ability and willingness to give their lives as a living heritage. One *thakur*, pointing to the respect he receives when he visits the villages once part of his father's estate, comments that respect is an enduring tribute to the sacrifices of royal blood that his family and ancestors made on villagers' behalf. Such sacrifices, he believes, have been an integral part of the Rajput way of life. Their symbolic summation is the *saka*, the battle unto death. Preparing for the *saka* (the cutting down), Rajputs donned the garb of ascetics, which showed that they intended to sacrifice their lives in accord with duty and with the reward of a place in warrior heaven. Today the *saka* remains a powerful symbol of caste identity and personal integrity and represents to all Rajputs the idea that sacrifice is both a natural proclivity and a moral imperative.

The ideal of sacrificing or giving one's life was linked with the duty to give throughout one's life.[18] As members of the royal caste, Rajputs were accountable for the sustenance and prosperity of those whom they ruled. Thus Rajputs have traditionally been addressed by the honorific *annadata*, "giver of grain." The survival of the conception of the Rajput as benefactor is exemplified by the popular adage that whereas a Brahman approaches a Rajput with his palms up (seeking alms), a Rajput approaches a Brahman with his palms down (giving alms). Rajputs enjoy explaining that their dispositional tendency toward generosity made them fit to rule even over Brahmans, their superiors in terms of caste purity. They also frequently contrast this generosity with what they see as the inherent greediness of *baniya*s, members of merchant castes. As one nobleman explained to me, the Rajput makes a better politician than the *baniya* because Rajputs are not naturally motivated by a desire

17. Ziegler, "Action, Power," 69. On the asceticism of Rajput warfare in ancient and medieval times see Kolff, "The Rajput."
18. Ziegler, "Action, Power," 69.

for personal profit; they strive for the welfare of those whom they govern.[19] These days the Rajput legacy of patronage has been preserved in some minimal ways, perhaps the most visible of which is the continuing Rajput sponsorship of various traditional festivals and rituals.[20]

In short, sacrifice and donation—yielding up life and property on behalf of subjects—are closely related elaborations of selflessness. They constitute endowments and commandments, representations of what Rajputs are and what they ought to be. They demonstrate the underlying assumption that whereas a Rajput is Rajput by nature, he becomes a realized Rajput, a valiant Rajput, through action in accord with his nature, action that develops his character.[21]

Just as Rajput men have retained the *saka*, women have retained the *sati* as a paramount source of inspiration in adapting to modern times and circumstances. In discussing the *sati* ideal and in describing their everyday lives, Rajput women speak of sacrifice and giving. They explain the *sati*'s death as the ultimate sacrifice, the *balidan* that follows a life full of sacrifices.

They believe that this death requires a life of sacrificial devotion to the husband. It consists of giving everything to him, to his family, and to those related to his family through blood or friendship. In this vein, Rajput women often mention the hospitality they offer invited visitors as visible evidence of their ingrained code of giving.

Hence though men and women share the ideals of sacrifice and giving, the contexts and contents of these ideals differ considerably. Rajput women translate the caste duty of generosity within their domestic context: a Rajput woman gives to her family as her husband gives to his subjects.[22] The inherent capacity and duty of Rajput women to give and sacrifice domestically constitute the basis for their claim to have the best prospects for becoming *sativrata*s. They say that the Rajput wife is incomparably devoted to her husband while he lives and so is optimally disposed toward following him when he dies. Moreover, by following

19. His conviction echoes the position of the Sanskrit Hindu legal texts, the *dharmashastra*s, which hold that the proper aim for a warrior (*kshatriya*) is *dharma* (law, duty, order), whereas the proper aim for a merchant (*vaishya*) is *artha* (material success).

20. Various royal and aristocratic families hold such festivals at their residences.

21. Ziegler, "Action, Power," 25.

22. Rajput women have endowed charities such as temples and girls' schools but have understood their families as their primary arena of giving. Gayatri Devi, a well-known member of the Jaipur royal family, told me of her frustration during World War II when she tried to convince some Rajput noblewomen to knit sweaters for Indian soldiers fighting in Europe. The women refused; it would be improper to give such things to strange men.

him in death she demonstrates to herself and others the sincerity and success with which she has lived as a *pativrata*.

In this way the *sati*'s death has served a validating function. Not every Rajput develops into a military hero (*vir*), and not every Rajput woman becomes a faultless wife. In fact, even though a woman who is faithful to and protective of her husband is called a *pativrata*, the term still states an ideal, one she can only approximate during her life. Furthermore, the extent to which a woman approaches this ideal is difficult, if not impossible, for her and others to assess. In her roles as wife and as Rajput a woman faces conflicts she must resolve. Choosing among priorities and interests often creates lingering uncertainty. Yet by dying as a *sati* a woman acquires the insight and confidence that she has done her duty and done it well.

This understanding of her accomplishment also reconfirms the presumption that becoming a *sati* is anything but an instantaneous and rash act. It is thought to constitute proof of the existence of character cultivated throughout life as an aspiring *pativrata*. To appreciate this fact fully we need to scrutinize the content of character. When Rajput women define *pativrata* or explain what a good Rajput woman is (the two, as we have seen, amount to the same thing), they often say, "a woman with good character (*accha caritra*)."

This character is not an abstract construct representing the sum total of excellent personal qualities. It is itself a quality. Moreover, it is a quality understood substantively. We speak of a good person, a person with integrity, as a "person of substance." Rajputs also say this but mean it literally. They think of a good person as having *sat*, a quality that is not abstract but concrete. It is a thing, a material developed through compliance with duty. In the context of women's duty, it refers to the moral fabric enabling a woman to become a *sati*, a woman incorporating *sat*. Thus Rajput women will say of a *sati* that she had tremendous *sat* in her body.

Sat is not an exclusively female quality. Carrying all the connotations of the English colloquialism "the right stuff," it also defines the realized character of Rajput males. *Sat* is the agent resulting from and catalyzing compliance with the Rajput code of military chivalry and administrative generosity. Understanding the term in both its female and male contexts is essential to constructing a fully nuanced meaning of the term as it applies in either context.

We can elucidate this term most economically by drawing on the *Nainsi ri Khyat*, a Marwari text that recounts a number of well known Rajput traditions. The text's version of the story of Guha, founder of the Guhils, beautifully illustrates the conceptual connection between *sat* and *sati* on the one hand and *sat* and male duty on the other.[23]

It will be recalled that when Guha's pregnant mother, who was returning home from a pilgrimage, learned that her husband had been slain, she determined to become a *sati* right away. She was dissuaded from doing so by a Brahman, who insisted that she first bear her child.[24] Some time after the queen had given birth to Guha, she desired to fulfill her intention to die as a *sativrata*. She asked the Brahman who had first counseled her if he would raise her son as a Brahman so that her husband's enemies would not be able to identify and slay the boy. The Brahman, however, was not eager to accept custody of the child. He objected that because the boy was a Rajput, he would grow up wanting to hunt animals and fight wars. That would be abhorrent to a Brahman such as himself.[25] He felt that in taking responsibility for the boy, he would be morally accountable for the consequences of un-Brahmanical activities in which the Rajput boy would doubtless engage.

The queen was sympathetic but said she could do nothing about his predicament, because burning was the result of her very nature. Having been a devoted wife, she could no longer control her urge to die as a *sati*. She managed to console the fearful Brahman, however, by assuring him that her son and his descendants would be well behaved because their Rajput character would enable them to act appropriately as wards of Brahmans, just as it would enable them to act as Rajput kings when the appropriate time arose for them to conquer territory and rule as kings:

> If I am burning because of my nature (*satsūṃ baḷūṃ chūṃ*), then the descendants of the family of this boy will be Rājās: they will pass ten generations (*pīḍhī*) following the manner of life of your clan (*kuḷ*). They will give you much happiness and prosperity.[26]

Citing this passage of the *Nainsi ri Khyat*, Ziegler notes that the word *sat* carries multiple related meanings, chief among which are "nature, essence; marrow; strength; virtue; courage," and it derives from the

23. Ziegler, "Action, Power," 113–15.
24. It is unclear whether the Brahman's reason is disapproval of self-immolation by a pregnant woman or hope that a pregnant woman might bear a son who would preserve her husband's line and inherit his title as king. This uneasiness over the idea of a pregnant *sati* is apparent in a story one woman told me about a *sati* in her family. She said that when the *sati* approached her husband's pyre, some people criticized her for intending to kill her unborn infant. In response, she grabbed a dagger from a bystander and carved the child out of her womb before immolating herself. The child died anyway, the story concludes, leaving unsettled the issue of whether a pregnant woman should die.
25. Being a vegetarian, the Brahman would wish nothing to do with hunting animals or with the bloody business of battle.
26. Ziegler, "Action, Power," 114.

Sanskrit *sattva*, meaning "true essence, the principle of being; substance, any natural property, quality, characteristic, disposition." He concludes that *sati* immolation "is part of the *Rāṃnī*'s [Rani's] code of conduct, inherent in her nature or quality of being, just as being a ruler is of her son's descendants who are of the substance and code of a Rajput and possess the potential to fulfill their codes."[27]

Here and elsewhere, the word *sat* has two distinct though related meanings. First, *sat* conveys a generic sense of "goodness at." Here goodness is tied to caste-affiliated virtue and duty. For men it means perfection of the duty to act as a Rajput and observe Rajput conventions. Guha's *sat* creates the urge to fight and hunt, but allowing this behavior violates the Brahman's code of conduct (*karm-dharm*).[28] Even if Guha and his descendants manage to control their urges to behave as Rajputs while hiding out at Nagda, a future generation is certain to reveal the Rajput character that its progenitors repressed. It will conquer a kingdom and found a line of rajas.

This generic use of the term *sat*, however, exists alongside the more specific meaning of *sat* as goodness, truth, and purity.[29] This same definition of *sat* is articulated in the Indian notion of the three *gun*s or qualities.[30] According to popular wisdom, *sat* is the virtue associated with Brahmans whereas *rajas* (passion, activity) belongs to Rajputs, and *tamas* (darkness, torpor) to *baniya*s.

Despite the formal distribution of the three qualities among highcaste groups, Rajputs with whom I conversed on the topic said that Rajputs have both *rajas* and *sat* and that both are essential to the performance of caste duty. It is tempting to speculate that this double identification arises from the fact that Rajputs are both warriors and rulers. As warriors they require *rajas*, but as rulers they require *sat*. A ruler who is good at being a ruler governs as a king who is generous and good, in accord with *sat*. Thus, the attribution of *sat* to Rajputs explains the frequently voiced Rajput contention that by caste tendency and duty they were best suited to be kings and are now well suited to be politicians.

This association of *sat* with Rajput character comports with Marvin

27. Ibid.
28. Ibid., 119.
29. Apte's Sanskrit dictionary defines *sat* as what is "real, essential, true" and as "good, virtuous, chaste . . . best, excellent" (*The Practical Sanskrit-English Dictionary*, rev. ed. [Delhi: Motilal Banarsidass, 1978] s.v.); Lalas lists very similar definitions under *sat* and under the related terms *satya* and *sac* (Sitaram Lalas, *Rājasthānī Sabd Kos*, vol. 4, pt. 3 [Jodhpur: Caupasni Shiksha Samiti, 1978], s.v.).
30. The *gun* theory is important in Samkhya philosophy, which Samkhya-inspired passages in the *Bhagavad Gita* have popularized.

Davis's findings in his study of caste rivalry in Bengal.[31] Davis says that the public perceives *sat* as dominant in Brahmans and *tamas* as dominant in *baniya*s, but *sat* and *rajas* as jointly dominant in Rajputs. Thus, returning to Rajasthan, for a Rajput to have *sat* does not mean that he simply embodies and manifests the *kshatriya* (warrior) quality of *rajas* (i.e., that he is "good at" *rajas*), but that along with *rajas* he embodies and manifests *sat*, which is why Rajput sons could live as Brahmans for seven generations.

In discussions of meat and wine this distinction comes out clearly. Both are appropriate fare for Rajputs but not for members of other high castes. Throughout India meat and wine are considered necessary for Rajputs because they build passion. They incite readiness for battle as well as the lust essential for intercourse, the source of children and hence soldiers. Furthermore, to have many sons Rajput men need many wives, which means they need a lot of sexual passion.[32] In sum, Rajputs embody *sat*, the quality informing good judgment and the benignity catalyzing discipline and control, in addition to *rajas*.

With this in mind, we can educe the generic and specific meanings of *sat* in the case of women. A look at women's attitudes toward eating meat and drinking wine gives us *sat*'s generic sense. As men do, Rajput women partake of meat and alcohol, but their consumption is far more moderate. In responding to questions about meat and alcohol, Rajput women stressed that whereas it is proper for Rajput men to imbibe quantities of liquor, women who do so tend to lose their dignity. As one noblewoman put it, "If a lady drinks too much, she will allow her hair to fall loose on her shoulders and she may say too much, both of which are unbefitting a Rajput woman." Loose hair and loose lips characterize a loose woman, the opposite of the *pativrata* and the Rajput ideal.[33]

It is not, then, surprising to discover that for Rajput women the pri-

31. Marvin Davis, *Rank and Rivalry* (New York: Cambridge University Press, 1983), 49, 51.

32. Carstairs reports the belief that meat and wine helped the Rajput build semen (*virya*) "and with it the qualities of courage and strength which its possession conveyed" (*Twice-Born*, 109). He records a villager's affirmation: "Rajputs are very lusty, Sahib. It is because of their food and their drink. It makes them so that they have to have their lust, poor fellows" (ibid., 188). The tale of the Sisodiya founder, Bappa Rawal, also exemplifies virility; he became a great warrior and king and had a hundred sons. While maintaining that meat and wine enhance strength and passion, however, Rajputs warn that overindulgence in food or wine brings on weakness and laziness, the opposites of strength and passion.

33. Even apart from discussions of alcohol consumption, Rajput women mentioned covering the head and soft speech as primary characteristics of a well-bred Rajput wife. Inattention to these conventions conveys moral and sexual laxness.

mary associations of drinking liquor and eating meat are sexual rather than martial. These women feel, as their husbands do, that wine and meat enhance fertility. They, however, have no need for military passion. As will be seen in chapter 6, the participation of women in battle has always been exceptional and undesirable because it has occurred only where men have been unable to fulfill their protective roles and then only under unusual circumstances. Thus for women the military justification for consuming wine and meat has been a pale one.

Nowadays many Rajput women drink very occasionally and perhaps only ceremonially. Some explain that younger women in particular find it unfashionable to indulge. Nevertheless, during wedding celebrations all women must accept the *manvar*, the ritual toast (as in fig. 7), for it celebrates the fertility of the newly married couple.[34]

Just as married women must accept *manvar* at weddings, they must also cease consuming alcohol and meat if they become widows. Because Rajput women do not remarry, they have no legitimate need for passion. Drinking is restricted to *pativrata*s, women whose husbands are still alive.

In following such Rajput customs as drinking alcohol and eating meat, Rajput women reveal the sense in which being a good Rajput equates with being a good woman. Meat and wine incline the Rajput woman to be a passionate and adoring wife. Taken in moderation they enhance personal virtue. In this way the generic sense of *sat* blends with the specific.[35]

Inasmuch as caste duty is primarily male duty, it is easy to see how among women the specific sense of *sat* predominates. Being a good woman may be facilitated by Rajput identity, but the norm directs behavior that is the task of all women, Rajput or not. Thus one common synonym for *sat* is the term *pativrata*.[36]

Sat, though defined in two ways, is a single substance. The story of Guha recounted from the *Nainsi ri Khyat*, as we have seen, explicitly states that the same *sat* manifested in the queen's death will be manifested in the son's desire to act as a Rajput. As a good Rajput woman,

34. In former days men also took opium as *manvar*. Conversations with and wedding photographs of nobles indicate that over the last twenty to thirty years this practice has gradually diminished.

35. Rajput women frequently used the term *gun* to classify *sat* but named no other *gun*s. Rather than *rajas* they spoke of the *raja ka caritra*, "king's character," which being brave (*bahadur*) is that of the hero (*vir*).

36. See *sat* in Lalas, *Sabd Kos*, s.v.; and *Nainsī rī Khyāt* (Jodhpur: Rajasthan Oriental Research Institute, 1960), 1: 2 n. 30.

the mother will die a *sati*; as a good Rajput male, the son will want to hunt and fight and will sire a line of rulers. To reiterate the queen's claim, "If I am burning because of my nature [*satsūṃ baḷūṃ chūṃ*], then the descendants of the family of this boy will be Rājās." In other words, since the queen has been a *pativrata*, her son's *sat* and her male descendants' *sat* will be reflected in their realization of the Rajput duties of conquest and rule.

This passage not only demonstrates the connection between *sat* in the sense of *pativrata* and *sat* in the sense of caste duty, it also clearly shows that dying as a *sati* validates previous actions. The queen feels conflict as to whether she should die when she first hears of her husband's death or after giving birth. Her death as a *sati* demonstrates the sincerity of her intention to die despite her decision to give birth before doing so. It shows that she has been a *pativrata* all along. From the moment of her marriage she has accumulated the *sat* required to follow her husband into the afterlife. Thus dying as a *sati* manifests the queen's *sat*, which shows her to be a *pativrata* (a good woman) and guarantees that her son's descendants will be kings (good Rajputs). *Sat* constitutes her character both as a Rajput and a woman. Moreover, it beautifully illustrates the identification of *sat*'s two meanings in its one material form.

This examination into the implicit meanings of *sat* allows us now to address the question of *sat*'s effect and function. *Sat* is essentially an autogenerative moral fuel. Produced by good activity, it generates good activity. In generating good activity, it also produces heat (*garmi*). Because of *sat*, the great warrior of times past, having fortified himself with opium or alcohol, charged onto the battlefield hot with battle frenzy.[37] If he was decapitated while fighting, his *sat* enabled him to continue fighting and even to kill his assailants before falling to the ground. He became a *jhumjhar*, a "struggler," a Rajput so perfected in character as to have transcended merely human heroism.

The *pativrata* also generates heat. As she fulfills her duties, she accumulates stores of *sat*. If she finds herself widowed, this *sat* becomes manifest. Her temperature rises. As her body heats, she experiences the urge (*bhav*) to die as a *sati* and makes a *vrat* to this effect. In the process she acquires superhuman powers (which are described below). Finally, hav-

37. Opium or alcohol were thought to enhance their natural battle fury. On alcohol consumption Carstairs quotes a Rajput village informant: "Every Rajput has two pegs of whisky before going to war, it is a general custom. Still it is this way" (*Twice-Born*, 188). See also Rudolph and Rudolph ("Rajput Adulthood," 179) on the use of alcohol and opium in celebrating war.

ing processed to her husband's pyre and taken his head in her lap, she spontaneously bursts into flames. The passion of her commitment to her husband consumes both their bodies.

A *sati*'s death reveals the *sat* that has resulted from and contributed to a woman's performance of prior sacrifices of selfish desires. The *sati*'s flames exhibit her perfected *pativrata* character, a perfection that complements, but is not synonymous with, the perfection of the warrior who dies in battle. The death of a *vir* is clearly a sacrifice to the *kuldevi*, his lineage protector. Although the *sati* undeniably sacrifices her life for her husband, it is not obvious from the narratives and comments of Rajput women whether she is thought to sacrifice herself *to* her husband, her family protector. This seems to me not simply a matter of language (*ko* and *ke liye*) but one of conceptualization, which is vivid in the case of the *vir* and vague in the case of the *sati*. Rajput women simply do not speak of *sati* sacrifice in terms of consumption; they usually discuss it in terms of validation (in life) and benefit (through death). Nevertheless, it is tempting to speculate about symbolism of the rituals described in narratives and conversation and to decipher possible underlying assumptions.[38]

Let us ponder for a moment the notion that the *sati balidan* represents a wife sacrificing herself to her husband. From this perspective the sacrifice is similar in kind to the sacrifices made by the *pativrata*, who leads a life of *pati ki seva*. This phrase, used often by Rajput women to explain the notion of wifely duty, means literally "service of one's husband," but it also means "worship of God." In Rajasthan as elsewhere, women say that one's husband is one's god; he grants salvation. If a woman worships her husband during life, it seems consistent that she do so at the moment of death. In ascending his pyre she appears to be offering herself up to him as a sacrificial victim.

This explanation, however, is not complete. Weighing against the exclusive assignment of such a meaning is the fact that the regular rituals a woman performs for her husband during his life (*vrat*s, *puja*s, *ratijagas*, and *dhok*) are ones she directs to deities for her husband, not to him. She worships them for her husband's welfare. Even at the moment of marriage, where the groom is worshiped as a god, the metaphorical

---

38. Because only few and widely scattered *sati* immolations have occurred during their lives, contemporary Rajput women base their ideas of ritual on narrative. I am not generally interested in the Brahmanical interpretations of ritual prescriptions, but rather in the assumptions Rajput women may hold given their notions of *pativrata*, *seva* (service or worship), and *balidan*.

aspect of husband as deity is retained; the wife treats her husband *as* a god, but she is perfectly aware that he is still—or at least also—a man. Moreover, no ritual performed during a woman's life formally depicts the sacrifice of a woman to her husband in the vivid way that Navratri depicts the sacrifice of a man to the *kuldevi*. The sacrifice of a *sati* to her husband is not a straightforward and unambiguous parallel to the sacrifice made in the ritual of battle.

The positions of the *sati* and her husband in the ritual of immolation suggest another set of associations. The *sati* is always described as dying with her husband's head in her lap. In taking her husband's head, the *sati* seems to be as much a recipient of sacrifice as she is its victim. At this awesome moment, the wife who sacrifices her life is becoming a supernatural being. The *sat* that she has gained through goodness manifests as power, the same sort of protective power wielded by the *kuldevi*. Moreover, even if not called a *devi*, the *sati* holding her husband's head seems reminiscent of the classic pose in which the Sanskritic Goddess accepts the head of a male sacrificial victim.

Although such connotations appear likely, they cannot stand by themselves, for they fail to convey the crucial notion of *sati* as self-sacrifice. Suggestive as the *sati*'s posture is of receiving a sacrifice, her dying with her husband's head in her lap also represents a certain tenderness. She has been, after all, his most intimate protector; now she is dying with a man she is assumed to have loved.[39] Moreover, because (as we shall see) the most venerated Rajput heroes have actually lost their heads in the sacrifice that is battle, the *sati* holding her husband's head would seem to imply that her husband is a hero. In this case the *vir* beheaded in the *saka* and the *sati* become parallel or joint victims. The man's death, however, is clearly an offering to the *kuldevi*, but the wife's sacrifice is at best indirectly associated with the *kuldevi*. Lacking verbal testimony or iconography to the contrary, we can assume that the *sati* sacrifices herself to the *kuldevi* only to the extent that she shares her husband's fate.

Another possible meaning of the ritual is that the sacrifice is not simply a sacrifice to someone but a sacrifice unto itself. By this I mean that it seems rather like the Rig Vedic sacrifice of Purusha (cosmic man), in which sacrifice sacrifices itself to itself that creation may occur.[40] The

39. Perhaps the most vivid depiction of this intimacy and tenderness I found is a stone that shows the *sati* reading to her husband from the *Bhagavad Gita* as she dies.
40. *Rig Veda* 10:90, the "Purusha Sukta." For a translated version, see R. C. Zaehner, *Hindu Scriptures* (London: Dent, 1966), 8–10.

sati, who joins her husband in the flames that she circumambulated with him when they married, loses her human body but becomes a being who produces family welfare and continuity. As a protector, she oversees its re-creation. Such an association is explicit in the *Dharmasindu* text.[41]

In sum, the *sati* ritual, which is known to women through household stories, not through personal observation, is rich with possible associations. These are not, however, the subject of women's own speculation any more perhaps than the underlying meaning of blood turning to wine is a subject of speculation for the vast majority of the Christian laity. In the narratives they tell women are simply less concerned with what *sati* immolation is than with who the woman is (a woman who has been good) and what she does (by way of practical benefits to her devotees). The proof of who she is and the protection she can provide lie in the flames that emerge from her body and accomplish the *balidan*.

For practical reasons the proof is usually assumed, not demonstrated. Before a *sati* ascends her husband's pyre, the pyre has likely been ignited. This sequence makes it impossible for witnesses to determine the source of the flames that envelop a *sati* and her spouse. Nevertheless, if the *sati* is a Rajput, the presumption will be that her intentions were pure and therefore without doubt it was her *sat* that consumed her husband and herself. Conversely, if the *sati* is not a Rajput, Rajputs will conclude that her intentions remain unproven and dubious.

There are, as we shall see, rare cases when the *sat* of a non-Rajput woman causes flames that are witnessed. These exceptional *sati*s are regarded as valid by all, including Rajput women. Lacking proof to the contrary, however, Rajput women regard the capacity to develop the stores of *sat* sufficient to transform a woman into a *sati* as overwhelmingly Rajput.

One last aspect of the identification of *sati* character as essentially Rajput is worth considering. The primary convention that Rajput women regard as responsible for the development of *sat* is *parda*, which, they say, has preserved their inherent modesty. Moreover, it has functioned as the preeminent symbol of their ethos and identity. Asked what distinguishes Rajput women from other women, they predictably respond, "Rajput women do not go out; they observe *parda*." *Parda* is the predominant means by which their *sat* is generated and stored.[42] As one

41. Paul Courtright, personal communication to author, March 1990.
42. Explaining *parda*, one woman said, "Many restrictions help us maintain our character." The vast majority of informants singled out *parda* as the critical distinguishing characteristic of Rajput women. Responding to the interview's request to describe the

noblewoman made clear, *parda* not only requires many sacrifices, it is itself a sacrifice. As she explained to me, "One thing about Rajput women—sacrifice is very important to us. We make a lot of sacrifices in our lives. Even the *parda* we keep is a sacrifice." Thus sacrifice builds character, which in turn makes further sacrifice possible.

The fact that most Rajput women identify *parda* as the institution most responsible for the realization of their character does not mean that they practice it now as their mothers and grandmothers did. When a Rajput woman says that she keeps *parda*, she may mean that she stays within the female section of the household; she may mean that she inhabits the entire household but does not go out in public; she may mean that she seldom goes out in public but is veiled and escorted when she does. To whatever extent individual Rajput women still practice *parda*, it remains a key symbol, a highly condensed representation of their basic values and way of life.[43] While locating the feminine within the household, it communicates the Rajput criteria for *pativrata* status: modesty and chastity, generosity and sacrifice.

In sum, dying as a *sati* is considered to be only the final consequence of a life dedicated to household duty. It manifests the moral substance that a woman has developed through the performance of duty. Paradoxically, it symbolizes both the perfection and the transcendence of duty. It transforms a woman who was once a *pativrata* into a *satimata*, a supermundane protector of family. The *satimata*'s character now requires scrutiny. Examining the *satimata* stage in the context of its ideological relation to the *pativrata* stage will then let us discern the theoretical contours of the *sativrata* stage that connects them.

THE *SATIMATA*: FAMILY PROTECTOR

Like the domestic *kuldevi*, the *satimata* is benevolent toward those under her guardianship—she is the very embodiment of goodness, *sat*.[44] To wish or do anything that is not ultimately good for her protégées is simply not seen as possible given her *sattvic* nature. Moreover the protective actions she performs are similar, if not identical, to those of the

---

character of Rajput women, informants focused on modesty (*sharam*, *laj*), a virtue they especially associated with *parda*, and on the institution of *parda*.

43. Ortner, "On Key Symbols," 1344.

44. Unlike a *pitr* or *purvaj* (ancestor), the *sati* does only good things. She does not make trouble: "*Taqlif kabhi nahim karti.*"

kuldevi. She appears in dreams in order to warn women of impending household crises. She comes to women to reprimand them for neglecting to perform proper ritual observances on her behalf. Furthermore, she provides protection to those aspiring to live as *pativratas* but withdraws protection in order to teach them when their efforts have lapsed. Although the *satimata* is good, she allows children to contract fever and cows' udders to wither if *pativratas* neglect her protection-securing rituals. When properly worshiped, she reverses the negative consequences of women's oversights. She restores sick children and cows to their previous health and reextends her protective shadow.

Not only does the *satimata* act like the maternal *kuldevi*, she also looks like her. As a result, women say that sometimes they are unsure whether the dreams or visions they have had are of *satimata*s or *kuldevi*s. If the message that the heavenly *suhagin* (*pativrata*) gives does not implicate her identity, women must consult a *bhopa*, a shaman, to ascertain it. All accounts of *satimata* visions describe a woman dressed in an auspicious color (red, pink, orange) of the very finest type of Rajput dress. She is inevitably bejeweled and beautiful.[45]

Some representative accounts women gave of appearances by *satimata*s demonstrate the standard circumstances under which a *satimata* makes herself manifest. The first account exemplifies the dream warning. One prominent noblewoman living in Udaipur described an appearance by a *satimata* in the dreams of her Brahman *purohit* (family priest), whose job it was to perform household rituals under her direction. The woman said that the *satimata*'s appearance coincided with the arrangements she was making for the marriage of her niece. She had intended to organize a *ratijaga* (night of singing) for the niece, but days slipped by and she had still not made the necessary arrangements. It finally dawned on her that she had left herself too little time to prepare for the *ratijaga*. She conveniently decided it would not be essential to perform the ceremony before the wedding. That night the priest received a dream of his patroness's *satimata*, who ordered him to make sure that the aunt undertook the preparations for the *ratijaga*. When he awoke, he set about fulfilling this command.

The circumstances of the *satimata*'s appearance are identical to those under which a *kuldevi* would appear. The story is standard in every way, except perhaps for the detail that on this particular occasion the *satimata* chooses to appear to a *purohit* in the service of a Rajput woman

45. As we shall see, the *satimata* is conceived as a realized *pativrata* (though technically she has passed that stage since her husband has predeceased her).

and not to the woman herself. Although usually a *satimata* appears directly to the woman in charge of ritual responsibilities, once in a while she may enlist the aid of an intermediary—sometimes a shaman, here a *purohit*, elsewhere a relative—to persuade her. The channel of communication that the *sati* uses is not thought to alter the content of the message.[46]

A second account illustrates the way in which a *satimata* compels a negligent woman to fulfill her ritual responsibilities by withdrawing a measure of protection. A woman tells of a time when her husband had taken ill. Soon after this a *satimata* came to him in a dream and said, "You have forgotten to venerate me." Just at that moment the hot-water bottle that he was using burst. The bursting of the bottle was a miracle (*camatkar*) attesting to the power of its generator. Here again the *satimata* appears directly to a man. The woman narrating the story, however, subscribes to the generally shared viewpoint that *satimata* worship is primarily the responsibility of women. The illness of a husband can only reflect badly on a wife whose foremost responsibility as a wife is to protect her husband. This and other instances in which a *satimata*, or a *kuldevi* for that matter, appears to a male but responsibility for a ritual lapse lies wholly or partly with a woman, support the hypothesis that a wife is accountable for any ritual negligence that occurs.

A third example of a *satimata*'s appearance illustrates the role a *satimata* takes in preparing a woman to meet an impending crisis. As in the case of such appearances by *kuldevis*, the typical crisis that occasions a *satimata*'s appearance is the imminent demise of a close relative. The *satimata* gives *darshan* (a vision) that will help a woman cope appropriately and productively when the crisis occurs. Here a well known Mewari noblewoman describes such an encounter:

> It is good when one's *satimata* appears in dreams. She brings peace (*shanti*). One time, a month and a half before my father-in-law died, I had a dream. In it my husband and I were in the *mahasatiyam* (cremation ground). The eleven *satimata*s of our family appeared and began to approach us. We were seated on a *chatri* [elevated cenotaph]. . . . They kept coming closer and closer. They came all the way up the steps of the *chatri*. One of the ladies said to my husband "Your *paddonti* will soon occur" [*paddonti* (promotion) refers to the ritual occasion on which a son takes over the *kul* and familial responsibilities of his deceased father]. Then all the *sati*s applied *kumkum* (saffron rouge) to our foreheads.
>
> Six weeks later, my father-in-law died.

46. I continue to explore the intriguing power of such intermediaries in my work on heroism.

In sum, the major purposes for which a *satimata* appears are those for which a *kuldevi* appears. She comes to encourage a woman to rectify a ritual blunder. Alternatively, she withdraws some of her protection to prod a woman into compliance with ritual responsibilities and then, if necessary, appears in a dream to verify that family problems are related to the lapse of ritual responsibilities. Finally, she reveals herself to prepare a protégée for assuming ritual and other responsibilities in conjunction with a crisis.

As we saw in chapter 3, the *satimata* does not make her will manifest by possessing protégées. One woman remarked, "*Satimata*s don't possess people: they're higher than *pitr-pitrani*s (ordinary ancestors)." Even when women consult *bhopa*s to interpret dreams in which *sati*s appear, a *bhopa* is not possessed by the *sati* but by a deity (almost always Bheru or Dharmaraj) who reveals to the *bhopa* a *sati*'s identity and purpose.

Concerning worship, the *satimata* is honored much as a maternal *kuldevi* is honored. In most places family members customarily go to their *satimata* and *kuldevi* to show respect (*dhok dena*) before leaving for a journey or when returning from one. In this way, they demonstrate that they are mindful of their guardians when crossing out of and into the guardians' jurisdiction. The *satimata* is also worshiped when a new bride enters a household. After she has visited the *kuldevi*, whose shrine is her principal destination after her arrival, the bride pays respect to other divine and ancestral spirits worshiped by her husband and his family. Foremost among these is the *satimata*. Women say that visiting the *satimata* is essential after coming to the new home because, if they ignore her, she may cause havoc. One *thikana* queen I came to know well, a very spirited and independent woman in her late twenties, told me that when she first went to her *thikana* she did not venerate the *satimata* right away. For various reasons she just kept putting it off. Several nights after her arrival, she had a nightmare: she dreamed she was being strangled. The next day she realized that the dream was a warning sent by the *satimata*, so she put on her wedding clothes and went straight to the *satimata*'s shrine to pay her respects. Afterward she had no recurrence of the dream. The *satimata* had been satisfied.

In addition to the occasions above, there may be other regular scheduled showings of respect or performances of *puja*. Often, however, the *satimata* is left alone except on days sacred to her. These days vary from family to family. In all families songs are sung in honor of Satimata (as we shall see, however many *satimata*s a family might have, it generally collapses them into one personality and refers to them in the singular) during the night wakes (*ratijaga*s) women keep to celebrate births and weddings.

Satimata worship may be done with the help of a trusted family *pujari*, but he is not essential.[47] In some families, women encourage other family members to join them in their *satimata* devotions. In some households women attend to these responsibilities by themselves. Other families even prohibit men from entering the *satimata*'s shrine (usually a room containing a *thapana*), because the *satimata* keeps *parda*. In one of the great *thikana*s outside Udaipur the family priest is forbidden to enter the *satimata* shrine. He must perform devotions to her from outside the shrine's closed door.

Along with the mode of worship, the place of worship varies among families. Some veneration takes place in the *mahasatiyam*. Its distance from the household poses problems for women who keep strict *parda* and cannot go out to the cremation ground. If women leave the *thikana* to go on a journey, however, they often order their drivers to stop near the *mahasatiyam* and from the car perform veiled obeisance to the *satimata* before proceeding.[48] More accessible is the *zanana*'s *thapana* (crude shrine), which is similar to the *thapana* dedicated to a *kuldevi* except that usually instead of a trident it shows a red handprint, which symbolizes the auspiciousness of a *pativrata*.

Then there are the *ratijaga*s, typically performed in the *zanana* courtyard. Rajput women join Dholhins (female drummers), Brahmanis (usually the wives of Brahman priests employed by the household), and Darogas (members of a caste of palace servants whose ancestral fathers were Rajput and ancestral mothers non-Rajput) in singing to *satimata*, *kuldevi*, and other members of the pantheon of family-protectors.

The most important way in which the *satimata* is venerated, however, is specific to *satimata*s. Protégées observe *ok*s (restrictions, customs) that are common to their family lines. These are established during the period just before a woman mounts a funeral pyre. I treat them in the following section, which examines how the *sativrata* stage links the ideals of the *pativrata* who venerates the *satimata* and those of the *satimata*

47. Zananas often employed female Brahmans—*purohitani*s (female *purohit*s) or *pujarani*s—to help with the *puja*. People often use the terms *pujari* (a person, usually a Brahman, responsible for offering *puja*) and *purohit* (a Brahman advisor) interchangeably; they do the same for the terms' feminized forms. I met one such Brahman woman, a widow employed in the Jaipur royal *zanana*, in that part of the *zanana* where a few elderly residents still maintained *parda*.

48. Located outside the bounds of the village or town, the *mahasatiyam* frequently offers more privacy than an exterior *kuldevi* shrine, which is usually found just outside the household.

who serves as the *pativrata*'s retrospective paradigm and prospective protector.

SATIVRATA: THE TRANSITIONAL STATE

The metamorphosis into a *satimata*, as we have seen, proves that the *sati* has perfected the *pativrata* role. Thus what the *satimata* was is what the *pativrata* should be. In graduating from *pativrata* status, however, the *satimata* becomes larger than the *pativrata* ideal. More than a paradigm, she is an autonomous and powerful family protector. Moreover, the *satimata* issues commands. She requires of her devotees not simple emulation of her protective services but obedience and faith.[49]

The *satimata* sets the terms of obedience before she in fact becomes a *satimata*, that is to say, between her vow of *sati* and her death. Unlike the *satimata*, who directs individuals through dreams or visions, the *sativrata* can communicate her will directly to the many who witness her procession. Having abandoned her old life and now standing on the threshold of a new existence, she attains the powers to compel her protégées and so change the course of their history.

The powers that she acquires in this condition are essentially two: the power to give a curse (*shrap*) and the power to confer a blessing (*ashirvad*). Because curses last many generations their impact is generally severe. Causing inconvenience, even tragedy, the *shrap*s are not easily forgotten. They become part of oral history.

Blessings, however, are soon forgotten. As is the case everywhere, devotees concentrate on their problems rather than count their blessings. Granting the happinesses that women would normally achieve with any luck—enough money, sons, a loving husband—blessings simply do not stick in the minds of their recipients' descendants. Although individualized blessings are not recalled, however, the general blessing that the *satimata* gives, the extension of her protection to the family line, is always remembered. This extension is symbolized by the *sati*'s imposition of an *ok*, a custom, practice, ordinance, that takes the form of a prohibition. As the *sativrata* prepares to die, she designates an *ok*, a special way in which she wishes to be honored. By reverencing the *satimata* as she wishes, protégées renew their end of the protective covenant.

---

49. Many women, of course, die before their husbands do and so could never directly emulate her.

The *shrap* and the *ok* are crucial elements in the establishment of *sati* guardianship. They form the foundation for the *sati*-devotee relationship.

THE *SHRAP*

If for some reason a *sati* is vexed at the time she is preparing to die, she pronounces a *shrap*. She curses one or more persons, usually close relatives, to suffer bad fortune and to have their descendants share their bad fortune for a number of generations. For example, there once was a *sativrata* whose *sasural* (conjugal household) for some unknown reason declined to provide a horse and a drummer (Dholi) for her procession to her husband's funeral pyre. A *sati* is supposed to process to the cremation ground in grand style. Because a proper procession requires these two things, the *sati*, furious, pronounced a curse. She said that from then on whenever her in-laws might have need of a good horse or a Dholi, neither would be available. The curse proved to be a tremendous hardship, for drummer and horse are essential to many ritual occasions, including weddings and coronations.

This curse is unconditional. The family has erred; it must suffer the consequences. Many *shrap*s, however, append to unconditional curses implicit and contingent curses. A good example comes from a Mewar estate. Many generations ago, the reigning *thakur* took a bride. After a while he found that he liked being married so well that he decided to take another wife. When he returned home after his second marriage, his first wife, enraged by jealousy, ambushed and murdered him. At that point the second wife took a vow to become a *sati*. Later, while preparing to mount her husband's pyre, she pronounced a curse that from then on no *thakur* of the family could be married to two women at the same time. Nevertheless, a few generations later a *thakur* disregarded the curse. Not long after the second wedding, he suddenly and mysteriously died.

Hence the curse described in this story imposed two related punishments, one explicit, the other implicit and conditional. The explicit punishment, the ban on polygamy, is itself severe. Rajput women often point out that in times past polygamy was necessary in order to ensure that at least one son would survive as heir. Because battles, illnesses, and court intrigues (including not a few poisonings) all took their toll on progeny, to have many sons was essential.

In addition, the curse contains an implicit "or else"; it portends secondary punishment if the restriction is flaunted. In the instance of the foolhardy *thakur*, that punishment was death. Family members do not know if disregarding the ban will always bring on death. They undoubtedly feel it is best not to find out.

Another good example of such a conditional curse is the story of a husband who fell off a roof and died inebriated. As a *sativrata*, his wife forbade all males in the family to touch alcohol—or else. Since that time, the women in that family told me, all men have abstained.

Whatever form such curses may take, they inevitably affect the lives of women. The absence of a good horse and Dholi means serious inconvenience for the *sati*s of later generations. It also represents interference with religious celebrations for which women are wholly or partially responsible, such as Gangaur, Tij, and Navratri.[50] The ban on remarriage of *thakur*s meant exposing the entire family to the threat of a lapsed lineage. Adoption, though accepted by Rajputs and frequent in Rajput history, has always been lamented as an undesirable necessity.[51] It has often disrupted family harmony, the preservation of which is a paramount responsibility of *pativrata*s. The ban on drinking has led women in the family to give up drinking, lest they tempt their husbands to resume the habit.

Often not the primary victims of the *sativrata*'s displeasure, women still share the consequences, for a woman must always share her husband's fate. It is a harsh one when the *shrap* is an infertility curse, by far the most common variety. Biologically, infertility is considered a woman's problem. If a husband is cursed to be heirless, his wife is understood to be infertile; however many women a man so cursed may marry, they will all be infertile. Thus the curse imposes a heavy burden of suffering on wives, who are denied the opportunity to bear sons or, in some cases, any children at all. Both fates are considered catastrophic.

In one case a *sati* caused a family to be barren for six generations, which necessitated many adoptions. In another, a *sati* gave a *shrap* that every third generation of the line would be barren. This curse, which has ended with the present generation, is assumed to have lasted seven generations. When a *sati* does not specify the duration of a curse, it is generally believed to fade after seven generations.

50. All these occasions celebrate the Goddess.
51. Six successive adoptions in the Udaipur line are attributed to a curse of infertility by the princess Krishnakumari, who was inadvertently engaged to suitors from two royal households. The insult of an alliance with one household over the other would have precipitated a war with the other, so Udaipur decided to avoid choice and allow its daughter to take poison. She did and pronounced her curse.

Up to this point the targets, whether primary or secondary, have all been members of a *sati*'s conjugal family. Although the most common targets of a *shrap* are members of the conjugal family, the focus may shift to persons who are or will be outside the *sasural*. One Mewari noblewoman told me that at her estate a *sativrata* uttered a curse that for three generations the first-born daughter of the household would never attain happiness or bear children. The effect of this curse meant that when the daughters married out of the family they took their misfortune with them. Trouble spread out from the in-laws' homes like an amoeba.

A second example of a curse that applies outside the conjugal family was told by another Mewari noblewoman. She said that once a man from her *thikana* had a daughter who became engaged to the son of the Maharana. Unfortunately, shortly after her engagement the daughter's fiancé died. The girl asked her father to take her to her fiancé's pyre, but the father was reluctant. He did not want his little girl to die.

The two argued on and on until the father, exasperated, agreed to help his daughter become a *sati*. He rigged a curtain around the outside of a bullock cart so that she could maintain *parda* during her trip. By the time he accomplished this, he had again become heavyhearted. He simply could not bring himself to drive her to her destination.

Miraculously, the cart started on its own and drove itself to the fiancé's cremation site. There in Udaipur, the girl circumambulated her fiancé's pyre seven times. In this way she married her intended.[52] Then she mounted the pyre and took her husband's head in her lap. Flames emerged from her body. Before dying, she pronounced a curse on her father's family. Today no one in the family recalls the nature of that curse. The narrator said that it lasted seven generations, then lapsed.

This story is particularly interesting for two reasons. First, it shows that no one, not even a father, may interfere with a *sati*'s plan to share the fate of her husband or even of her betrothed; from the perspective of the bride-to-be, at the moment of engagement she is his.[53] Second, it reveals that the nature of the curse is no longer important to the family. What matters is that engagement itself institutes a tradition of venerating the *satimata* and of receiving the *satimata*'s protection. She becomes

52. In the central ceremony of a Hindu wedding the groom and bride circumambulate a sacred fire. Here the bride circumambulates an unlighted pyre.

53. After an engagement is broken by either side, the groom will face no difficulty in becoming engaged to another girl, but the girl may well face great difficulty, for her engagement to marry is a commitment of fidelity to one man alone. On this situation in Bengal, see Fruzetti, *Gift of a Virgin*, 35.

the family's guardian. Since the time of the curse, the *satimata* has du-
tifully protected the family against harm.

Whether a *sativrata* curses her husband's family—the frequent tar-
get—or other relatives and their families, she utters a curse that is taken
to be benevolent and protective. The *sativrata* intends her curse as a
lesson to those whom she loves. She wants to deter them from making
future blunders.

At times, however, a *sativrata* curses persons with whom she shares
no ties of blood whatsoever. Then she punishes without providing protection. To outsiders she is malevolent and vengeful. The following story
provides rich illustration of this point.

> At my father's estate there is a *satimata*. When she was alive she was a kept
> [local English for a kept woman] of one of my ancestors. She was a Gujar
> [from an agrarian caste, which is lower than the Rajput]. In those days all
> the *thakur*s had to stay many months of the year in Udaipur in order to serve
> the Maharana. The *thakur* from our estate died while he was in Udaipur. By
> the time the news of his death reached the estate, his funeral had already
> taken place. A *sati* is supposed to burn with her husband's head on her lap.
> Because this was not possible, the Gujar girl, who had determined to die a
> *sati*, fetched her lord's turban (*pagri*) so as to immolate herself with that on
> her lap.
>
> The family's *purohit*, Nai [barber], and Dholi [drummer] [all three figure
> in the procession and ritual] refused to believe that a mere consort would
> seriously consider becoming a *sati*. The sister of the deceased *rao sahib* [the
> *thakur*] taunted her: "My brother is dead and you have taken your bath and
> put on your finery?"[54] The consort called the *purohit*, Dholi, and Nai, but
> they refused to come. Nobody from the family showed up for her procession.
>
> The kept [woman] then went to the family cremation ground. She took
> the turban and a coconut as an offering to God. She prayed and her body
> began to burn by itself. The people who happened by saw by this that she
> was a true *sati*. Everybody came running to watch.
>
> The *sati* was so furious with the "sister-in-law" [the king's sister] for teas-
> ing her that she cursed her, saying, "You and all future daughters of this
> family will have no husbands. Because of this you will have no sons. Also,
> you will have no wealth." Everyone was stunned. The crowd pleaded for
> mercy. Moved, the *sati* changed the curse so that the sister and future daugh-
> ters of the family would be without one of the three items mentioned. If a
> daughter had a husband and wealth, she would have no son. If she had a
> husband and a son, she would have no wealth. If she had a son and wealth,
> she would lose her husband. This curse lasted for seven generations.
>
> In our generation we are on the margin. I have only one son but I have a
> husband and enough money. My family has complete faith in Satimata.

54. She took the purificatory bath (required before processing to a pyre) and put on
auspicious *pativrata* garments.

Whenever we go to the *thikana*, we pay our respects to her [the implication: the *satimata* is now pleased with the family].

The *satimata* also cursed the *purohit*, Nai, and Dholi. To the *purohit* she said, "In each generation your family will have only one son and he will be half-cracked [an imbecile]." This is still true of that family. To the Nai she said, "Your family will not have sons." This also has held true. That family has always had to adopt. To the Dholi she gave a curse that was really not too much of a curse. She said, "If you or your descendants are playing your drum at one end of the village, people will not be able to hear the music at the other end of the village." This has remained true to this day.

This story exemplifies ways that a *satimata* may condemn nonrelatives who cross her. The pronouncements she makes upon them are not tempered by the mercy that she intends toward family members. The fact that she sees them as outsiders is emphasized by the character of the curses she directs toward them. She tailors her curses to relate to the performance of caste duty. Hence the Brahman, whose duty is to learn and teach philosophy and ritual, is condemned to bear the knowledge that his male descendants will be few and afflicted by imbecility. The barber, many of whose ritual functions take place during childbirth ceremonies, is deprived of male children. Finally, the drummer and his descendants will be diminished in their capacity to make music. The *sativrata* renders them incapable of performing the very services they failed to provide her when she needed them.

In short, the *sati* can devastate nonrelatives who anger her. Such acts do not cause Rajputs to think of her as having a dark side. The "good mother"—*sati mata*—may cruelly destroy others who injure her family or who insult it by interfering with its proper performance of tradition. She seeks vengeance against enemies just as the heroic *jhumjhar* seeks vengeance as he pursues enemies who have decapitated him.[55]

We might ask whether the *satimata* has a dark side, at least from the perspective of nonrelatives who have crossed her. Tradition does not really address this question. In all the stories of *satis*' curses I gathered during my research, not one explained family misfortune as a result of other people's *satimata*. Family misfortune is regularly explained by one's failure to perform proper *puja* to one's own *satimata*, not by the power of someone else's *satimata*. This misfortune is never understood as final or complete; if its duration is unspecified, it is assumed to lapse after seven generations. *Satimata*s simply do not ruin their relatives by

55. On the pervasive motif of revenge in Rajput culture, see Hitchcock, "Martial Rājpūt," 12; and Ziegler, "Action, Power," 79–80.

blood and marriage. They punish their "naughty children" but do not destroy the lot of them.[56]

We might also ask whether, narrative and ideological exegesis to the contrary, Rajput women "really" or "deep down" think of a *sati* as exacting revenge on her own family for the submission required of her when she was a *pativrata*. This question too is hard to answer. Whenever I tried to suggest the notion of spite (one that seemed to me an obvious aspect of a curse) I found myself being corrected. One elderly woman refused to discuss *sati*s with me any more; she felt a suggestion like this was insulting to her *satimata*.

If *sativrata*s have felt vengeful toward their families, their feelings are simply not interpreted as such by their families, who pass traditions of *sati* veneration down through the generations. A curse may in fact accomplish vengeance, but a *sati* cannot be seen as intending vengeance because self-serving intentions belie the very definition of *sati* and *pativrata*.[57] A *sati* who curses out of spite would not be seen as validating her life as a *pativrata*, a woman who sacrifices selfish desires on behalf of her husband and his family. An idealized representation of *sat*, she is seen as benign toward those who are her own.[58]

Given this notion of protecting "one's own," the story narrated above is especially interesting in that it provides a rare example of a non-Rajput woman who becomes a *satimata* for Rajputs. The family that doubted her vow's sincerity not only accepts this Gujar woman as a valid *sati* but venerates her. When she erupts into flames, the family comes to realize that she has made a proper vow, which unfortunately means that her curse too will be valid. Because the Gujar woman is a

56. It would be interesting to ask members of other castes whether their families have suffered from the curses of Rajput *satimata*s. Because I was interested in the perceptions of Rajput women, not others, I did not undertake this task, which would be a fascinating though time-consuming one. Recently people have celebrated *sati*s (many from non-Rajput castes and most from eastern Rajasthan) in new *mela*s (fairs), which most Rajput women dismiss as non-Rajput or unnecessary—Rajput families have their own *sati*s. I came across stories of miracles attributed to these *sati*s, but not curses. Journalists and academics have stressed the novelty of these *mela*s, which seem to be more populist and politically charged than the private Rajput *sati* veneration; see *Manushi* 42–43; and *Seminar* 342. Cf. my brief description in chapter 6, note 5, of the Jauhar Mela at Chitor, a festival distinct from the family traditions of Rajput women.

57. The following chapter explores the *satimata*'s intentions in detail.

58. Coccari also notes the attribution of unequivocal goodness to the *sati*s of Banaras. She speaks of the "pure and uplifted character of the Sati." She concludes: "The enshrined Satis in the Banaras area are idealized, honored and revered, yet do not seem to evince the powerful ambivalence which would make them more riveting objects of devotion" ("Bir Babas," 124–25).

consort of a family member and thus part of the household, she mag-
nanimously grants the family her guardianship.

The question arises, how was the Gujar woman able to become a
sativrata? One conjecture can be dismissed immediately. Being the consort of a Rajput did not transfer the Gujar into a Rajput. The Rajput
community would not have accepted her children as Rajputs. They
would be Darogas (also called Ravana Rajputs), who constitute an en-
dogamous caste of palace servants.[59]

Rather, the answer has to do with living in a Rajput environment. By
associating intimately with Rajputs, especially her Rajput lover, the Gujar woman became Rajput-like. While a consort, explain the Rajputs
who worship her, she learned to behave as a Rajput wife does. In other
words, through her loving devotion to her lord she attained a higher
moral and physical makeup. She acquired large reserves of *sat*, the sine
qua non of a *sati*.[60]

Such a thoroughgoing transmutation is, as has been stressed, unusual. A non-Rajput woman's association with her lord does not by itself transform her character. The perfection of the *pativrata* role is difficult even for Rajput wives. How much less likely it is for a consort,
who lacks not only Rajput caste but also the benefits and privileges of
wifehood. Thus, more typically, the women of another Rajput family
have discredited the death of a non-Rajput consort of an ancestor. Although their family has commemorated her death with a marker, it says
that it does not reverence her as a *sati* and has suffered no harm on this
account.

Paradoxically, because the Rajputs think it unlikely that such a consort would accumulate the *sat* sufficient to become a valid *sati*, they recognize her as a particularly powerful paradigm. Having received fewer
advantages than her married harem mates, she can demonstrate more
gratitude than they can. Overcoming an inherent disadvantage, she
comes to represent the epitome of *pativrata* selflessness. In this she compares closely to very young Rajput wives who die as *sati*s. Lacking the

59. Often Rajput men took women from other castes as consorts and sometimes as
wives; Rajput women married only Rajput men. During medieval times the offspring of
Rajput men and consorts were not accepted as Rajput, but those of Rajput men and lower-
caste wives occasionally were (Ziegler, "Action, Power," 52–55). More research is needed
on where and when the marriage of a non-Rajput woman legitimized her offspring as
Rajput. Contemporary Rajputs disapprove of all marriages between Rajputs (female or
male) and non-Rajputs.

60. On personal mobility in the traditional Rajasthani context, see ibid., 21–26.

status and privileges of their senior co-wives and having a newer attachment to their husbands, they therefore show greater gratitude in becoming *sativrata*s. If the youngest wife is the only wife who takes *sati*'s *vrat*, she puts her elders to shame. Her glory stands in heightened contrast to their petty insincerity.[61] Becoming a *sati*, the youngest wife, like the sincere consort, illustrates the very purest of intentions.

Ignored or vexed, a *sati* is a dangerous woman. The nature of her wrath, however, must be interpreted according to its targets and the intentions she holds for them. Even the consort and the young bride, only partially or newly integrated into a household, can prove earnest *sati* guardians. What qualifies them is the unreserved love and respect they have given those men to whom they have dedicated themselves as *pativrata*s.

THE OK

Whether or not a *sativrata* pronounces a curse on the family (or families) she will protect, she invariably confers a specific means by which they can communicate their reverence for her. This is the *ok* (custom). *Ok*s may ban the use of certain items or the performance of customary *pativrata* activities.

The most common restriction designated by a *satimata* is of designated colors of clothing. Typically, these shades are of pink or red, the colors worn at the time of marriage. For example, because of one *satimata*'s pronouncement, Jhala Rajputs have had to give up red wedding dresses for green ones.

Also common is a prohibition on the *pilya* (literally, yellow), a deep yellow half-sari head covering with a red border and red tie-dyed speckles that women wear in the period following childbirth. Hence when women of many lineages emerge from the seclusion that is mandatory at childbirth, they must substitute for the *pilya* some other attire. That restrictions on red shades and the *pilya* dominate the *ok*s for clothing is telling. Red is the color of passion, the *pilya* the color of fertility. Both represent auspiciousness.

The second most common prohibition is on types of jewelry. The item restricted is inevitably some ornament associated with marriage.

---

61. The youngest wife's enhanced virtue and power emerges in stories I collected. One example tells of a maidservant from a Mewar Solah Thikana who drinks water from her young mistress's purificatory *sati* bath; the water magically compels the servant to join her mistress on the cremation pyre but others restrain and save her.

An unmarried girl wears a minimum of jewelry in order not to draw to herself the attentions of men. A wife, on learning of the death of her husband, breaks the glass bangles she is wearing and gives away the remainder of her wedding ornaments. Because remarriage is not considered an option for Rajput women, widows wish to discourage men's attention by forsaking ornamentation. Although nowadays these restrictions are slightly relaxed, most unmarried girls and widows wear little, if any, jewelry.

Examples of jewelry *ok*s are plentiful. The most common bans the noisy ankle bracelet (*gughari*), a chain to which many tiny square bells (*caurasi*) are attached. The jingling of these bells is considered alluring. Many Indian poems tell of a lover whose anticipation of a tryst with his beloved is heightened by the tinkling sound of her approaching footstep. Here also the interdicted item is associated with auspiciousness. The anklet symbolizes marriage; the woman awaited in poetry is married to someone else.

Other *ok*s preclude the wearing of specific kinds of arm bangles. The most frequently prohibited bangles are of ivory, either natural-colored or red-dyed, that a bride receives at the time of her wedding. Some women may wear red but not the natural shade. For other families the natural is the acceptable hue. In a number of households, the bangles prohibited are thin glass bracelets with tiny facets. Because these facets sparkle in the sunlight, they are thought particularly captivating. The same holds true in other families for bangles with gold inlay or gold painting. Moreover, gold symbolizes affluence, which enhances the symbolic value of the bangles' auspiciousness. Finally, many families observe *ok*s that prohibit various shades of glass bangles. Some families do not wear red ones. Others must forswear purple or green. All these shades, like the items themselves, represent auspiciousness.

Although most of the *ok*s connected with dress involve clothing and jewelry, one unusual *ok* bears mention in passing because, more radically than any other prohibition, it ties an *ok* to auspiciousness. This is the ban on *sindur*, the red powder worn by married women in the parting of their hair. Not only the quintessential mark of a *pativrata*, *sindur* is used in the worship (*puja*) of deities. A denser symbol of auspiciousness could not be found.

All the *ok*s discussed thus far apply directly to women. A second class of prohibitions applies to women through the children in their charge. In this case the *ok*s apply to women not as wives, or potential mothers, but to those who have already had the good fortune to bear children.

This class of *ok*s largely prohibits the use of baby cradles, though there are isolated instances of other child-related *ok*s. A notable example is the *ok* prohibiting mothers in one family from dressing their children in clothing until the children have gone through their hair-cutting ceremonies.[62] It means that children are supposed to go naked during the first months, even the first year, of life.

The overwhelming majority of *ok*s, then, apply to women in their auspicious roles: wife and mother. Curiously enough, a *satimata*'s ban on designated auspicious items is itself auspicious; observance of the ban brings a devotee under the protection of the *satimata*, the ultimate *pativrata*. The *ok*, which never lapses, establishes a permanent relationship between the family and a *sati*. The honoring of prohibitions represents continuing acceptance of and appreciation for a *satimata*'s protection. Moreover, observing *ok*s is an important means for the *pativrata* to accumulate *sat*. Whereas the curse is something that she must suffer, the *ok* allows her to endure a curse, to face the hardships and disappointments of life, and to advance in her aspirations toward meeting the ideal that the *sati* embodies.

Up to this point I have discussed the *shrap* and the *ok* as distinct features of a *sativrata*'s power and her devotees' response. Often, however, the relation between *shrap* and *ok* is an intimate one. This is true when the curse is conditional. In the story narrated above, when a *sati* cursed her *thakur* husband (the one murdered by his first wife) and all his reigning descendants, she simultaneously established an *ok*: the abstention from multiple marriages.

A second illustration of the association between *shrap* and *ok* is presented by the following story from an Udaipur estate.

> One time a husband and wife from our family were playing *caupad*.[63] The wife was winning. The husband was irritated by this and joked that he would kill her brother and father. She became angry and wrote a letter to her brother and father to send soldiers to attack her husband. The soldiers came. There was a big battle in which the husband was killed. The wife became a *sati*. She made the *ok* that no husband and wife should play *caupad* together.

Though this account has no explicit mention of a *shrap*, the family understands that a curse has occurred. The *sati* intends to teach the family a lesson; her *ok* implies an "or else." The story relates no instance of violation, but the family assumes that to do so would be perilous. Ig-

---

62. The hair is usually offered to a goddess (a *kuldevi* or sometimes a village goddess) or, less often, to her attendant, Bheru Ji.
63. This Indian board game looks like a cross between chess and parcheesi.

noring an *ok* conjoined to a curse is simply more dangerous than ignoring an *ok* in isolation. The consequence of violating an isolated *ok* is only the *satimata*'s withdrawal of a modicum of protection. If the family renews its observance, the protection resumes. By contrast, if a *sati* utters a prohibition when she is angry (when stating or insinuating a curse), the consequences of violation may be much greater, and perhaps irreversible. The nobleman who married and should not have, received no second chance. By punishing the individual, the *sativrata* instructed the family, the preservation of which is always her foremost interest.

The relation between conditional *shrap*s and *ok*s is so close that the words are sometimes used interchangeably. A woman may say that a *sati* was angry and imposed an *ok*. When asked if this means that the *sati* pronounced a curse, the answer will be, yes, obviously (*zarur*). The conclusion that the *sati* must have been angry may, however, be deduced. If punishment for violation of an *ok* is known to be severe, the *ok* is thought to involve a curse. Thus the grounds on which a curse is adjudged to have occurred are either the initial motivation of the *sati*, anger, or the consequence of an *ok*'s violation, a severe punishment, which indicates anger.

Conveying a fuller sense of the variety of forms that *shrap* together with *ok* can take is this final example of *sati* narrative. One time a wife was preparing to die as a *sati*. She tried to persuade her co-wife to join her. The co-wife responded, "I'd love to, really, but you see I have all these dishes to do. You go on ahead." Unimpressed by the flimsy excuse, the *sati* forbade all the household's women from doing dishes at night so that they would be free to tend to more important responsibilities. Because becoming a *sati* is the expression of ultimate devotion, the work that was used as a reason for not becoming a *sati* is interdicted.

In this story, as in so many others, the activity banned by the *ok* is an auspicious activity: no good *pativrata* leaves the dinner dishes undone. I have stressed the connection between *ok* and auspiciousness throughout. I now wish to clarify the rationale behind banning auspicious activities, from the wearing of certain clothes to the doing of dishes at night. First, although given items and activities are auspicious, their usage or performance is inauspicious in specific contexts. Anything that should be associated with being a *pativrata* but that becomes meaningful in itself—and so potentially, if not actually, harms a husband—is no longer acceptable. The excuse that a devoted wife must do the dishes rather than die as a *sati* simply will not do. It is meaningless. Playing *caupad* with a husband in order to entertain him is not a valid activity if it brings about the husband's death. Finally, the donning of clothing, jewelry, and cosmetics symbolic of *pativrata* status is not acceptable if a woman is not prepared to sacrifice these symbols of household life when her husband dies.

This explanation, however, is but half the answer. Although becoming a *sati* is an affirmation of the auspicious role of the *pativrata*, it results in death. The *sati* is auspicious but death epitomizes inauspiciousness. The activities connected with death and the items worn at death or explicitly prohibited at the time of death are necessarily associated with death. However blessed, death is inescapably a tragedy.

Furthermore, the *sati*'s immolation is part of a double death. There is the death of the *sati*, an intentional death, and there is the death of the husband, a death utterly non-normative from the female point of view. Even where the male sacrifices his life in battle and thus attains the glory and honor that are the goals of the Rajput warrior, his death is inauspicious for his wife and family. Women's religious rituals and women's household tasks are directed toward protecting the husband against such an untimely end. Thus death as a *sati* is characterized by inharmonious associations. The act of immolation is meritorious; the reason for the act is not. In sum, becoming a *sativrata* is on one level auspicious—hence the potency of the beneficial *ok*—and on another inauspicious—hence the dangerousness of the *sati*'s wrath.

The strangely liminal condition of the *sati*-to-be specifies the *sativrata*'s double nature. The *sativrata* is a woman who has lost her husband but is not a widow. She is neither still in this world nor beyond it. During this marginal and fleeting existence her power of *sat* culminates and becomes manifest.[64] She has renounced life but is not yet dead. In this she resembles the *sannyasi*, the ascetic who has renounced the world but continues to live in it. As the *sannyasi* has symbolically performed his own funeral rites to symbolize his freedom from social responsibilities, the *sativrata*, having learned of her husband's death, has taken a vow to die, which relieves her of her duties as wife and mother. Out of her devotion springs the will to renounce the rules that in life are inseparable from devotion. That is to say, she renounces her status as a *pativrata*, which, in the absence of a husband, is meaningless, in fact impossible. Nevertheless, in becoming a *sati* she is affirming her erstwhile status as a *pativrata* while she transcends it. In this time of suspension and renun-

64. For the classic structuralist perspective on marginality, see Victor Turner, "Betwixt and Between," in *The Forest of Symbols*, ed. Victor Turner (Ithaca: Cornell University Press, 1967), 93–111.

ciation, the *sati* is both powerful and dangerous. Her decisions to apply her powers to bless and to curse are understood to derive from a vantage point of transcendent wisdom born of renunciation.

The ambiguity of the dutiful wife whose husband has died shows up in accounts of *sati* processions.[65] In some the *sati*, having first broken her bangles, gives away all her precious jewelry. She is performing the actions of a widow, acknowledging that her husband has died and that she is no longer a wife in the normal sense. She goes to the pyre devoid of ornamentation. This scenario, the basics of which my informants often described, matches the perceptions of Robert De Nobili, an early seventeenth-century Jesuit missionary who reported from Madurai on the *sati* immolations performed by wives of a deceased monarch. In narrating the story of one particular *sati*, he says:

> Then she rose . . . and went to the river, where she bathed, and put on a cloth dyed with saffron; she distributed her necklace, ear-rings, and arm-rings among her relations, came close to the pit, round which she walked once, speaking to each of her acquaintances, and then, raising her hands, jumped with a cheerful face into the fire.[66]

As in many other Rajasthani narratives, this description of a *sati*'s death shows a woman who wears jewelry until she is ready to ascend the pyre, but it lays emphasis on her giving her jewels away. Similarly, many Rajput women make much of the fact that the *sati*, no longer the wife of a living husband, renounces her most precious possessions. In such descriptions renunciation connotes widowhood.

In other *sati* accounts, emphasis rests not on renouncing jewels but on wearing them, at least until immolation is imminent. In this vein, Rajput women note that a *sati* prohibits auspicious jewelry, clothing, and cosmetics because she is wearing these at the time of her sacrifice, not because she gives them away before her sacrifice. Some women believe that *sati*s wear their jewels into the fire. Others emphasize that their families' *sati*s dress up in the finery that *pativrata*s wear.[67] Putting on

65. Dennis Hudson's compilation of *sati* ceremonies includes prescriptions by the nineteenth-century Bengali ritualist Raghunathan: "Let those women, not widowed . . . being wives, ascend . . . to the proper place . . . (and) enter the fire with the body of their husband." Cited as "Translated by Yogendra Chunder Ghose, editor of *The English Works of Raja Rammohun Roy*, compiled and published by Eshan Chunder Bose, 2 vols., [Calcutta, 1885], Vol. I, footnote one, pp. 353–54, translation slightly modified," in Hudson's annotated "Examples of the Ritual Act of Sati."

66. From Vincent Cronin, *A Pearl to India* (New York: Dutton, 1959), 53–54 in Hudson.

67. See the account given by John Scudder, a Protestant missionary in the 1820s, as quoted from May Pauline Jeffry, *Ida S. Scudder of Vellore*, Jubilee Edition (Mysore City:

wedding dresses or *pilya*s, two common subjects of *ok*s, these *sati*s act
as *pativrata*s, as is implied by the *sati* act. But the narratives give stress
to renunciation with minimal reference to the technicality of widowhood. Wearing jewelry into the fire or giving it up—either act conveys
renunciation.

In accounts of *sati* immolation the symbolism of widowhood may be
pronounced or minimized, but the interpretation of the *sati* ritual is
bound by the concept of widowhood. The symbols of sacrifice may be
those of widowhood that in turn draw on *sannyas*, ascetic renunciation;
unmediated, they may stress *sannyas* or simply imply widowhood. The
underlying premise remains: before she ascends the pyre, the *sati* is either both wife and widow or neither wife nor widow. The two formu-
lations employ the same discourse. Both reveal a mutually implicating
tension between auspiciousness and inauspiciousness.

The auspicious items and activities tied to the *sativrata*, whose status
is ambiguous, remain auspicious. But their usage or performance is inauspicious because it indicates bad intentions: it reveals a lapse in the
vow of the *pativrata*, which is the very foundation of the *sati* transformation. This distinction between the auspiciousness of the items and
activities and the inauspiciousness of their usage or performance is subtle and vital. And, as we shall see, it illuminates the tradition of *sati*
veneration.

In sum, investigating *ok*s has divulged the deeper aspects of *sativrata*
character. It has provided a symbolic basis for interpreting the *sativrata*'s goodness and dangerousness. Moreover, in detailing the transition
that the *sativrata* stage represents, it has elucidated the conceptual connection between the *pativrata*, who sacrifices personal desires to fulfill
those of her husband and family, and the *satimata*, who protects the
husband and family directly and also indirectly, by helping the *pativrata*
to protect them. Finally, it has shown how the *sativrata*, not yet a fully
transcendent being, publicly communicates with those whom she intends to protect. Manifesting her *sat*, she demonstrates that her acquisition of *sativrata* power results from a cultivated attitude of selfless sacrifice, only the final expression of which is the sacrifice she will make on
her husband's pyre.

In the course of describing the basics of *sati* transformation, I have

---

1951), 9–10 in Hudson. Some informants said that *sati*s wore their finery into the fire,
except their bangles, which were kept and put into a bundle with the ashes and bones and
then were stored in a domestic temple.

presented two fundamental propositions. I have stated that the *satimata* is a paradigm that integrates within a wholly domestic context the competing aspects of the Rajput woman's identity as a Rajput and as a woman. This integration is a reflection of the goodness, the *sat*, that the *satimata* realized while she herself pursued the ideal of the *pativrata*.

Second, I have characterized the *satimata* as a protector who protects her family members, even when she curses. To aid protégées she issues commands that establish customs, which condition her continuing protection and provide means for veneration. On the basis of these propositions, chapter 5 explores the motivations women have as they interpret the *satimata*'s orders and assimilate the paradigm of duty that she represents. Its overarching purpose is to examine the paramount role of intention in the protective actions that *pativratas* perform.

Satimata Tradition

The Role of Volition

With *sati* veneration, it is clearly the thought that counts. This is true whether we observe the *satimata* who harms a family in the short run to help it in the long run or whether we consider the women who revere a *satimata* to avoid her wrath and gain her blessing. In both cases we must assess intention and motive; without such an assessment, some behavioral aspects of *sati* tradition fail to make sense. Pursuing the *sati* ideal, women act in ways that seem contrary to the ideal and yet are interpreted by other women as supportive of the ideal because of the valid intentions that guide them. My aim here is to explain how it is that in certain motivational contexts women can pursue the *sati* ideal while not observing *ok*s, not obeying their husbands, and not dying as *sati*s.

NOT OBSERVING *OK*S

As we have seen, one way Rajput women reciprocate the protective services that *satimata*s render is to honor *ok*s, customary observances. Pursuant to their *satimata*'s request, they renounce the performance of a specific activity or the use of a special item. When we compare and analyze *ok*s as religious symbols, we must pay close attention to the explanation of *ok*s that Rajput women offer. Rajput women do not ponder patterns of similarity and difference—they may know only the *ok*s observed in their own homes. Nor do they contemplate levels of symbolic meaning. Most commonly, they simply say that observance of *ok*s "shows faith in Satimata." Though simple, this answer is helpful; it travels a good distance toward explaining some of the peculiar ways in which *ok*s are practiced or, perhaps more accurately, not practiced.

Rajput women stress faith to such an extent that in many cases their observance of an *ok* does not necessarily require the practice of the *ok*. What is prohibited becomes permitted if respect (*samman*) for the *sati*'s wishes is retained. Many women who say they obey *ok*s but in practice use what they should not, explain that they may do what is prohibited because they show respect for their *satimata* in an alternative way. They conclude that if they acknowledge *ok*s and express faith, then they may avoid the inconvenience associated with that *ok*. There are various ways in which women manage *ok*s so as to minimize inconvenience and yet show due respect. They often conclude that they may use a prohibited item if it is not purchased or if it is not actually owned by the family. Renounced by the family, it may be used if it comes from a source outside the family. Thus, for example, the woman whose children were prohibited from wearing clothes before their hair-cutting ceremonies could allow her children to wear clothes borrowed from outside the family or given to the family. In this situation and in many situations like it, the assumed source of prohibited items will be natal families of daughters-in-law.

This is not to say that all families observe only the spirit and not the letter of the *sati*'s injunctions. In some families cradles are prohibited outright. Yet in most, cradles may be borrowed or accepted as presents. The same holds true for interdicted items of clothing and jewelry. Some families practice complete abstinence. Others borrow or accept the items as gifts. Still others reject the idea of borrowing or receiving gifts but will permit use of a banned item if a member of the family provides a token payment for it. Such is the case in the family to which vermilion (*sindur*) is prohibited. Family members cannot purchase vermilion directly but can receive it from others who have bought vermilion if in return they hand over a small sum, usually a rupee. In one case, a woman circumvented the problem of not being able to use a cradle for her baby by giving her family's *satimata* a miniature silver cradle in lieu of the abstinence imposed by the *sati*'s *ok*.

Borrowing prohibited items, receiving them as gifts, providing only token financial consideration for them, or replacing them with alternate sacrifices may all seem like too convenient ways of getting around prohibitions and so subverting a *satimata*'s purpose. Such cynicism is unwarranted. Women's purpose in obeying *ok*s is to sacrifice in honor of the *satimata* that in turn she might protect their husbands and help them protect their husbands. If the intent to honor the *satimata* is present and marked by some form of observance, then the *satimata*'s will is not frustrated. In short, if the spirit of self-sacrifice is preserved and combined with proper respect and worship of the *satimata*, then all may be thought proper.

The conclusion to be reached: devotion to the *satimata* and devotion to the husband whom she protects require not mere abstinence but active, mindful renunciation. If the spirit of sacrifice is present, then the act may be adapted. Not empty ritual, it is believed, but mindful renunciation will please the *sati* so that she will give protection and help the *pativrata* perform her job of protection.[1] The renunciation practiced by attention to *ok*s parallels the renunciation practiced by the *sati* at the time of her cremation.

When a *pativrata* decides to reject or abandon an *ok*'s observance, she must substitute an alternative observance, which will enable her to show respect for her guardian while allowing her to do things she judges essential for a *pativrata*, such as clothing her children and providing them with cradles. This motif of disobedience true to the spirit of being a *pativrata* is not, however, confined to the observance or, rather, non-observance of *ok*s. It is a motif that pervades the stories told about famous *pativrata*s and about *pativrata*s who become *sati*s. Such stories provide context for an adequate interpretation of intent and sacrifice in the *sati* scenario.

NOT OBEYING HUSBANDS

The *sati*, we have seen, renounces *pativrata* status while she reincorporates the *pativrata* ideal on a supernatural level. As a protector, the *satimata* is the preserver of family fertility. Because of her death as a *pativrata*, she is especially empowered to promote birth. Her incorporation of the mutually dependent processes of birth and death makes her a compelling symbol. Through self-sacrifice the *satimata* acquires power over the most basic life processes.

In a parallel way, the *pativrata* too brings together self-sacrifice and birth. The *pativrata* is the very embodiment of chastity, itself a form of renunciation. It is clear from the stories women tell and the explanations

---

1. On the notion that intention is more important than action see Gold, *Fruitful Journeys*, 297–98, on pilgrimage; and Bennett, *Dangerous Wives*, 49, on *puja*.

they offer for the primacy of chastity that it represents the female coun-terpart of male celibacy (*brahmacarya*). Chastity presupposes both re-nunciation and fertility: it assumes active sexuality within the confines of marriage. What is renounced is not sexuality but unwifely sexuality. What is affirmed is the fertility of the family line, and hence of *kul* and caste. Furthermore, to set this notion in its broader context, what is de-nied is not the self per se but those self-centered impulses that are by definition unwifely. The role of wife and mother requires expression of sexuality as a duty, one that a Rajput woman can and should assert herself to pursue.[2] Wives speak frequently of the importance of attract-ing one's husband by wearing flattering clothes, plenty of jewels, and sweet perfumes.[3]

Marital fidelity, the most fundamental aspect of the *pativrata* role, gives us a model for other acts of renunciatory assertion. When a woman sacrifices in order to fulfill a duty, her acts may appear, out of context, radically insubordinate and just plain bad behavior. In other words, beginning with chastity and extending to the other duties of a wife, the ethic of protective sacrifice is not simply a negative, self-effac-ing role. Many women I interviewed commented that performing a *pa-tivrata*'s role requires wisdom, for women must often make hard deci-sions. The duty to sacrifice always needs interpretation. Sometimes a woman must even decide whether obedience to her husband is a service or a disservice to him. Rajput lore is full of examples of *pativrata*s who become *sativrata*s after they controvert their husbands' orders and in this way help them and their families, whose welfare depends on the proper performance of wifely duty.

We have had a glimpse of this duty to controvert male wishes in the discussion of curses. The *sati* who curses her wine-loving husband and the *sati* who curses her previously married husband both act in ways seemingly incommensurate with the ideal of the *pativrata*. Both women, however, find that their husbands have exercised bad judgment. Al-though alcohol and polygamy are recognized as permissible for Rajput

2. Throughout India sexual intercourse is understood in the first instance as a female need and its satisfaction as the duty of husbands; see, for example, Carstairs, *Twice Born*, 73; the discussion of "the lustful bride" in Shulman, *Tamil Temple Myths*, 141, 166–76; and O'Flaherty, *Śiva*, esp. 141, which quotes the divine yogi, Shiv: "This girl with her magnificent buttocks must not come near me. . . . Wise men know that a woman is the very form of Enchantment . . . the destruction of ascetics."
3. Rajput women tend to regard their peers in general as having a unique beauty and allure. When asked to describe Rajput women, informants often noted Rajput women's facial features, which they considered particularly refined and aristocratic-looking. Many correlated these attractive features with the need for *parda*.

men, the men are expected to drink and marry responsibly. Women who have married into the families of these *sati*s adjudge the *sati*s' curses to be justified. The curses are tailored to ensure that men will learn their responsibilities as men.

It may here be objected that these interpretations of *sativrata*s' commands are only rationalizations used by women to serve their own agendas. But this is precisely the point. Women believe that the curses convey commands that women are bound to fulfill or to see that men fulfill. The very fact that women interpret curses bolsters their own authority as wives and mothers. As family-protectors they explain and enforce the family-protecting orders that *satimata*s give. A clear example of this is the way women in the family whose *sati* prohibited men from drinking alcohol today enforce their *sati*'s will and also provide an example by their own abstinence.[4]

Although men venerate *satimata*s, their wives perform the majority of *satimata* rituals. Women understand *shrap*s and *ok*s as expressing the will of their predecessors, which they interpret and enforce. Women are the primary tellers of *satimata* tales and performers of *satimata* ritual. When men participate in *satimata* worship, they seem not to alter the meaning of the rituals and stories that women in the family share.

In short, *satimata*s' *shrap*s and *ok*s confer authority on women, who at times use their authority to protect their households in apparent deviation from the norm of wifely obedience. Sacrificing their personal desires (such as the desire to please their husbands), they may legitimately demand that *satimata*s be properly propitiated and that their pronouncements be honored. It is always a woman's responsibility to make her husband tend to all his ritual duties, for these duties contribute to his welfare, the preservation and promotion of which are his wife's sworn responsibility. This correlation between the renunciation of selfish wants and the duty to make men do what they ought extends to many contexts.

Exemplifying the general notion of renunciation as entailing a positive formulation of female duty are the following stories, which tell of women controverting male wishes to promote male duty, as they understand it. Many of these stories recount successful attempts by Rajput women to goad or trick men into performing their duties as warriors. In

4. See Harlan, "Sati Veneration," in "New Light on Sati," ed. John Stratton Hawley. Many women do not like their husbands to drink much alcohol; they consider alcoholism a problem in their community particularly because Rajput drinking is sanctioned by tradition. They often say that problems of adjustment caused by disinheritance have caused many men to become depressed and drink too much.

one story that women love to tell, a husband, wishing he were with his wife rather than in the battle then raging around him, abandons the field for his fortress. Having been told of the approach of her husband, however, his wife directs a servant to have the fortress gates locked tight so that her husband will not be able to come home. The sad soldier's only option is to return to battle.

In a similarly popular story among Rajput women, a husband comes home in the midst of war and goes to see his wife and mother. The mother tells her daughter-in-law to prepare some food for him. The wife, who is outraged by her husband's cowardice, bangs her cooking pots as she prepares his meal; her mother-in-law, also furious, scolds her for handling the kitchen utensils too noisily. In a voice loud enough to ensure that her son can hear, she calls into the kitchen, "You mustn't frighten my son. How the sound of clanging iron terrifies my timid little son!" The mother-in-law's insinuation that iron kitchen utensils banged together sound to her son like clashing swords, which frighten him, is of course highly insulting. Angered, the son returns to the battlefield. Hence despite an ostensible respect for the warrior's desire to stay home, the wife and mother manage to drive him out into the battlefield, where he risks his life instead of his honor.[5]

Rajput women tell many other stories in which women are credited with shaming their husbands into doing their duty.[6] In one, a woman from one of Mewar's biggest *thikanas* tells her maidservant not to bring her cowardly husband coals for his pipe in an iron container because iron might remind him of the weapons he so fears. Having fled battle, the man does the honorable thing by committing suicide.

Stories such as these articulate a norm of positive renunciation. The mother or wife sets aside her desire to gratify her loved one and secure his safety. In both instances, the woman acts as a wife of the family and a perpetuator of the family line. She sacrifices her personal happiness—predicated on the safety of her husband—in order to support his role as a performer of male/caste duty.

The principle that guides these stories combines with the *sati* ideal in the two following popular legends that I here consider together for pur-

5. Among the exemplary mothers who shame their sons into battle is one who says to her faint-hearted son, "You've drunk my milk, now slay the enemy." This recalls the story of Guha, whose mother says that if she has *sat*, then her son and his descendants will be successful kings.
6. Rajasthani folklore frequently uses the motif of women motivating warriors (Kothari, "Epics of Rajasthan," 15). One *thakur* expressed the same notion of motivation: "Our ladies tell us what we should do, otherwise we cannot do it. It's the mother's job to tell the son to kill, to die, to fight in battle."

poses of comparison. Women often recited them to me during my stay. The first, the story of Hari Rani,[7] involves a woman who is not a *sati* in the narrow sense of the term: she does not immolate herself on her husband's pyre. In fact, she kills herself while her husband lives and faces no imminent danger of death.[8] Nevertheless, she is called Sati Hari Rani and is invoked in discussions on *satis* because her death is seen as a direct manifestation of her *sat*. Rather than recount one of the many detailed and elaborate accounts of this famous story I include here only the bare bones essential to its paradigm of duty. This course is particularly appropriate as most Rajput women know only the story skeleton and base their interpretation on it. The narrative from an interview with a Mewari *thakurani* is a good example:

> Hari Rani had just been married to the Lord of Salumbar [one of the major estates of Mewar] when he was summoned by the Maharana to help repulse an attack by Aurangzeb. The husband was so enamored of his new bride that he had great difficulty pulling himself away from her to go and fight. Barely managing to leave her, he could muster no enthusiasm for the upcoming battle. When he reached the palace gates, he sent word back to Hari Rani that she should send him some souvenir to take to war with him so that he could feel she was by his side. Without hesitating, the devoted wife drew a sword and sliced off her head so that he could take that with him. When a maidservant delivered the head to him, he affixed it to his saddle and, inspired by his wife's example of devotion, rode off to do his duty as a soldier.

The second story is that of Ruthi Rani or the Angry Queen. A typical version of this tale was told to me by another *thakurani* from Mewar.

> There was once a very beautiful princess of Jaisalmer. Both Jaipur and Jodhpur wanted her in marriage. There was almost a war, so many kings wanted to marry her.
> The Maharaja of Jodhpur forced his presence on her father. They signed a treaty, one of the conditions of which was that the Maharaja would have the hand of the Jaisalmer princess. The father, however, managed matters so that the groom's *gaddi* (wedding throne) would be precariously perched over a hidden pit. Thus when the groom attempted to sit down, he would fall to his death.
> Having discovered this plot, the daughter sent a maid to warn her betrothed that he should test the *gaddi* with his sword before sitting upon it. She also pleaded with her father not to carry out his plan, but to no avail. At

---

7. "Hari" (Haḍi) is a feminized patronymic, indicating that the father of the queen (*rani*) was from the Hara *shakh* of the Cauhan *kul*.

8. In this she resembles the *sati* who dies in *jauhar*. The *jauhar sati* dies before or while her husband fights what appears to be an unwinnable battle. By dying, she frees him from worry about her welfare and saves herself from the possible shame of rape by triumphant enemy forces.

the ceremony, the groom tested the *gaddi* and its seat fell into the pit below. Another *gaddi* was set upon a safe spot and the ceremonies were completed.

After the wedding, the groom went to the bridal chamber. His wife was preparing for her wedding night in a back room. The groom sat waiting for her. Strong drink and dancing girls had been provided for his entertainment. Having waited some time and consumed some wine, the groom grabbed one of the dancers, sat her on his lap, and began to amuse himself with her. Just then the princess entered the room. Disgusted, she turned and left.

Having seen his wife's beautiful face, the groom became impassioned. He pleaded with her to stay, but she kept on walking. Then she sent him a message that because he was so impatient that he could not wait for her even a short time, she had decided not to join his harem. (He already had many wives.) He hoped she would change her mind, but after seven days he decided he had better go home. The queen's family tried to convince her to go with him, but she refused. Because she was now a queen of Jodhpur, the Maharaja left with her a suitable staff of servants.

Two or three years passed. The queen was still angry, even though she knew her husband's behavior was typical of kings. About that time, the Maharaja found it necessary to go to war. He sent Ruthi Rani a message asking her to come to him before he faced battle. Reluctantly, she agreed.

When the queen's procession neared Jodhpur, the Maharaja sent her a message that he would soon be out to greet her. Meanwhile, a Caran caught sight of the entourage and sang out a song (*doha*). In effect he said, "We thought that this woman was beauty and pride incarnate, but now we see that she is just an ordinary woman." Her anger rekindled, the queen returned to Jaisalmer.

The Jodhpur Maharaja was killed in the battle. He had left orders that were he to be slain, his head should be sent to his angry wife. Upon receipt of the head, the queen immolated herself as a *sati*.

Both stories exemplify willful disobedience by women. The wives shame their husbands and subvert their husbands' intentions. Women nonetheless hold them up as exemplary *pativrata*s. Their strong willpower—an attribute that many Rajput women see themselves as possessing—enables them to make men do the right thing.[9] Like the wives in the stories of the locked palace gates and the clanging dishes, these brides force their husbands to behave in ways contrary to their personal whims but commensurate with their status as Rajputs. In most of the stories presented, the motive that women have in chastising their hus-

9. Rajput women frequently stress their insistence on proper behavior. One said, "Even if marriage is *suli*—torture by impalement—you must be willing to perform your duties." Another explained, "We Rajputs have very strong willpower and the guts to face all our problems. In the old days, Rajput men married three or four times, but the wives didn't fight with one another because they had guts." Still another extended this notion of willpower to control over others. "Because of their will," she said in English, Rajput women get what they want done, "by hook or by crook."

bands is patent. They want their husbands to fulfill their duties as warriors. In the final story, however, the motive is complex and less clear. Ruthi Rani gives her husband two rebuffs. The context of each is important.

With the first rebuff, Ruthi Rani reacts against what she understands to be improper behavior on the part of her groom. As the noblewoman who narrated the story commented, it is not wrong for a king to toy with damsels—that is to be expected. What incenses Ruthi Rani, she went on to say, is the lack of respect the king shows for her as his wife. As a bride determined to make herself as alluring as possible to her husband, the queen takes time to be bathed and adorned. When she is ready to give herself to her husband, however, she finds that he has allowed a mere dancing girl to upstage his bride. The king's behavior is insulting; it demeans her sense of wifely duty and dignity. Although such actions are appropriate to a Rajput king under other circumstances, here they are offensive, which is why she becomes so angry.

The second half of the story demonstrates that by withdrawing from her husband's company, Ruthi Rani proves that she will not allow him to forget his transgression: the Maharaja must not be allowed to confuse the place of wife and concubine. Especially striking is the story's ending. Still lovesick, the king finally persuades the queen to see him before he goes off to war. It was, after all, customary for women to see their husbands off and so inspire them as they left for battle. Nevertheless, when the queen hears the biting criticism of the Caran, whose caste duty is to sing of the Maharaja's achievements in order to expand the Maharaja's glory and power, she determines to rebuff her husband a second time. Were her reason mere vanity, however, doubtless she would not be held up as an exemplar. To interpret this renewed rejection we need to focus on two elements, the symbolic character of the bard and the connection between the queen's arrival and the inception of battle.

First, the bard. Presumably the song he sings is designed to protect the king's honor. His purpose is to bar the queen from the king's residence. If she enters, she impoverishes her pride, a pride based on her relationship with her husband and a pride that has been instructive, if painful, for her husband. Making this especially vivid is a variation on the bard's advice that the husband of one of my informants narrated to me in poetic (*doha*) form. Wishing the wife to go away, the bard sings, "If the queen keeps her pride, she loses her husband; if she keeps her husband, she loses her pride. These two elephants cannot be chained in the same stable."[10] That the bard intends the queen to choose pride and sacrifice her intention to be with her husband is apparent, for he discourages her from proceeding.

Second, the war. Its outbreak means that the queen arrives just as the king should leave home. I heard no specific commentary on this circumstance but speculate that the queen's arrival might threaten the king's resolve to do battle. The other narratives show the danger that a king's preoccupation with his wife can prove to the king's duty and his kingdom's welfare. In this instance, the king's infatuation with his very beautiful and long-inaccessible wife may well distract him.

Thus the story offers the queen an excellent reason to turn back. Her goal in coming to Jodhpur is to do her duty as a wife by supporting him in his performance of military duty. When she realizes that her decision to come to Jodhpur will not achieve that end but rather defeat it, she determines to withdraw. Her goal has remained constant; her means of arriving at that goal has changed along with her destination. That the king thinks his wife a virtuous woman is demonstrated by his order to have his head sent to her after his death. The delivery of the head suggests the king's expectation that his wife, being virtuous, will become a *sati* by immolating herself with his head on her lap.[11] His expectation is fulfilled. The queen's death manifests the purity of her heart and the strength of her wifely devotion.

All these stories contribute to the conclusion that wifely sacrifice is a positive duty. Self-denial produces protective power. In form always yielding, a wife may either conform to or rebel against her husband's will. These tales describe women's sacrifices as affirming and reinforcing husbands' performance of Rajput duty. They repeat the message: a Rajput woman must support her husband's caste responsibilities, for these are the source of his honor, which defines his highest self. Even if supporting a husband's Rajput responsibilities means pushing the husband

10. In his version of the story, Ruthi Rani, who still had not showed her face to her husband, lived apart from him in Ajmer. When Sher Shah was marching toward Jodhpur, a Caran sent a message to Ruthi Rani to join her husband there. She was going to go, but her husband's first wife told a Caran (the nephew of the first one) to dissuade Ruthi Rani from coming; he recited to Ruthi Rani the "elephant" *doha* above. Seeing its wisdom, she decided not to go. When her husband was killed, however, she led the charge against Sher Shah and then died a *sati*.

11. A friend suggested to me that the king's act seems spiteful. Spiteful or not, the king's order to have his head delivered seems to assume his wife will be a *sati* and serve as encouragement for her. It rather neatly parallels the way Hari Rani expects and encourages her husband to do his duty.

into certain death on the battlefield, the Rajput woman is supposed to do so, for it is a shameful thing to have a cowardly husband. The paradox occasioned by her failure as a *pativrata* to protect his life is then symbolically resolved by self-immolation. This act, as we have seen, verifies her purity of intent.

Because Rajput women see their caste as enabling them to best approximate the feminine ideal, they understand their duty to help their husbands perform Rajput duties as especially stringent. Thus whereas Rajput duties are understood as in the first instance male,[12] the female duty to sacrifice is conceived with reference to Rajput male duties. In other words, it interprets and justifies itself in terms consistent with and supportive of the general Rajput ethos of sacrifice. The female duty to sacrifice combined with the Rajput ethos of sacrifice make for a mandate of non-compromise. As a middle-aged noblewoman remarked, "If husbands prove cowardly, we Rajput women break our bangles, just as widows do." There seems little room for negotiating the issue.

This resolute courage characterizes the stories. Hari Rani does not hesitate before decapitating herself with a sword; its use is particularly appropriate as she wants to encourage her husband to use his sword in battle (fig. 25). She sacrifices herself that her husband might cut down his enemy. Ruthi Rani also does not delay: she sacrifices the life of a normal wife to teach her husband to behave properly and honorably. Behaving honorably herself, she heeds the bard's advice to stay away from her husband as he prepares for battle. Moreover, her sacrifice of self and protection of honor remain conceptually entwined with the fundamental abstinence that is chastity. Ruthi Rani is a paradigm of sacrificial chastity, a notion with important implications for the ethos of protection.

When women speak of chastity, they commonly use the words *sharam* and *laj*, both of which translate as shame and modesty. The terms themselves show that chastity does not simply mean restraint from extramarital sexuality: that may be taken for granted. Objectified as the *parda* (curtain), chastity informs and structures the entire code of wifely duty. As it fundamentally represents the expression of sexuality in support of a husband, so, in the appropriate context, it connotes the shame or modesty to renounce a woman's pursuit of personal desires,

12. Caste duties follow a division of labor set out in the classical legal texts (the *dharmashastras*) and popular wisdom; men perform specific caste duties while women have common duties, those of wife and mother. Asked what Rajputs do, both men and women nearly always refer to the tasks of Rajput men: ruling and fighting.

हा
डी
श
त
क

वीरांगना हाडी

—नाथूसिंह महियारिया

25. Hari Rani sends her husband her head as a memento (cover from a poetic narration of the deeds of Hari Rani; by permission of Pratap Sinh Mahiyariya and Himmat Sinh Ashiya).

even desires to please a husband, if these do not aim at helping him act as he should. Sacrifice and the consistent controversion of male desires found in *satimata* and *pativrata* tales are not the mutually exclusive behaviors that they appear to be. Their source is the chaste devotion of a *pativrata* and their goal is the protection of honor.

The chain of connotation does not end here. Chastity as protection not only preserves male honor (gained through the performance of male duty), it defines female honor. The chaste wife is the honorable wife. At the expanded level, chastity takes on a reflexive character: because wifely chastity depends on male protection and control of the *zanana*, male and female honor are mutually dependent. Both the wanton wife and the wife violated by an invader destroy a husband's honor, for a husband is duty-bound to preserve his wife's honor. Her dishonor degrades him until he exacts revenge.[13]

The terms may be reversed. A man who suffers a humiliating death in battle robs his wife of honor. The slain warrior is deemed humiliated if scalped, for scalping insinuates that the victim's wife has been or will be violated. This humiliation stems partly from the connotation of castration that scalping carries.[14] But it also conveys the idea that the soldier slain and stripped of his manhood is incapable of protecting his wife. The wife of a man so humiliated is herself stripped of honor unless his scalping is avenged.[15]

In sum, the *pativrata*, a term often rendered in English as "chaste wife," is a woman whose chastity serves as a foundation for the overall fidelity she realizes by protecting her husband's life, duty, honor. These in turn depend on her husband's performance of his Rajput role as a protector.

To articulate the norms explicit and implicit in ancestral *sati* stories we have looked at them in relation to one another and in the context of other nonancestral, thematically similar stories. Now let us examine the way in which the *sati* stories, both ancestral and nonancestral (i.e., "popular"), are construed as paradigmatic. Granted that these stories convey normative messages, can we assume that they directly represent illustrations of *pativrata* behavior? No and yes.

The *pativrata* stories, even the stories of Hari Rani and Ruthi Rani,

13. On revenge, see Ziegler, "Action, Power," 79–80; Hitchcock, "Martial Rājpūt," 12.
14. Ziegler, "Action, Power," 79–80.
15. A family member or the warrior himself could kill the scalper. As we have seen, a great warrior (*jhumjhar*) exacts revenge for death itself.

who become *sati*s, focus on the proper behavior of *pativrata*s during extraordinary circumstances. These women act in directly paradigmatic ways. *Pativrata*s admire the way these two behave and refer to them as women whom they would like to emulate. The ancestral *sati* stories told in chapter 4, however, focus not on *pativrata* performance but on the *sativrata* stage, in which the normal conditions of life and the normal rules of behavior are suspended. The power that the *sati* demonstrates during this period has been built up by conformity to the *pativrata* paradigm. The use to which this power is put, however, transcends the code and the capability of the *pativrata*.

For example, each *sati* appears in public for all to see. Furthermore, she may address whom she will. She may bring destruction, albeit instructive destruction, upon her *sasural* or she may damn the houses of those who have offended her. Obviously no wife would interpret such actions as options for herself. The *sati* is no longer simply human. It is superhuman power that makes her curse and *ok* efficacious. In the *sati*, *sat* has overflowed the boundaries of human being and surpassed the capacities of human reason.

Specific acts performed during the *sativrata* period are not, then, to be understood as exemplary in any literal sense. Nevertheless, the *sati*'s general behavior is normative in two important ways. First, the scenario is normative. Becoming a *sati* is only the culmination of a process of *sat* accumulation. The woman's act of dying reveals a life that has followed the *pativrata* ideal just at the moment when she transcends the ideal. The *sativrata* who is no longer a *pativrata* inspires women to be *pativrata*s.

Second, and perhaps less obvious, is the *sati*'s formal affirmation of the dual pattern of protection and controversion. The *sati* protects the family line directly, through blessings (corresponding to the wife's fulfillment of her husband's desires), or indirectly, through curses (corresponding to the wife's denial of her husband's desires when they will rob him of honor). Her curses are not to be emulated by *pativrata*s, but the model of controversion as an occasional aspect of female duty to support male duty is normative for them. The angry *sati*'s example is a paradigm of constructive rebellion, that is, denial consistent with the *pativrata*'s code of sacrifice, denial of the sort practiced by Hari Rani and Ruthi Rani.

This abstraction begs the interpretive question: how and when are women to decide whether insubordination is warranted? Although the *sati* paradigm legitimizes controverting male desires, it must be regarded in the context of a common understanding of male desire and male duty as usually synonymous or, at least, harmonious. If a *satimata* pronounces a curse, it is often because a family member has indulged personal desire at the expense of duty. Whatever the reason for the curse, all members assume it is a justifiable means for righting a wrongful situation. They know that even if the curse does not seem just to them it must be just; the *sati* knows best.

The motives of an ordinary woman are always less evident. However far such a woman may have progressed toward incorporating the *pativrata* ideal, she is understood to be susceptible to self-serving rationalizations, which reveal that her desire and duty (not her husband's) have taken separate paths. One of the worst accusations that is made of a woman is that she willfully manipulates her husband for selfish ends. Such manipulation is seen as the source of nasty court intrigues in times past and of devastating family quarrels today. In Rajasthan, as elsewhere in India, contriving wives are seen as spoilers of family solidarity. Hence the presumption to know better than a husband, to control him, or to disobey his wishes is prima facie arrogance. As the stories show, only when the desires of a husband are patently misguided is controversion warranted. As one noblewoman puts it, a *pativrata* "seeks to be beyond reproach." She and other Rajput women speak of their duty to avoid drawing criticism from their husbands' families. The wisdom of controversion must be salient, self-evident. Given the stress women put on the *pativrata*'s duty to obey, sacrifice of a husband's wishes should be an anomaly in the course of daily sacrifices that fulfill a husband's wishes. All sacrifices are done in the interest of duty. Thus a *satimata*'s curses do not legitimize particular acts of rebellion but demonstrate a conviction that gives positive form and meaning to the roles women play as women. Conditionally, they give authority.

For Rajput women, then, the *sati* is a symbol encompassing paradigms of conformity and rebellion, however contextualized. Within the parameters of the *sati* paradigm, rebellion is not a violation or rejection of duty but rather another mode of realizing it. The duty of the *pativrata* is to support male duty but not necessarily male desires, as the lore so aptly illustrates. Female duty applied as obedience or disobedience is understood as sacrifice; in the broad sense sacrifice is the lot of the *pativrata* as it is of the Rajput man.

Moreover as I have stressed, Rajput women believe that their Rajputness enables them to carry out their female duties. Rajput blood predisposes Rajputs to proper intentions and devoted service; it enables men to sacrifice for the realm and enables women to sacrifice for the family. Female service does not, however, restrict itself to household affairs. It is concerned with preserving the proper delineation between household and nonhousehold (male) affairs. If a husband or son does not respect the division between these spheres, his wife's or his mother's task is to educate him; hence the stories of Hari Rani's decapitation and the wife who ordered the palace gates to be locked.

This rule of separation is reinforced both by stories such as these and by the actual division of the household into male and female quarters. A man's entry into the *zanana* commences a visit. The male is a guest who comes for a specific reason, food and drink, the attentions of his wife, or the companionship of his mother and sisters. Once his needs are fulfilled, he is expected to return to male quarters and male company. If he lingers too long in female company, women may eventually shame him into leaving by taunting him or giggling at him. Extensive habitation of the *zanana* is considered emasculating and, so, non-Rajput.[16] Thus Rajput status is understood to connote ideal manliness as well as ideal femaleness. Caste identification delineates the separation and describes the mutual support of the two.

That women and men ultimately equate the ideals of gender and caste does not mean that they apply their shared ethic of protection in consistent, harmonious ways. The problem of priorities remains. The *satimata* stands as the embodiment of *pativrata* duty, which encompasses the norms of service to a husband through obedience and service to a husband through doing what is best for him. When the twin mandates of service contradict each other, a *pativrata* will have to use her judgment to assess which path *pativrata* duty will take. Although the wisdom of disobedience should be patent, the fundamental rule being obedience, a *pativrata* will have to make decisions that seem disrespectful—she may even shame her husband and show him her anger—which is one reason why status as a genuine *pativrata* may only be validated retrospectively.[17] Because this problem of priorities differs from the problem we saw in preceding chapters, a brief comparison of the questions of priority in *sati* and *kuldevi* traditions will be useful.

The *kuldevi* chapters demonstrated that women do not always reach the same solutions to conflicts between the female conception of Rajput

16. For an interesting illustration of this point, see Ziegler, "Action, Power," 81–82.
17. Women seem most vociferous in challenges concerning alcohol consumption and accompanying raucous behavior. We will hear more about their assessments in chapters following.

duty as it applies to the household and the general conception of (male) Rajput duty as it applies to the *kul* or one of its subdivisions. *Kul* tradition requires loyalty to its *kuldevi*. Nevertheless, some women may understand their natal family's *kuldevi* as better able to serve the functions assigned to the conjugal family's goddess. The rebellion—or compromise—intended by those women to support male service contradicts the male-defined notion of support of male service. In this case there is a conflict between the *kul* expectation and the female interpretation of duty.

In the case of *satimata* worship, however, this conflict tends not to arise. The *satimata* is an ideal: she is a *pativrata* so complete in her realization of duty as to have transcended *pativrata* status altogether. Her independence as a supernatural being is predicated upon her perfect conformity to female duty through her support of male duty. Worship of the *satimata* is not a *kul* duty; it is a family duty. Moreover, it is preeminently a female duty. The *satimata*, unlike the *kuldevi*, is overwhelmingly a household phenomenon. The neglect of a *satimata* or the incorporation of new *satimata*s into household ritual will not directly threaten the *kul*.

This is not to say that conflict cannot arise from interpretation of *satimata* myths and performance of *satimata* rituals. Rather, it is to say that *satimata* worship occurs within a conceptual framework of support of male duty, so that conflict arises within the conceptual parameters of female duty. The *satimata* is identified with the household first and last. The *kuldevi* is identified with the battlefield originally and the household derivatively. Thus, with the *satimata* no question of caste versus family loyalty is possible. The *satimata* serves the separation of male and female spheres of duty and equates the latter with service of the former. She is perceived as a resident of the *zanana*. Rising out of the *zanana*, she is the apotheosis of female sacrificial support. By contrast, the *kuldevi* is an utterly transcendent deity who descends to the battlefield. She is worshiped differently in the *mardana* and the *zanana*. She is both the animal goddess of battle and the *suhagin* goddess of home. Moreover, to the extent that she is both warrior goddess and household goddess, she incorporates and demonstrates the tensions that may arise between perceptions of male duties and female duties. These tensions create and are reflected by the temptation to split her functions and worship her as two *kuldevi*s.

The observable effect of the delimitation of *satimata* jurisdiction is the flexibility attending her worship. There is no competition possible among *sati*s. Whereas there must always be only one official *kuldevi*, there are many possible *sati*s. The greater the number, the prouder the family that performs their devotions. If *sati*s are imported through weddings, so much the better. Of chief importance in the context of *sati* worship is the *sati* scenario, which states the realization of the feminine ideal. Each *sati* is revered because she conforms to the scenario, which proves the purity of her heart. Hence all *sati*s easily merge into a unitary *satimata* personality. And so, when women say that they place their faith in Satimata, they are not selecting one from among many. They are affirming the functional equivalence of all.

In no way does this equivalence mean that the stories of individual *sati*s cease to be important. Quite the contrary. Each story exemplifies and affirms the paradigm. Moreover, the conclusion that *sati*s do not compete one against another does not suggest that *satimata* worship cannot catalyze conflicts concerning female responsibilities. We have seen that the *satimata* scenario can legitimize rebellion as a mode of conformity to the principle of duty. What noncompetition affirms is that *satimata*s are understood as representing female duty supporting male duty. Their example makes lucid the idealized harmony between the two. The *kuldevi* comes with competing male-oriented (*kul*) and female-oriented (family) myths of origin. The *satimata*'s origin is always the same: flames erupt from the internal fire of *sat* kindled by a lifetime of service as a *pativrata*.

Thus, whereas *kuldevi* tradition reveals tensions between conceptions of male duty and conceptions of female duty, *satimata* tradition demonstrates tensions between female duties to serve the desires of men as they are and to serve the needs of men as they should be. Women must venerate *kuldevi*s as protectors but emulate *kuldevi*s directly as *pativrata*s. They must venerate *satimata*s as protectors, but understand *satimata*s as onetime *pativrata*s whose footsteps can be followed. Therefore compared to the *kuldevi*, the *satimata* is an intimate protector; she guards households she has chosen, not an entire *kul*, whose members may be scattered far and wide over Rajasthan, and perhaps beyond. While she resides in heaven by her husband's side, she is yet ever accessible to her protégées. The *sati* stands for a scenario of *sat* accumulation, the internal dynamic corresponding to and resulting from performance of the *pativrata* role.

To conclude, all stages of the *sati* scenario demonstrate the conviction that a Rajput woman's duty toward her husband may require violating his wishes. As women's myriad stories of *shrap*s and *ok*s and of brave women and cowardly men reveal, the Rajput woman is duty-bound as a Rajput and as a woman to do what is best for her husband. This usually means obedience but occasionally means insubordination. The correctness of the dedicated woman's action is not the form of her action but rather the intention that guides it. That intention must conform to the general assumptions that attend her status as a *pativrata* and her desire to revere, if not enact, the example provided by the *sativrata*.

NOT DYING AS *SATIS*

I have spoken of the process of becoming a *satimata* as one more or less confined to the past. And yet, alongside the tradition of venerating *satimata*s who died on their husbands' pyres decades or even centuries ago, exists an emerging tradition of worshiping new *satimata*s who, oddly enough, have not actually died. In introducing these *satimata*s who, though living, are explicitly likened to the classic ancestral *sativrata*s, I hope to show the extraordinary extent to which intention, not mere action, governs the conceptualization of the *pativrata* ideal and the *sati* transformation process. The new, living (*jivit*) *satimata* tradition evidences an impressive continuity of values.

The living *satimata* is a woman whose husband has died but who has not been able to join him in the afterlife. The most famous example is Bala Satimata, who tried to immolate herself about forty years ago but was prevented from doing so. Another is Umca Satimata, who said she never tried to immolate herself because that action would have hurt her family.[18] Her great devotion to her husband, she told me, made her a *sati*. Both living *satimata*s have died, Bala Satimata a few years ago and Umca Satimata just recently. But their followers continue to venerate them and to enlist their aid in solving problems. The two are thought still capable of performing miracles.[19]

From the time of their husbands' deaths, both Bala Satimata and Umca Satimata, like the other living *satimata*s for whom I have information, stopped requiring the normal necessities for survival.[20] The liv-

18. Family members and other persons who facilitate a *sati*'s self-immolation can be tried as accomplices to what is legally construed as suicide.

19. Bala Satimata's death occurred just after I returned from the field and Umca Satimata's occurred during the copyediting of this book. It is too soon since their deaths to attempt a study of the ways in which deceased *sati*s of this type will be venerated. At present devotees of Bala Satimata and Umca Satimata are debating the particulars of ritual veneration.

20. I have limited information on three other living *satimata*s, one Rajput and two Caran.

ing *satimata* remains in this world but is no longer of it. She is no longer a *pativrata* in the standard sense of the term, nor is she technically dead. She breathes yet requires no food, drinks no water, and needs no sleep. The fuel that keeps her alive is *sat*, the internal heat that she has accumulated as a *pativrata*.

The living *sati*'s survival and her superhuman powers, the consequences of her accumulation of *sat*, compare formally to the ascetic yogi's survival and miraculous skills. These result from his cultivation of *tapas*, another kind of spiritual heat. Like the yogi, the living *sati* gains her powers through renunciation. Moreover, as she continues to live without food or water, her position compares even more closely to the penance-performing yogi, for her power to live without external nourishment is also the source of her continuing spiritual powers. Thus, for the *sati*, living abstemiously is both the result of a lifetime of renunciations and the continuing cause of her effectiveness. *Sat* and *tapas* appear to be similar, perhaps even overlapping, categories of spiritual heat.

Besides the fact that the classic *satimata* has died and the living *satimata* has not, the most notable distinction between them is that the traditional *satimata* is worshiped by families of her relatives and other families she designated through *ok*s and *shrap*s, whereas the living *satimata* is worshiped by Rajputs and others who designate her as a guardian. Thus the living *satimata* is venerated in the homes of many unrelated women. Because they can still see and talk to her, they can consult her as a teacher; they refer to her as guru.

Both Bala Satimata and Umca Satimata enjoy enormous popularity in western Rajasthan. Bala Satimata lived outside Jodhpur. Her immense following includes many Rajput and non-Rajput women from Udaipur. Umca Satimata lived in the small town of Umca, a few hours' drive from Udaipur. She was not a *satimata* as long as Bala Satimata was (she lived for about a decade after her husband died) and had fewer followers than Bala Satimata, but she enjoyed a special popularity in and around Udaipur, the chief area of my investigation.

Of the handful of such *satimata*s in Rajasthan, Bala Satimata is by far the best known. I compiled this account of her life from a number of interviews with Rajput women.

> When Bala Satimata was a young woman, her husband died. She intended to die a *sati* but was prevented from doing so by her family. To keep her from making repeated attempts to take her own life, her relatives locked her in a room. Every day they would slide a tray of food under the door. Every night

they retrieved the tray, only to find it untouched. Finally, fearing that the woman would die of hunger and thirst, they unlocked the door and went into the room to check on her. To their astonishment, she appeared perfectly healthy. Her human needs had miraculously vanished. Since that day, about forty years ago, Bala Satimata . . . remained in the same condition, healthy but independent of human needs.

In addition to this widely known story of Bala Satimata's transformation, many women tell stories about the powers Bala Satimata demonstrated. The following account, told by a woman who belonged to the extended royal family of Jodhpur, shows how such stories are taken to demonstrate the status and strength of living *satimata*s.

> One time, the royal family of Jodhpur wished to test Bala Satimata to see if she truly lives without nourishment. The family invited her to stay in one of its residences. While she visited, it posted guards to see that she received no food or water. Despite the severe heat that Jodhpur endured during her stay, Bala Satimata consumed not a single drop of water. And, of course, she ate no food. Had she been an ordinary mortal, she would surely have died in a couple of days. She remained strong because of her *sat*.

Because of Bala Satimata's abstinences and because of the miracles that her *sat* enabled her to perform, this foremost of *satimata*s became famous throughout Rajasthan and attracted many disciples and patrons. Many people came to visit her, including members of the Jodhpur royal family and pilgrims from various parts of Rajasthan. Since her death her poster has become omnipresent in Jodhpur and common in the homes of her Udaipur devotees.

The story of Umca Satimata is less widely known.[21] She was so devoted to her husband that after his death she could no longer eat, drink, or sleep. Although some of the Rajput ladies I interviewed assume that she attempted to die as a *sati*, as I have mentioned, Umca Satimata denied this. She said that she never tried to die as a *sati* but very much wanted to be with her husband, whom she loved. She attracted so many devotees that when she visited Udaipur in December 1984, large crowds assembled to pay their respects and receive her blessing.

Like classic *satimata*s, Bala Satimata and Umca Satimata are understood to have accumulated *sat* through devotion to their husbands. Because of the purity of their intention to protect their husbands, they accumulated the reserves of *sat* necessary to perform miracles (*camatkar*s) for the benefit of their protégées. As the classic *satimata*s do, they most

---

21. In 1985 informants said she had been a *satimata* for less than ten years.

often perform miracles of healing. A young Udaipur noblewoman narrated a typical example.

> Bala Satimata was visiting the town where my mother's elder sister lived. Although my auntie was a devotee of Bala Satimata, she was ill and could not get out of bed to go and see her. She had been vomiting constantly. She was too weak to move.
>
> After some time people began to pour into my auntie's house. They were all followers of Bala Satimata. Then Bala Satimata herself came into the house and asked, "Why don't you get off your bed and come with us?" Then she said, "There's nothing wrong with you. You're just making excuses for not coming." Satimata put her hand on my auntie's head. Just then all her pain went away. She got up and followed Satimata out the door.[22]

Here Bala Satimata cures by laying her hands on her devotee. In other cases she does so by giving to afflicted persons water she has blessed. This holy water is understood to cure diverse ailments.

A second power possessed by living and classic *satimata*s alike is the promotion and management of fertility. To both Bala Satimata and Umca Satimata is attributed the capacity to cure barrenness. Umca Satimata is known to have granted the gift of a son to a prominent Udaipur Rajput woman who had previously borne only daughters.

Finally, living *satimata*s share with classic *satimata*s the power to grant other protective blessings. All *satimata*s, as former *pativrata*s, attempt to protect families from all varieties of disaster. Happiness, like health and fertility, is essential to the family. Thus when one Udaipur noblewoman saw her family plagued by misfortune and acrimony, she sought the protection of Umca Satimata. She tells the story.

> Before my family began to live in the *haveli* in which it lives now, it had two previous owners. One was a Kayasth.[23] When our family moved here all sorts of trouble began to happen. The head of the family died and there was great hostility between his two sons. After a time the sons wouldn't even speak to each other. There was great tension in the house.
>
> At that time I went to Umca Satimata and asked her why this was happening. Satimata said, "There is a stone in the driveway of your *haveli*. People are always driving and walking over it disrespectfully. It is frequented by the spirit of a Kayasth who used to live in the house." Satimata told me to prepare some food (*bhog*) on a tray (*thali*) as an offering to the spirit and

22. A Caran acquaintance related a similar *camatkar*. He took his ailing mother to Bala Satimata to be cured. Too weak to walk from the station, she went to Bala Satimata's ashram in a cart. The *satimata*'s blessing gave her strength to walk back to the station.

23. The Kayasth is a high-ranking caste whose members often served Rajput kings as economic managers and political advisors (See G. N. Sharma, *Social Life in Medieval Rajasthan [1500–1800 A. D.]* (Agra: Lakshmi Narain Agarwal, 1980), 93–94.

then to have someone take it to a lake. At the lake the person was to empty the food into the water and then walk away without looking back.

My family prepared the *thali* as an offering. Then two men took it to the lake. The man carrying the *thali* experienced great changes in his body temperature—the spirit was within him. Both men emptied the food into the water and left without looking back at the lake.

After this the trouble disappeared. As Umca Satimata had predicted, the stone became vacant and harmless. It was the strength of her meditation on the problem that led to this.

Although this story illustrates the motif of protection that pervades *satimata* stories, it diverges from the stories of classic *satimata*s in a crucial respect: context. Traditionally, the protégée of a *satimata* gained protection for her family by observing *ok*s, giving *dhok*, participating in *ratijaga*s, and heeding warnings received in the dreams and personal appearances. In the story above, however, and in the case of the auntie who was cured by Bala Satimata, the relationship between *sati* and devotee is not ritualized or episodic but informal and ongoing. As we have seen, compared to the classic *satimata*, the living *satimata* is accessible. Whereas the classic *satimata* appears only when she wills, the living *satimata* is available at any time. When needed, she can be approached and, more important, asked direct questions.

Because of her availability, the living *satimata* has another advantage over the classic *satimata*. Whereas the messages of the classic *satimata* may be vague, expressed as they are in the symbolism of dreams and in the mystery of visions,[24] the messages given by the living *satimata* are straightforward. Moreover, not only can women receive specific instructions to face periodic problems, they can also become students of the *satimata* and so learn how to avoid or handle future problems.

Both Bala Satimata and Umca Satimata have ashrams (spiritual retreats that contain hostels for extended stay), where devotees can come to receive blessings and to learn. During my interview with Umca Satimata I learned that she taught two basic lessons: the ways of the *pativrata* and devotion to God. Umca Satimata would not enumerate her teachings on the *pativrata* ideal during my visit. Rather, she invited me to stay with her for two weeks in order to learn the secrets of *pativrata* devotion. Because my schedule would not permit this (I was about to leave India), I asked if she could not tell me a few of her thoughts on the subject. She responded that such wisdom cannot be gained through mere listening: it must be demonstrated, absorbed, and applied. Though Umca Satimata would not say why watching her activities would dem-

---

24. Such dreams and visions may require the interpretive services of a *bhopa*.

onstrate how to be a *pativrata*, she implied that through watching her perform her daily regimen of meditation on and service to God I would learn about the devotion and discipline necessary for *pativrata* service.

This connection between service to a husband and service to God leads us to another major way in which the living *satimata* differs from the classic one. The living *satimata* sees herself not only as a guru who instructs and in return receives devotion but as a *bhakt*, a devotee of God. When Umca Satimata, for example, was not with her devotees (*celas*), she worshiped the nameless, formless God whom she came to know through her guru.[25] Moreover, she taught her visitors to respect and love God, that they might live better lives and be better people.

What is particularly interesting about the fact that the living *satimata* practices and teaches devotion to God is that Rajputs understand *bhakti* yoga as an activity befitting widowhood. They consider preoccupation with God suitable for a woman whose husband has died and understand God to be the only proper recipient of the amorous affections she would normally have bestowed upon her husband were he alive. Zealous *bhakti* may distract *pativratas* from their proper duties as good wives but is an appropriate and beneficial occupation for those who can no longer perform as *pativratas*.[26]

Highlighting the idea that the living *satimata* is in some sense a widow is the fact that she employs the symbolism of widowhood. In the manner of a widow she wears a white or mud-colored *sari* and shuns embroidery and ornamentation. Moreover, her abstentions from food, drink, and sleep—which result from her liberation from human needs—are precisely the behaviors expected of a widow, who should perform ascetic penances. In sum, unlike the classic *satimata*, whose symbolic association with widowhood is fleeting and uneasy, the living *satimata*, whose appearance and behavior are appropriate to a widow, dwells among the living for years even though she is a *satimata*, one who has rejected widowhood.

Called a *satimata*, the living *satimata* compares symbolically to the classic *sativrata* (described in chapter 4). Actually, the living *satimata* combines into one the ultimate and penultimate *sati* stages. As a *sati-*

25. She referred to him as Dayal Ji; he may have been a follower of the *bhakt*, Dadu Dayal, or this saint himself, who spent much of his life in Rajasthan. He taught a combination of Hindu and Muslim ideas, and stressed the unity of God, whom he called "Guru" (G. N. Sharma, *Social Life*, 235–37). On Dadu, see Winand M. Callewaert, "Dadu and the Dadu-Panth," in *The Sants*, ed. Karine Schomer and W. H. McLeod (Delhi: Motilal Banarsidass, 1987).

26. Fruzetti points out that in Bengal *bhakti* is not necessary for *pativratas* (*The Gift*, 13).

mata, she gives warnings and performs acts of healing. As a *sativrata*, she may wield *sativrata* power, though the nature and extent of this power remain relatively uncertain and undefined. The living *satimata* is certainly seen as capable of pronouncing curses on those who fail to show her proper respect. Late in my interview with Umca Satimata, the Rajput friends who had accompanied me to her ashram expressed anxiety that my barrage of questions might irritate her and eventually incite her to pronounce a curse on us.[27] Apart from this, however, I never came across any mention of curses pronounced by living *satimata*s. As yet, cursing is not customary.

Nor have I heard of living *satimata*s imposing *ok*s. As far as I know, Bala Satimata and Umca Satimata are the only living *satimata*s who have died, and I know of no *ok*s that have been associated with them as yet.[28] Traditionally a *sati* imposes *ok*s just before she dies to allow a ritualized form of communication with her protégées after her death. Until more living *satimata*s die, we cannot know whether the imposition of *ok*s will become a feature of their veneration.[29] Here tradition remains incipient.

In any case, the tradition of living *satimata* veneration incorporates many of the elements of the classic tradition. It also expands and modifies it. Even as the living tradition adapts the classic, it preserves the centrality of intention that underlies the older tradition, while lifting the importance of intention to a new level. The classic *satimata* tradition stresses intention to the point that *ok*s need not necessarily be practiced if they are acknowledged symbolically. If *ok*s are remembered by substitutions or adaptations (e.g., borrowing an item instead of abstaining from its use), then the *satimata*, pleased, continues her protection. Thus for the *pativrata* the intention to observe *ok*s, which represent her commitment to her *satimata*, bridges the gap between belief and practice. The living *satimata* tradition stresses intention to the extent that a woman no longer needs to die in order to become a *satimata*. All that

27. She told me I was her first foreign visitor and seemed a little nervous. She did not, however, become irritated. Rather, she demonstrated considerable patience and hospitality, which culminated in a large vegetarian meal.

28. I understand that Bala Satimata and Umca Satimata were cremated. I had wondered whether, since devotees consider them to have slowly burned themselves away by living on *sat*, they might be buried as some ascetics are. The ascetics are thought to have burned away their social selves when they cremated their sacred threads and therefore not to require bodily cremation.

29. I have heard of no *ok* being observed by the followers of Bala Satimata or Umca Satimata. Because they are not familial *sati*s to most of their devotees, any *ok*s they imposed would not be simply ancestral custom as *ok*s have tended to be.

really matters is that a *pativrata* possess an unwavering desire to sacrifice the self in order to join her husband in the afterlife. For the *pativrata* whose husband has died, the intention to become a *satimata* is of itself transformative.

This emphasis on the efficacy of intention is an idea integrally associated with caste. Umca Satimata attributed the passion of her devotion to her husband while she was a *pativrata* to the fact that she was a Rajput. She said that she was a *satimata* because of her *sat*, which she felt comes easily to Rajput women. Undoubtedly, because she was a Rajput and other Rajput women perceive her to have had a natural advantage in cultivating the *pativrata* role, her transformation into a *satimata* is particularly credible. As the story of Bala Satimata and the Jodhpur royal family demonstrates, initially some Rajputs may have doubted Bala Satimata's transformation, the idea of living *satimata*s then being new. Now the Rajput community is comfortable with the premise that a woman can become a *satimata* without dying, and such suspicions have not attached to other Rajput *satimata*s. This, at least, has been the case with Umca Satimata. I never heard of Rajput women testing her powers. Whereas in times past *sat* was manifested by conflagration, which was assumed spontaneous in the case of Rajput women, it is now assumed present when Rajput *satimata*s thrive without food, drink, or sleep.

The same cannot be said about non-Rajput living *satimata*s. Addressing reports of such individuals, Rajput women often show their traditional skepticism. Not one woman interviewed listed a non-Rajput living *satimata* as a recipient of their veneration. Rajputs invest their devotional energies in worshiping the various protectors whose intentions they can discern or, in the case of Rajput *sati*s, simply assume.

Thus, this examination of *ok* observed in the breach and *sati* stripped of death has emphasized the paramount role intention plays in the worship and emulation of *satimata*s by *pativrata*s. Whereas death is the traditional validation of life as a *pativrata* (or, for men, life as a warrior), death is not essential if alternative validation is available. Such validation is provided by caste. Just as Rajput caste verifies the emergence of *sat* even when internal flames of *sat* cannot be distinguished from the lighted flames of a pyre, so it verifies the emergence of *sat* even when a living *satimata*'s daily regimen is not monitored by skeptics.

The *satimata*, classic or living, and the Rajput caste in general share a duty of protection, which requires the sacrificing of self or selfish desires on behalf of others. The Rajput male performing his duty as a soldier is idealized in the warrior-turned-ascetic who sacrifices his life in the *saka* in order to preserve the realm. The Rajput woman performing her duty as a *pativrata* is idealized in the *sati*, who sacrifices her life on the pyre to preserve her husband's honor by showing her devotion.

To Rajput women the *sati* stands for the strength necessary to sacrifice throughout a lifetime. Although dying as a *sati* is no longer a popular path, the *sati* remains a powerful ideal informing Rajput women's understanding of their own roles as wives. As in the past, she inspires contemporary Rajput women, who desire not to die as *satis*—to have their husbands predecease them—but rather to protect their husbands as accomplished Rajput *pativratas*.

In concluding it is helpful to review some of the claims made about the relationship between Rajput *satis* and their protégées. Like that between *kuldevis* and women, the relationship between *satimatas* and women is both reciprocal and paradigmatic. It is reciprocal in the sense that *satimatas* give women divine protection in return for devotion and veneration. It is paradigmatic in an oblique or contingent way. *Satis* and *kuldevis* tend to perform services of which ordinary women are incapable. They miraculously revive dying soldiers-husbands and protect them against diseases and other calamities. Women can only protect in mundane human ways. They emulate *satimatas* and *kuldevis*, however, by performing analogous but limited services for their husbands. They follow the examples set by supernaturals by protecting their husbands to the best of their abilities. Thus, in accord with their interpretations of these examples, they emulate obliquely.

There is an important exception to this generalization. As we saw, because a *satimata* passes through a *sativrata* stage, in this brief period she performs activities, specifically ritual activities, that are directly paradigmatic. These activities are normative, though not obligatory, for a woman who finds herself in the *sativrata*'s situation of incipient widowhood. Direct emulation of a *sativrata* is contingent in the sense that it is context-specific. For the *pativrata*, the *sativrata* can only be a conditional model because becoming a *sati* should not be intended a priori. Unless or until a husband dies or is about to die, the sole normative feature of the *sati* scenario is the spirit of devotion it illustrates. The *satimata* is not revered because of protective services she rendered when she was a *pativrata*. A good wife's services are expected, not exceptional. What women admire is the *sati*'s sacrificial inclination, which encourages and fortifies them in their performance of everyday duties.

Thus for the woman whose husband still lives, the *sativrata*'s actions are only obliquely directive: as a *sativrata* gives away her possessions because life without a husband has made them meaningless, so a well-intentioned, ordinary wife eschews selfish pleasures and delights only in those things beneficial to a husband. The *sativrata*'s actions are directly paradigmatic only for the woman who has lost or will soon lose her husband and thus is in a position to become a *sativrata* herself. In either case, the *sativrata* transcends and validates the experience of the *pativrata*.

This concept of transcendent validation serves as a point of departure for an investigation of the nature of human heroism. The following chapter explores the norm of protection by comparing normative and heroic actions found in popular legends about Rajput women. The women who perform heroic deeds are deemed among the finest exemplars of Rajput womanhood, yet the deeds they perform require suspensions of socially shared rules and entail context-specific reversals of ideal relationships. These figures are revered rather than worshiped; the attraction they hold lies not in the general but in the particular episodic protective services they perform. Our objective is to discern another angle on the protective norms of caste and gender by investigating the character and logic of admiration.

CHAPTER 6

The Heroic Paradigm

Padmini

Padmini had character and purity; she died by *jauhar* [immolation].

I admire Padmini, who died in Chitor. One has to die anyway, so why be humiliated?

Being a *pativrata* is like what Padmini did. She died by *jauhar* rather than allow herself to be accosted by the Muslims. She was very brave. . . . The heroines from Mewar are especially brave, each in her own way.

——*Comments of three noblewomen*

It would be tempting to deduce that just as a Rajput hero is one who superbly fulfills his duty as a soldier, so the Rajput heroine must be one who superbly fulfills the role of the *pativrata*. We have seen that Rajput women understand Rajput status as that which enables them to be incomparable *pativratas*: they interpret their capacity to perform *pativrata* action as qualitatively superior to that of other women. Thus it would seem reasonable to suppose that those women adjudged best among Rajput women (*sab se acchi* Rajput *nariyam*) most perfectly, most mechanically, execute the *pativrata* role.

But they do not. As we shall see, what is striking about the exemplars of Rajput womanhood is their transgression of fundamental *zanana*-linked law. Nevertheless, although heroines' behavior violates *pativrata* standards, it ultimately validates the *pativrata* paradigm. A widely admired woman is simply stated to be good (*acchi*) and to have good character (*accha caritra*) both in spite of and because of her exceptional behavior.

Rajput women are quite consistent in responding to the twofold question: who are the best exemplars of Rajput women and why are

those women good? The names of Padmini and Mira Bai overwhelmingly predominate. Commonly, respondents gave both names. When
these two began to recur regularly, I decided to ask for evaluations of
them, whether or not all respondents included them in their lists. (Respondents almost always included at least one.) These evaluations together with the other evaluations made of all exemplars listed demonstrate that both Padmini and Mira Bai, in quite different ways, reject the
pativrata role and reaffirm the *pativrata* paradigm. They also show that
rejection and reaffirmation are vital to the admiration they inspire.

Interestingly enough, although all women understand Padmini as an
illustrious *pativrata*, almost all deny that Mira, though virtuous, can
properly be called a *pativrata*, at least without altering the ordinary
sense of the term. Comparing these women will help us discover the
parameters of the *pativrata* concept and deepen our understanding of
the protection it conveys. This task begins with an account of the Padmini legend. What we should note from the account below, which is a
composite of narratives recited by those interviewed, is that although
Padmini dies a *sati*, she deviates from the *sati* scenario as we have understood it. Her sacrifice is preceded by a sequence of actions atypical
of *pativrata* behavior.

THE TALE OF PADMINI

Padmini, a queen of Mewar, was renowned for her incomparable
beauty. Ala-ud-din, the notorious Afghan invader, determined to take
Chitor and capture her. His initial charges proved unsuccessful, but lust
spurred him on. Finally, frustrated, he submitted a compromise: he
would withdraw his troops if he could be allowed but a glimpse of the
fair lady's face. The Maharana consented but stipulated that to protect
Padmini's modesty, the Muslim would only be able to see her face reflected in a mirror. The offer having been accepted, the queen was taken
to a palace in the middle of a large tank. She stood next to a window
with her back toward the outside. Ala-ud-din was placed in a building
at the edge of the tank, from which considerable distance he was allowed to catch a fleeting glimpse of Padmini's reflection in a mirror,
which was held up to the queen for a few seconds. Far from satisfying
his desire, this vision inflamed it. He decided to double-cross the Maharana and make Padmini his own.

Because the Muslim had arrived in Chitor alone and thus demonstrated his faith in Rajput honor, the Maharana felt compelled to return

the compliment by personally accompanying him back to his camp. When they arrived, however, Ala-ud-din took his escort hostage and demanded Padmini as ransom. The Rajput army could not contemplate such a trade. To ask the queen to compromise herself would contravene the Rajput code of honor, which protects women. Padmini herself ordered that the trade be executed but, having sized up Ala-ud-din as no man of honor, also plotted an ambush. She sent Ala-ud-din a message consenting to his terms provided that she be allowed to bring along her belongings and attendants. He agreed. Then the queen ordered many curtained palanquins, which were designed to transport ladies-in-waiting, to be filled instead with soldiers. Because the soldiers who were to be concealed in this way knew they would not be able to defeat Ala-ud-din's powerful army, they prepared themselves to die in a battle of honor, a *saka*.

When the palanquin procession reached its destination, Padmini asked Ala-ud-din that she be permitted to bid farewell to her husband before leaving him. Having agreed, the Muslim took his bride-to-be to the place where her husband was held captive. As soon as the Maharana's location was known, the Rajput soldiers sprang upon the Muslims and liberated the captive king. In the uproar, both Padmini and her husband managed to escape. Padmini was whisked back to the palace, while the Maharana fled for the hills. Because it was clear that his forces would lose the battle, he retreated so that he might plot an assault on Ala-ud-din at a later more promising moment. Back at Chitor, seeing that the Maharana's forces faced defeat, Padmini led hundreds (some say thousands) of women to the vaults under the palace, where they committed *jauhar*, mass immolation.[1]

In general, *jauhar* is understood to accomplish closely related purposes. To begin with, it preserves female virtue.[2] The noblewomen

1. This representative narrative is a condensation of what Tod gives as two episodes. In Tod, Ala-ud-din takes time to recoup his losses and then begins another attack. *Jauhar* follows this attack, in which the Maharana is killed. No respondent mentioned two attacks or the circumstances surrounding the Maharana's death, which is central to Tod's detailed account (*Annals and Antiquities* 1:212–16). Tod identifies Padmini's husband as Bhim Sinh, but official palace records at Udaipur identify the king as Ratan Sinh. Bhim Sinh belonged to the collateral branch of the family at Sisoda.

2. In the *Rājasthānī Sabd Kos* the first definition of *jauhar* is "jewel" (*ratna*). The second is "proof" (*pramana*) of the "character" (*svarup*) of a sword as seen by fineness of the striations in its iron. The third is "quality, beauty, character" (*vishesta, khubi, gun*). The fourth is "the mass burning of live Rajput women on a pyre when their husbands, wearing saffron, are about to lose their fort to the enemy, so that the enemy cannot get them." The fifth is the "pyre" (*cita*) where such burning occurs. The final, sixth entry ties the "rite" (*kriya*) of immolation of anyone (*kisi*) to the motive of "revenge" (*pratikar*) for

quoted at the very beginning of this chapter said, "Padmini had character and purity; she died by *jauhar*." As noted previously, Rajputs have been keen to protect the purity of Rajput blood. Because conquest brought with it the likelihood of rape, they have seen conquest as a threat to family integrity and caste identity. Until now, another woman commented, the purity of Rajput blood has not been diluted. She said that with society changing, that might happen in the future, but said she was proud that "blood-mixing" really had not happened to any appreciable extent as yet.

Jauhar also promotes caste duty, which is symbolized ultimately by the *saka*, the "cutting down" that ensues. It inspires soldiers to fight unto death, for they have nothing left to lose.[3] Although *jauhar* often precedes the death of a husband (or a wife's knowledge of the death of her husband), women who so die are referred to as *sati*s. Hence, as a heroic strategist, Padmini enables her husband to face his enemy in battle and then, as a *sati*, prompts his courage and promotes his honor.[4]

Two matters concerning the Padmini narrative merit immediate attention. First, although Padmini is a *sati*, she is not simply assimilated to the category of *satimata*. True, Padmini is a *satimata* to Sisodiyas. But when Sisodiyas speak of their *satimata*, they do not single out Pad-

---

injustice. (It presumably applies to immolations of others besides the Rajput women mentioned in the fourth definition. This is interesting because women sometimes say *jauhar* punishes enemies by depriving them of the opportunity to satisfy their carnal desires). *Jauhar* shares basic associations of *sat*. Like *sat*, it refers to quality and character; like *sati* it is proof (of female character and goodness). The link between "gem" and character appears to be the same made in English when we refer to someone as a "real gem." In short, the primary meanings denote character; the derivative meanings refer to the rituals that demonstrate it.

3. Women's renditions usually mention no children or elderly persons. As we saw in the tale of Guha, a child (unborn) raises an issue of conflicting loyalty that Rajput mythology resolves in various ways. In one myth a *sati* first cuts her unborn child from her womb. In other stories, women die pregnant or with their children; heirs are smuggled away but everyone else perishes in flames. I saw only one miniature painting of the Padmini *jauhar*, which depicts women dying together—no children or men. The issue deserves historical study. The point of the Padmini myth told by women, however, seems to be the sacrifices made by women for the encouragement of men.

4. The enabling function of women's *sat* is somewhat like the motivational aspect of *shakti*, the female power discussed widely in literature on women and goddesses in India. My Rajput informants did not invoke *shakti* in discussions of *sati*s or heroines. They describe the Goddess or a *kuldevi* as being Shakti (a Sanskritic epithet) or having *shakti*, but they overwhelmingly speak of *sati*s, heroines, and ordinary women as having and seeking *sat*, understood as substantive virtue and power. Informants understood what I meant when I spoke of *shakti* but themselves employed the term *sat* when talking about women's duties, powers, and goals. *Sat* is the term they employ when they describe themselves and their motivations in admiring and worshiping *kuldevi*s, *satimata*s, heroines (and heroes and other deities). See the discussion of *sat* in chapter 5 and that of *jauhar* below.

mini from other *sati*s. Self-immolation is the basis for the worship she receives as one of the *sati*s whose identities merge into the integrated *satimata* personage. What causes Padmini's name to be remembered and revered is not just the mode of her death but the manner in which she lived her life.[5] Two women thus summarized their sentiments: "I admire Padmini because she was very clever; she showed the Muslims that!" and "I like Padmini because she met danger when her husband wasn't around to protect her."[6]

This is not to downplay the importance of Padmini's death: it is the climax of the Padmini narrative. One Rajput woman noted that when Padmini leaves the palace to attack Ala-ud-din, "her body becomes hot with *sat*," which clearly foreshadows her death as a *sati*. Acts that make her story something more than a *sati* scenario, however, are the rescue she plots and the ambush she directs. To execute her plan she abandons her household and takes to the battlefield. For these reasons she is revered even by Rajputs (and others) who do not worship her as a *satimata*.

Second, Padmini's heroic action contravenes a cardinal rule. Padmini leaves *parda*. The story builds toward this event and dwells on its significance. The mirror incident, in which Padmini shows her face to Ala-ud-din, portends this trangression. The stereotype of the lustful Muslim is well known to Rajasthani mythology. When the villainous Ala-ud-din sees the reflection of Padmini's face, it is a foregone conclusion that desire will defeat honor and he will conspire to ravish her. The bargain he strikes is thereby transformed from an end in itself to a means of conquest. Furthermore, while the belief that Padmini's body becomes hot when she exits the palace shows that Padmini does not thereby abandon her virtue, it also stresses that she deviates from custom. Her dramatic departure emphasizes that the state of affairs in Chitor has become so

5. At Chitor there is an annual celebration of heroism known as the Jauhar Mela. Rajputs parade through Chitor to honor the courage of their ancestors. Although the festival focuses on *jauhar*, it does not bear a specific *sati*'s name. It takes place on the anniversary of another *jauhar*, but most Rajputs I know assume it celebrates the *jauhar* led by Padmini. Its organizers intended the festival to commemorate all three sacks and *jauhar*s at Chitor—they chose the anniversary they did because it is a time when neither students nor farmers are busy. Although the procession commemorates the bravery of Rajput ancestors, it also occasions fiery political speeches and protests against the lawmakers in Delhi for grievances related to the loss of political power.

6. Almost without exception the women who mentioned Padmini said they admired her because of her bravery. The only woman who made a negative remark about Padmini said that although she was brave, "Padmini should have committed suicide early on; that way there would have been no need for a war!" In other words, she could have done even more for her husband.

perilously chaotic that only Padmini, a woman, can save it. Chitor must suspend its own law to reestablish the order that the law is intended to preserve.

Thus Padmini's departure is richly symbolic and movingly dramatic. In going out to war (over and over, women specified that she went out [*bahar*] to fight), she disregards female custom and performs male duty. Treading on male territory she assumes her husband's command. Hence Padmini is heroic not because she fulfills the codified role of the *pativrata* but because she departs from it to assume another, more urgent, role. When Padmini leaves the household and thereby inverts the relationship between her husband and herself, she abandons the behavior normally incumbent on a *pativrata* while pursuing a purpose in accord with *pativrata* duty. This inversion is verified by the story sequence. While Padmini's husband is concealed as a hostage in Ala-ud-din's camp, Padmini leaves her concealment to lead her husband's army. Once she has served in her husband's place to rescue her husband, she retreats to Chitor, which reinverts her inverted status.

Finally, self-immolation proves that her intentions have been pure. She has transgressed boundaries solely to protect her husband and not for self-aggrandizing purposes; she acts for her husband, not herself. The *pativrata* role encompasses and ultimately revalues violation as consistent with its purpose. It cannot, however, arbitrate the immediate contradiction. Women say that Padmini is a *pativrata*, but they also say that she is brave (*bahadur*) enough to have defied *pativrata* convention by going out among men. Thus there exists both conjunction and disjunction between Padmini's heroic action and the role of the *pativrata*. Both are meaningful. They constitute the experience and the end (goal) of conflict. It seems that because Padmini substitutes for her husband, she exempts herself from the rule of support synonymous with the *pativrata* role, but because she dies as a *sati*, she shows that she also fulfills the support function she transgressed. In sum, when Padmini crosses back into the *zanana*, she is not mysteriously "absolved from the sin" of leaving the *zanana*. Her reentry symbolically, not logically, states both the opposition and consonance of her actions, which have a single intention. Intention is, as always, key.

The symbolism of conflict and conjunction is predominantly spatial. We have seen how protection is located within spheres. The protection offered by *pativrata*s, be they divine (maternal *kuldevi*s), semidivine (*satimata*s), or human, has its source within the boundaries of the *zanana*. We have also seen that integral to female protection is support of male duty, which is performed on the battlefield. While that support is a mode of protection that accompanies a husband outside the household, it is predicated on the partition of *zanana* and *mardana*. Women defend honor by remaining in the *zanana*. *Parda*, we have seen, not only builds among men the esprit de corps essential for army life; it preserves and enhances the modesty and purity of women.[7]

Parda, then, represents and cultivates the character of women and men. As their character flourishes so does their reputation, the stuff of which heroism is made. When women acquire *sat* through chastity, they build good reputations. The reputation of a wife protects and furthers the reputation, and so the honor, of her husband. Because reputation is understood to reflect honor and is thus inseparable from it, female chastity, symbolized by *parda*, strengthens the character of both women and men and reinforces their respective duties of protection.

Yet Padmini, like other military heroines, abandons *parda*. When she leaves the female sphere, she no longer functions as a supporter of male duty; she becomes a performer of male duty, which is the very foundation of her heroism. Thus it is not insignificant that in speaking of Padmini Rajput women often remark that they admire her not simply because she was a *pativrata* but because "she fought like a man." Padmini's stepping out of the *zanana* constitutes an inversion of feminine and masculine as well as a transformation from housewife to heroine.[8] Such an act is not good in itself. It is good in the context of a highly undesirable state of affairs in which a husband, through death or other incapacitation, cannot carry out his martial duty, a duty predicated on the royal-caste responsibility of protection. Only in such a case may a woman substitute for her husband in order to protect him and, if he is still alive, enable him to protect as his caste responsibility demands.

This point emerges from the "two elephants" variation on the Ruthi

7. The *sat* that women and men inherit through the blood they increase through appropriate behavior. This notion is illustrated in one *thakurani*'s claim that "because Padmini and the other heroines like her had good blood, they could fight." Padmini's character, developed by being a *pativrata*, gives her the ability to perform her husband's tasks. Recall that in the Guha story, the *sat* of the mother dying as a *sati* enabled her male descendants to conquer a kingdom. Recall also that in the stories in which women shame their men into fighting, the *sat* of the mother or daughter encourages the son or husband to fight (myth variants often interchange wife and mother).

8. A heroine (*virangana*) takes a masculine role in various Indian myths and legends. On the use of "male attire, as well as the symbols of male status and authority, especially the sword," see Kathryn Hansen, "The Virangana in North Indian History," *Economic and Political Weekly*, 30 Apr. 1988, 26–27. An interesting, if partial, South Indian parallel is the Madurai heroine Minakshi, who is trained as a prince (here the heroine does not die but becomes the spouse of Shiv).

Rani story mentioned in the previous chapter. Well before the bard tells Ruthi Rani she must choose between pride and her husband's affection, she ponders whether to lead an army against her husband's enemy while her husband lives. Ashamed that her husband has not led an army to challenge his enemy sooner, she thinks of doing so herself. A bard warns her that if she fights, people will ridicule her husband and destroy his honor, so she chooses not to fight. She leads forces against the Muslims only after her husband's death.

Substituting for a husband is the basis for a woman's heroism. The act is not obligatory but supererogatory and presumably for this reason is deemed heroic. The transgression it entails can be recommended only indirectly by the rare examples of exceptionally courageous (*bahadur*) women who face the horrors of battle in violation of their normal and normative code of behavior.

That this violation is conceived as such is clear from two attendant assumptions. First, a hero attains a status that ought to be permanent, and a heroine achieves a status assumed temporary. Individual heroes are worshiped at individual shrines constructed in their honor;[9] heroines, we have seen, are worshiped only as *satimatas*, in which case they lose their individual identities. Death both validates the inversion undergone by the heroine and confirms *pativrata* status. In sum, a heroine is admired for her violation but worshiped (if worshiped; the Rani of Jhansi, we shall see, is not) without reference to violation, or for that matter to any other distinguishing acts preceding *sati* immolation.

Second, female heroism is exceptional and personal. The heroine enters the battlefield unattended by other heroines; other women remain where they should, at home. Thus the heroine has sole charge of her destiny as she battles for the realm. Temporarily transcending the model of spatial support that the *zanana* offers the *mardana*, she works alone in a world turned chaotic. Her inversion is task-specific: she is to catalyze a restoration of order. Once she has set the process in motion, she will resume her proper place among other women in the *zanana*.

The threat of conflict looms large in the story despite the understanding that it is ultimately resolved. The conflict Padmini faces is symptomatic of a more general dilemma. The idea that only Padmini can accept the villain's terms and thus save the king, the protector of the realm, underscores the aforementioned conviction that where conflict has caused order to disintegrate, it may take a woman to restore it. Such is

9. See, for example, Sontheimer, "Hero and Satī-stones."

the case with the cosmic conflict described in the *Devimahatmya*. There, when demons have so demolished the world order that the gods are powerless, the Goddess steps in to set things straight. I never heard women explicitly liken the Padmini story to the *Devimahatmya*, but even without an implicit comparison the texts reveal a common understanding: when the world has turned topsy-turvy, a female might be able to turn it right side up.[10]

Closely related to this conclusion is the observation that Padmini's departure from *parda* and assumption of male duty are occasioned by opposition stated in the narrative between the male duty to protect the realm by fighting and the male duty to protect the realm by protecting women.[11] Honor prevents men from relinquishing either goal and so paralyzes them. Only when Padmini takes charge are men delivered from their dissonance. Thus Padmini's inversion not only handles the dilemma of competing *pativrata* responsibilities, it enables men to act and thereby catalyzes a battle for restoration.

In sum, restoration of order means that conflict has been resolved and that conflict had existed. If restoration has been effective, actual, not apparent, conflict must have been overcome. This being so, what is to be made of the symbolism of Padmini's return to the *zanana* and of the conviction that her *pativrata* status has not been interrupted or diminished? Two thoughts come to mind. On the one hand, women clearly assume that the military heroine crossing out of *parda* internalizes the (sexual) control that *parda* symbolizes. It would seem she takes *parda* and the *sat* it has built with her and so is not judged immodest. Perhaps this thought explains why some variants on the Padmini and Hari Rani stories describe the heroines' faces as still veiled, though most I have come across describe heroines as out of *parda* and without veil (*ghunghat*) or mention no veil.[12] (Presumably a veil would make fighting especially troublesome.) In any case, the internalization of *parda* is verified by her death as a *sati*. Even where death occurs not through fire but

---

10. The notion that a woman, presumably weaker than a man, is especially able to demonstrate Rajput heroism brings to mind the theme of the youngest *sati*, mentioned previously, who is the ideal *sati*; she is the weakest, having had the least opportunity to accumulate *sat*. People dwell on the beauty and fragility of Padmini, presumably because she is so much weaker than one would expect a soldier to be. Cf. Beck's parallel finding that people identify with the youngest sibling in South Indian folk narratives (*Three Twins*, 35).

11. On the male duty to protect a woman and the preservation of honor, see Ziegler, "Action, Power," 80.

12. See also Ann Grodzins Gold, "Stories of Shakti" (paper presented at the Association for Asian Studies Annual Meeting, Washington, D.C., March 1989), 15.

in battle, it verifies internalization, for the heroic Rani of Jhansi, who is felled while fighting, bears the *sati* epithet.[13]

On the other hand, when a woman leaves the household she implicitly assumes male purpose and duty, so that the person outside *parda* is perhaps not quite the person who was inside it, although the outsider still intends to return once her task is accomplished. In other words, the person who conforms to the *pativrata* paradigm may be thought of as not really leaving the *zanana* and its *parda*; while absent from the *zanana* and performing male duty, the heroine may be not quite herself. Her intentions and so her honor would remain veiled by *parda*, which is located at home. Reentry would then signal a symbolic confirmation of the *pativrata*'s continued presence in the *zanana*.

In either case, it seems to me, the heroine gains a mode of control generally attributed to men. The chastity she has exercised in the *zanana*, chastity protected by males and protecting them on the battlefield, now empowers and protects her as she sets out for war. Her chastity protects her person as she fights for her husband; as she fights for him she is able to protect the chastity of her person.

The heroine's internalization of *parda* and assumption of male identity conjointly reveal a further valence of boundary symbolism. This is the idea, widespread in Rajasthan as elsewhere in India, that marriage merges the discrete male and female into a single symbolic personage. The notion that a woman is part of her husband pervades Indian classical and popular culture. A man needs a wife to become whole. Without one, he cannot perform essential Hindu rituals. This idea finds expression in the familiar image of Ardhanarishvara, Shiv as half himself and half his wife, Parvati.[14] In commenting on the behavior of Padmini and other heroines, a *thakurani* from a leading Mewar estate made explicit reference to this image. Having said that these women were *pativrata*s and that being a *pativrata* is a woman's highest duty, she said: "I'd give my life for my husband [also]. You can defame God but not a husband. I am half his body; I'd do any sacrifice for him."

If we apply this notion, substitution for the husband could also represent merging with him. The heroine, having united with her husband through performance of his role, becomes the recipient of her own

13. Summarizing her assessment of this queen's character, one woman stated, "The Rani of Jhansi was very brave and had good character. She was a lady but she had to come out of *parda* to fight!"

14. I am grateful to Dennis Hudson for bringing up this point in discussions of chastity and heroism.

power. She acts for him; he acts through her. Her passage into male space transforms her so that she is both heroine and masculine, or at the very least male-like.

This transformation of Padmini's power as she enters the battlefield would seem to emphasize the functional androgyny indicated by staging a military ambush. During this time of disorder, in which customary segregation is suspended, Padmini's performance of her husband's military duty (as strategist and commander) points to the ultimate theoretical harmony of segregated roles. At the same time, the symbolic merging of sexual identities represented by Padmini qua soldier, woman as performer of male caste duty, points to their differentiation in ordinary experience. Padmini's crossings out into battle and back into *parda* show that the suspension of custom is not final. In the end she resumes her traditional role as is expected. In fact, her crossing out carries overtones of the ritual crossing out of a *sati* on the way to the pyre.

Recall that when Padmini leaves the palace, her body becomes hot with *sat*. It is at this precise point, the intersection of inner and outer spheres, that *satis* traditionally symbolize their intention to die as *satis* by placing their handprints of wet vermilion on the entry gates. Thus the observation that Padmini becomes hot with *sat* as she emerges from the palace likens her crossing into the battlefield to the crossing that a *sativrata* makes as she processes to the cremation ground (*mahasatiyam*). That she is a *sati*—she is full of *sat*—is clear.

It is tempting to draw out the analogy by suggesting a further comparison between the *sati* procession and Padmini's caravan procession. In the case of the *sati* procession, a woman is understood to be going to the *mahasatiyam* as a bride to be joined once again with her husband: the fire is the basis for both the marriage ceremony and joint cremation.[15] At the same time, the *sativrata* is technically a widow and the conjunction of bride and widow symbolism expresses the power she possesses and the fear she inspires through her capacity to curse. Padmini is recognized to feign a dowry-carrying procession toward marriage (or perhaps marriage of sorts) with her enemy while truly advancing toward reunion with the Maharana, her husband. Her journey appears to emphasize her fidelity in marriage. Her mission is to liberate her husband in order to enable him to fight, although it is clear that the Rajputs cannot win against the Muslims, who vastly outnumber them.

15. Hence some *satis* wear wedding dresses. Moreover, as we have seen, a betrothed woman who circumambulates her financé's funeral fire and ascends it, becomes wife and *sati*.

Given this situation, Padmini's procession portends imminent widowhood; it is a prelude to *jauhar*. Hence the bride-widow elements of
sati symbolism fall easily into Padmini's procession, though their presence is not necessary to prove the significance of the fundamental *sati*
analogy stated by Padmini's manifestation of *sat*.

The fact that Padmini will die a *sati*, although no actual *sati* procession is possible under the circumstances, is plain from the time she dis-
ingenuously agrees to Ala-ud-din's terms.[16] From this perspective, Padmini, whose *sat* is manifest, is a *sativrata*. She is transformed not simply
from wife to heroine but to *sati* as well. Neither conceptualization will
suffice independently. Although Padmini is like a *sativrata*, she does die
a *sati*; although Padmini is a *sati*, she engages in exceptional behavior
that does not literally conform to the *sati* scenario.

Perhaps the best way to conceive the mutuality of the two perspectives—Padmini the *sati* demonstrating normative *pativrata-sati* behavior and Padmini the soldier exhibiting extraordinary heroic behavior—
is to think of one as the mirror image of the other. The mirrored representation is exactly what it reflects, its equivalent. It is also the opposite
of what it reflects and therefore reflects in faithful denial every detail it
reproduces. And so the heroine is a *sati*, which is why her *sat* manifests.
But she is also like the *sati* in that she plays a perfect (heroic) counter-
part, which carries the charge of her story's dramatic emphasis on transgression, both normative and locative.

This transgression, however harmonious with her purpose, is symbolically reversed when Padmini crosses back into *parda* and resumes
the custom of segregation deemed necessary in society. This reentry is
understood as the most proximate prelude to death. As Padmini's departure for the battlefield is meaningful in terms of a *sativrata*'s procession, so her return to the fortress connotes and points toward crossing
into fire, which is a salient purpose of reentry. The fortress then takes
the place of the *mahasatiyam*. The husband being alive, *jauhar* occurs
where the husband has lived rather than the place where he is to die.

What, we might ask, would have happened if the Rajputs had won a
quick, decisive victory? Would Padmini then have had no need to kill
herself? Would not reentry then be robbed of half its meaning and symbolize not legitimation but aggregation? Would Padmini still have been

---

16. In one woman's telling of the tale, Padmini wears a wedding dress to the ambush.
In another's, Padmini dresses for battle (presumably as a man) and then puts on her wedding dress when she returns to die a *sati*. In both, wearing a wedding dress is preparation
for *jauhar*.

a paragon of virtue? Such questions force issues not to be forced. Symbolism is meaningful relative to the situations in which it is found. To alter its premise or artificially expand its context is to invite unsound speculation. Moreover, even to conduct interviews to determine what would have happened if only this or that element of the story were changed, would mean asking respondents to disrupt the relations among story elements and damage the narrative's integrity. In the Padmini story, death makes sense of the events it follows. It confirms the reversion of the transformation essential to female heroism, even if individuals interviewed do not expressly articulate this notion in equivalent terms. As myths are social institutions, their meaning cannot be wholly explained by individuals called upon to dissect them.[17] The efficacy of the symbols they comprise exists within the arena of social consciousness, elements of which individuals may not be consciously aware. Thus the question to be posed is not whether death is required and if not, what then; rather, it is what death means where it occurs and then, in a similar vein, whether its occurrence has a meaningful pattern elsewhere in the culture's myth and ritual.

We have seen already that death validates purity of intention in the Padmini story and, more generally, in the immolation ritual. Death as a *sati*, a true *sati*, proves purity of the heart. Given the analogy and equation of the Padmini story and the *sati* scenario, we have concluded that death as validation both justifies what has preceded the story's climax and catalyzes and constitutes that climax. It is, however, legitimate and advisable to inquire whether such a death is typical of stories that tell of situations similar to the one Padmini faced. The context of a symbol is defined not only by the story in which it is found but by those stories utilizing the same thematic and symbolic elements. The stories must be drawn from the same social element. Still, not any old myth available from that element will suffice. Preliminary relevance must exist not in the mind of the researcher but in the minds of the storytellers. Thus here I invoke only those myths chosen by Rajput women as bearing on the question at hand: the exemplification of good Rajput character.

Given this limitation, I find it significant that the myths told by Rajput women conclude with the death of the protagonist. Even Mira, whose behavior bears little obvious resemblance to that of the heroines discussed in this chapter, dies a legitimizing death. Death is an essential

17. Victor Turner, "Symbols in Ndembu Ritual," in *The Forest of Symbols* (Ithaca: Cornell University Press, 1967), 26–27.

aspect of all their stories' meanings.[18] To illustrate this point it will prove fruitful to compare the Padmini story with the stories of the only other exemplars whose stories are mentioned with any regularity.

CASES FOR COMPARISON:
THE RANI OF JHANSI AND HARI RANI

The first of these exemplars is the Rani of Jhansi, the widowed queen who died fighting the British following the Indian Mutiny of 1857. Although the historical reasons for the queen's battle are complex, the basic grievance the queen had with the British was their failure to recognize her adoptive son's claim to the throne. She took to the battlefield in order to protect her husband's estate and regain her son's inheritance. Having strapped her son to her back and mounted a charger, she fought her way to fame and glory in an unwinnable skirmish.

Curious from our perspective is that the Rani of Jhansi was not a Rajput but a Brahman and was married to a Maratha, facts of which many Rajput women are unaware. Some of those who know she was not a Maratha maintain that she nevertheless illustrates the character a good Rajput woman possesses. Both groups of respondents have varying degrees of unfamiliarity with the Rani of Jhansi's legend. Unlike the case of Padmini, there is no standard version known to Rajputs. Thus their telling of the tale is often particularly improvisational. For example, some women assume that the Rani of Jhansi died as a *sati* when it became clear she would lose to the British. The logic behind this assumption is apparent. As the queen's intentions were selfless—she fought as her husband in protecting the welfare and status of her son— she died a *sati*. For those women who believe that she must have retreated from the battlefield at the last moment to immolate herself, the Rani of Jhansi is literally a *sati*. For those who know that the queen was slain on the battlefield, she is a *sati* by analogy. In either case, her death is adjudged unselfish sacrifice. It manifests her goodness, her *sat*. It therefore accomplishes what self-immolation accomplishes: it validates her *pativrata* status.[19]

18. In this respect the heroines' deaths resemble martyrdom. There is, however, a crucial distinction in that martyrs are remembered as heroic individuals as a result of their deaths, whereas these heroines are celebrated because of their behavior while living. Their deaths are far more commonplace than their lives.

19. The Rani of Jhansi was a widow for quite some time, a fact of which many women are unaware. They take her husband's death as a more immediate catalyst for hers.

The Rani of Jhansi is not a *satimata* for any Rajput family. She is not worshiped; she is admired. Once again, the basis for the admiration she receives is her leaving home to perform her deceased husband's duty. Thus "she fought the enemy," as one woman explained, "and did everything once her husband died." Having taken on her husband's role as an administrator, she now assumes his place on the battlefield, which dramatizes her transformation. It is the militant, equestrian image of the Rani of Jhansi that is enshrined in public memory. It fits easily into the conceptual framework already articulated. Much is made of her leaving home. When she does so, she goes armed with sword and shield. Her venture into battle demonstrates her bravery, and her death, even if it is known to have occurred on the battlefield, reveals the purity of her motive. Moreover, her death serves as a second crossing (a crossing back into *parda*), for it establishes her as a *sati* and verifies her life as a *pativrata*.

The second and final illustration is provided by Hari Rani, who, we have seen, is understood as *sati*-like. By slicing off her head with a sword, she liberates her husband from concern over her welfare and enables him to fight valiantly on the battlefield. Her act thus resembles *jauhar*. She bears the epithet *sati*, but it is by no means sure that she is worshiped as a *satimata*. No Hara Cauhan women I interviewed mentioned her as a *satimata* when asked about their families' *satimata* traditions. Like other Rajput women who named her as an example of a good Rajput woman, they usually referred to her as a *sati*, this epithet not establishing a separate tradition of *satimata* worship. Their *satimata* remains an amalgam.

What is particularly odd about the Hari Rani narrative is that the queen sacrifices herself very early in the story sequence. She marries, then dies to help her husband. Her abrupt exit would seem to belie the observation that the military heroine is remembered not for her death but for her action. Such a conclusion, however, is unwarranted. First, Hari Rani's death is an unusual action per se. She does herself in though nothing indicates that her husband will perish on the battlefield. Moreover, she dies by the sword, the instrument she wishes her husband to use. The mode and meaning of her death are notably specific: they are not simply assimilated to the *sati* mold.

Futhermore, Hari Rani's participation in the story does not end with her death. The king of Salumbar, emboldened by the bravery of his wife, straps her head to his saddle and charges out the palace gates to gain glory as a warrior. The symbolism here is patent: when the king leaves his castle, his queen goes with him. She not only catalyzes (supports) his courage, she *is* (substitutes for) his courage. Hence Hari Rani meets the common criterion of crossing out of the palace and into the battlefield. Her face exposed to all beholders, she leaves *parda*. Yet she does so in inverted order: she dies, then fights.

The king's attachment of the queen's head to his saddle stands as a succinct reversal of the Rani of Jhansi's act of strapping her son to her back. The Rani of Jhansi fights bodily but with the spirit of her husband (the courage of a man, which is symbolized by his heir). Hari Rani lends her spirit (the courage of a man, possessed by a woman) to her husband, who fights bodily. What is essential, evidently, is not the logical order of the crossings (Hari Rani dies in the *zanana* before going to the battlefield) but the symbolic value of those crossings. Although Hari Rani has severed her head, she enters the battlefield a human, not a supernatural being. As a heroine, she fights after her death, which has already verified that she has been a *pativrata*.[20]

Hari Rani's doubly inverted heroism—crossing out (like other heroines) plus crossing out after death (unlike other heroines)—occurs in the context of male heroism. Rajputs conceive of female heroism, as we have seen, in masculine terms and recognize a likeness between the heroines and heroes, who are the devotional counterparts of *satimata*s. There is a special similarity between the heroine and the type of male hero known as *jhumjhar* (struggler), who continues to fight after his head has been severed. *Jhumjhar*s figure among the most illustrious of heroes because their surfeit of *sat* enables them to fight fiercely before succumbing to death.

Many Rajput families have preserved their *jhumjhar* myths. Although these myths are a varied lot, their outlines closely resemble the pattern of the following accounts, taken from interviews and chosen for inclusion here because together they demonstrate the alien and domestic settings *jhumjhar* plots can assume.

> The Rao Sahab Maha Sinh was engaged in war with the Muslim Ranbajkhan. The Rao Sahab had a custom of granting a boon to someone every morning. Ranbajkhan's mother came to the king's court disguised as a Bhil woman and asked of him the boon that in the upcoming battle her son be allowed to strike the first blow. The king, thinking her son an ally, assented.

20. One woman said she appreciated Hari Rani for facing up to adversity and sacrificing for her husband: "She gave her head for her husband. She's my favorite—I'd like to be like Hari Rani. She was so brave not running away from hardship." Another noted that Hari Rani was bold and so she fought by making her husband fight. Typically, these informants assume Hari Rani was present, as her head symbolically indicates.

Then the Bhil woman revealed her identity [as a Muslim], but the king had already given his word and was honor-bound by it.

When the battle began, Ranbajkhan charged toward the king and with a single slash of the sword removed his head. The king, outraged by the twin insults of trickery and decapitation, fought on brilliantly until he had revenge in the form of Ranbajkhan's head. The decapitating blow he dealt also split in half his enemy's elephant and elephant-saddle. To this day we worship the Rao Sahab's sword and shield on Dashara.

The *jhumjhar* we worship was the eldest grandson of the king (*thakur*). He was very religious and routinely stayed up all night in one or another village in the realm in order to attend performances of Pabu Ji.[21] The grandson's uncle was jealous that the boy was heir to the throne. The uncle told the grandfather a lie. He said that the boy bedded strange women during his nocturnal excursions. The grandfather was furious. He gave the uncle permission to assassinate the boy.

The first thing the uncle did was to tell the lie he had told to the grandfather to the boy's wife. Hurt and angry, the wife retreated to her second-story bedroom, where she bolted her door so that her husband would not be able to come to her after returning from his nightly outing. When the boy came home and ascertained the state of affairs, he resigned himself to sleeping in the ground-floor courtyard. The uncle had foreseen that this would happen and had hidden himself nearby. When his nephew fell off to sleep, he leapt out from his hiding place and bound the boy to his bed. Three or four accomplices then ambushed the captive. The uncle sliced off his nephew's head, but the boy managed to rise and while still tied to his bed slew his assailants before falling to the floor.

As these stories illustrate, the *jhumjhar* may lose his head through battle or palace intrigue. To die fighting is not a misfortune; it is the goal (*virgati*) of all Rajput warriors. Nevertheless, to die of decapitation whether on the battlefield or at home is degrading: it violates the warrior's physical integrity, which is inseparable from his moral integrity.[22] Such humiliation can be erased only by revenge. A surfeit of *sat* enables the *jhumjhar* to survive the loss of his head long enough to avenge with interest the insult paid him. Before dying he kills at least a few, and perhaps many, enemies. This revenge takes victory from the hands of his slayers and immortalizes his valor.

At the most immediate level, the comparison between Hari Rani and the *jhumjhar* takes the form of contrast: one fights with bodiless head, the other with headless body. This comparison, however, is reductionistic, for while the *jhumjhar* fights headlessly, he still uses his head.

21. Performances of the epic of Pabu Ji, a Rathaur hero, are still given by husband-and-wife teams, which travel throughout Rajasthan to sing of the hero's exploits.
22. Ziegler, "Action, Power," 80; and Marriott and Inden, "Ethnosociology," 228.

Though severed, it functions as it should. It continues to allow the *jhumjhar* to see: it focuses and directs the courage springing from his heart. In like fashion, Hari Rani's head continues to function past the point of its severance. No longer attracting the king and distracting him from his duty, it inspires him to attack his enemies and so save face, which would have remained lost had he been allowed to continue doting on his bride. Moreover, it enables him to gain a reputation for bravery.

There is in this scenario an unmistakable mergence. It is the queen whose head is severed, but it is the king whose body avenges the loss of his queen. The king's motivation to fight is heavily charged with revenge. His wife, his protégée, has lost her life because of the enemy; therefore the enemy must suffer.

Literally speaking, of course, the queen's death is not the enemy's fault. Death is her idea. Her motivation also fits in well with the *jhumjhar* scenario. Let us look more closely at *jhumjhar* symbolism. When a *jhumjhar*'s head survives its body, it may roll a great distance in order to achieve an auspicious destination, which is then marked by a shrine. Similarly, Hari Rani's head travels about to attain its end, her husband's glory. This comparison also hinges on the male-female inversion, for Hari Rani's head does not animate the body from which it is severed but the body to which it is offered—the body of her husband. The symbolism of three types occurs: substitution, combination, and sacrifice.

First, Hari Rani's head serves for her husband's. The queen can substitute to the extent that she does because she is part of her husband, which her metaphorical transformation into a *sati* has already shown. Second, while her ashes and his do not commingle, her head accompanies him and gives him strength. It is because the queen is with him that her husband has the power to fight; they act as one. Third, as *sati* immolation is a sacrifice, so is decapitation: the queen offers her head on a silver platter, the instrument worshipers use to present offerings to deities.[23] Because her death results from her desire for her husband's success, it is, as sacrifices are, creative and empowering. It sustains and enables. In so doing, it protects the husband and his soldiers by causing him to do his duty, that is to say, by making him pursue the course of heroism ordained for a Rajput warrior.

In sum, the dying-then-fighting sequence of the Hari Rani story makes sense within the context of male heroism. Female heroism must occur within the male sphere. This notion justifies the battle-related use

23. On the ambiguities of *sati* immolation as sacrifice, see chapter 4.

of the queen's head. Once victory is attained, Hari Rani's head is retired. It is again identified with its proper discrete body because Hari Rani is conceived as a *sati*, a status logically established prior to battle. Furthermore, she is not worshiped for her heroism, whereas *jhumjhar*s are worshiped as the quintessence of heroism. There is no class of heroine stones. Hero stones commemorate the deeds and lives of heroes, and *sati* stones commemorate the deaths of women.[24] Heroes and *sati*s are worshiped as natural counterparts. Their complementarity externalizes the role separation that is symbolized by the curtain between the *mardana* and *zanana*. This complementarity does not preclude the celebration of female heroines, who are revered precisely because their actions do not fit (are not limited by) the social framework.[25]

There is to the *jhumjhar*, as well as to the *sati* and particularly to the heroine, a pervasively liminal aspect. The period that extends from the *jhumjhar*'s decapitation to his collapse parallels that time between a *sati*'s *vrat* and immolation. Both the *jhumjhar* and the *sati* pass from strictly human to superhuman states, yet their marginal periods continue to reflect male and female roles. The *jhumjhar* fulfills his male duty so well that he exceeds it and so gains the power to fight on and destroy his enemies; the *sativrata* fulfills her female duty so well that she exceeds it and so gains the powers to bless and to curse, that is, to manage, her household. In both cases, a surfeit of *sat* occasions a transformation in consonance with the concept of duty insofar as duty translates in terms of role fulfillment, that is, with reference to acceptable and laudable actions. To the extent that the heroine partakes of *sati* symbolism, she conforms to the role-specific conception of duty. Yet she goes beyond the boundaries of role fulfillment defined by compliance with its rules.[26] She receives admiration because of what she does. Yet what she *does* Rajput women understand—as we must—in terms of what she *is*.

Hence we must resort to the vocabulary of virtue. Rajput women hold that Padmini, the Rani of Jhansi, and Hari Rani are good Rajput women because they are brave (*bahadur*) and because they have good character (*sat*). To reiterate a crucial point: their actions are not good

24. A *jhumjhar*, like other heroes, is worshiped in the form of a stone relief image of a warrior on horseback, placed outdoors on a village boundary or near the village well. If a *jhumjhar* has no stone, the household keeps a small metal image of him in a wooden box or basket. When a hero's wife dies as a *sati* the couple sometimes shares a stone.

25. On saintly virtues as inimitable, see John Stratton Hawley, ed., *Saints and Virtues* (Berkeley: University of California Press, 1987), xvi–xvii, passim.

26. For highly productive discussions of rule compliance versus duty fulfillment I am indebted to David Wills.

per se. Indeed, considered out of context, their actions offend conventional wisdom and its rules and obligations. Heroines transgress but receive admiration. The appropriate question to ask is not, is what they were doing good? It is rather, in doing what they did, were they good women?

THE HEROINE AS GOODNESS

At this juncture let us recall that goodness, character, is both substantive and normative, substance and norm being mutually dependent and reciprocally transformative.[27] We have already seen how what one *is* gives value to what one does (the Rajput *sati* is assumed valid, the non-Rajput *sati* is suspect), but we have also seen that what one *does* establishes what one is (the Gujar *sati* is scrutinized for motive, but in the case examined, found valid; all valid *sati*s are deemed by the mode of their deaths to have been *pativrata*s). Given a substantialist orientation toward character,[28] we might ask what ethical implications can be gleaned from the heroine's change of identity.

In gaining and sharing a male identity, the heroine remains the same person, the same woman, guided temporarily by the norms appropriate to male behavior. In so doing, she identifies with her husband, which is the purpose of each individual *pativrata* but represents an ideal unreachable by the ordinary *pativrata*. The identification that the heroine achieves illustrates what Marriott and Inden call the "particulate" nature of the individual.[29] The adoption of the male role demonstrates a combination of the essences of two persons deemed for other (social role-performance) purposes individual. Identified with the male, the heroine represents an ideal and realizes it although and because the ideal controverts social categories. Thus the heroine, the person, is good both because she is who she is—not an individual in the typical sense of the term, but an individual identified as merged with another, her husband—and because her actions as a heroine demonstrate, symbolize, and proclaim her attainment of who she should be.

The transformation of identity is symbolized by action (the bearing of male weapons, the performing of male responsibilities) but the import

27. Marriott and Inden, "Ethnosociology," 228, passim; Ziegler, "Action, Power," 23–25.
28. Marriott and Inden refer to the South Asian perception of persons as "unique composites of diverse subtle and gross substances" ("Ethnosociology," 232).
29. Marriott and Inden use this concept to analyze caste (ibid.), but it is also helpful in considering gender identification.

of such action is its validation of intention. Without appropriate intention, such a transformation is a masquerade. As I emphasize repeatedly,
the symbolism of transformation refers to the subjective as well as the
objective state. The heroine who is a *pativrata* does not make sense in
terms of social classification; she makes sense only in terms of motivation.

Thus we must understand virtue as the heroine incorporates it. The
heroine possesses bravery, which her conduct validates. That conduct is
symbolic; it has a preordained set of meanings and commands a context
consistent with the character it illustrates. Because symbolism depends
on setting for meaning, symbolic action must fall within a comprehen-
sible pattern. Isolated actions neither communicate nor instruct. Therefore the individual performing an isolated act cannot be paradigmatic,
either directly or obliquely. What makes sense of a narrative's symbolism is the pattern the individual enacts, alters, or refutes by substituting
or combining it with another pattern.

In order to understand female heroism it is essential to compare and
contrast pattern illustrations, each of which contributes to the pattern's
meaning over time and at any particular moment for one particular person. We comprehend the story of Padmini by comparison with the *pativrata-sati* scenario from which it deviates and with the female heroic
scenario, which like the myths of Hari Rani and the Rani of Jhansi it
exemplifies. What is especially interesting is that it affirms the identity
and necessity of good character, established not through specific actions
but through intent, symbolically validated by death.

And so although technically deviant, heroines are exceptionally good
persons, persons whose characters instruct and inspire over the course of
time through the medium of personal interpretation. As narrators draw
on these exemplars over and over again, they tell us much about the
ongoing creative tension between religious tradition and socialization.
They embody and illustrate *sat*. Through admiration of the possessors
of *sat*, narrators vivify the past that inspires them.

In both veneration of *sati*s and admiration of heroines, then, women
praise the accumulators of *sat*. This does not mean they themselves want
to become heroines any more than it means they want to become *sati*s.
The *sati*s and heroines they admire are overwhelmingly figures from the
Rajput past. Rajput women see them as models that can help women be
mindful of *pativrata* responsibilities. We may find it difficult to think of
these models as empowering women to perform their domestic roles,
but Rajput women do not: the sacrifices of these women made them into
great, superhuman beings. Rajput women see themselves as women who

do not go out but who perform sacrifices at home for the sake of husbands and families. They still admire the spirit of those whose *sat* becomes manifest in sacrificial fire; its inspirational force appears in the comments of many of the women whom I interviewed. One woman told me stories of Padmini, Ruthi Rani, and Hari Rani and went on to describe a relative who carried out a suicide pact with her husband during the 1950s when her husband was severely depressed by the disinheritance after 1947. The woman who narrated these stories saw her relative as a good woman but did not consider her a *sati* because the relative's fear of being a young widow seemed to be her motivation, not truly selfless devotion. This narrator told me of another woman who died in the same period who is considered a *sati* because she had the proper motivation.[30] She considered that *sati* to have died in a transitional period, however, and does not think *sati* immolations are valid today.

Another woman who described her favorite heroines then told me that circumstances have changed but "there is something about fire that still attracts Rajput women." She said that they still cannot but gaze into the fire and feel an urge to join it. By this, I believe, she meant that although the practice of *sati* immolation has changed, women still have *sat*, which their shared attraction to flames demonstrates.[31] Viewing it as both inherent and cultural, a nobleman also mentioned this temptation to me and recited for my instruction a well-known *doha* about a spectator who sees a lion (Rajput) drawn to a fire but fearfully skirting around it and then sees a Rajput woman drawn to a fire and fearlessly mingling with it. The narrator used this verse to back up his point that Rajput women are actually braver, more heroic, more virtuous than their men. He then recited one of the stories in which a woman shames her man into battle (the story of "the sound of clanging iron" in chapter 5) and concluded that even today, "Whatever we [men] do, it is our women who make us do it." It seems such stories and the one about Hari Rani remain poignant to women today. They dramatically illustrate the widely shared belief that through giving up the self, women gain character and power.

In sum, the exemplars of *sat* are paradigms for *pativratas*, who seek to protect their husbands and families. Rajput women understand the duty of protection to encompass their caste and gender responsibilities. As women and as caste members they act by protecting their husbands'

---

30. That woman's shrine is found on the airport road in Jodhpur.
31. Her description reminded me of the temptation to jump some people describe when they stand at the edge of a cliff or tall building.

lives and by pushing their husbands to perform their duties. Referring to and passing on paradigms of protection, these women conserve and contribute to a mythical tradition that makes sense of and gives meaning to the ever-imperfect character of social convention and social life. Identifying with the heroine, the ordinary *pativrata* accepts and affirms the necessity to internalize social control through sacrifice, which is how women perform their protective role.

Relating good character (*sat*) and the duty (*dharm*) of protection is bravery, which women see as a disposition toward sacrifice. All heroines and *sati*s are brave (*bahadur*) Rajput women who "do not run away from hardship," as one woman put it.[32] This bravery gives kinetic force to goodness and catalyzes protective sacrifice, which preserves life and welfare. It effects fulfillment of a preconceived protective duty, performance of which is the paramount external index of character. As I emphasized, duty is not expressed in specific action, although certain acts such as religious fasts or marital obedience are thought prima facie to accord with it. It is expressed in terms of intention, which is why moral exemplars are emulated despite their violation of approved conduct. Bravery animates a selfless intention to sacrifice, be it that of personal desires by a *pativrata* or of life by hero, *sati*, or heroine who is ultimately a *sati*.

The heroines we have considered conform to a pattern of protection that functions when the standard social pattern of protection breaks down. Just as the duty of the warrior is to protect the realm and the duty of the wife is to protect her husband as he protects the realm, the responsibility of the heroine is to protect where ordinary protection no longer suffices. Where society is threatened from without and customary defenses prove inadequate to their task, the interiorization of the social order—metonymically represented as *parda*—by the heroine, who comes to perform the tasks of men, sustains the social and moral order.

Padmini and the rest affirm the *pativrata* paradigm just as certainly as they violate the *pativrata* role. Because of their character, they are called *pativrata*s and judged the best among them. Our attention now turns to the other figure frequently listed as being among the best of Rajput women, Mira Bai. We must discover the curious logic by which Mira, who also violates the *pativrata* role but is not herself called a *pativrata*, is interpreted obliquely to affirm it.

32. One woman noted that Mewari women are especially brave; she said women living in Jaipur could never have done what Padmini and the others did.

CHAPTER 7

The *Bhakt* Paradigm

Mira Bai

I like Mira because she gained enlightenment (*moksh*). She wasn't a *pativrata*, though. She didn't sacrifice for her husband. But in my estimation, she had taken Lord Krishna as her husband before she married. . . . I think what she did was not wrong because she did it out of devotion. Maybe she sang in the streets, but at least she sang only songs of devotion.

Mira left everything because of her *puja*. I can't comment on that. Well, she shouldn't have left. Rajput ladies are very much tradition-minded. They are expected to mind their homes.

Mira was very dedicated [to Krishna]. She abandoned every-thing, whereas a Rajput woman living in a family must per-form her duties. A Rajput woman wouldn't dare to go out; everybody can't be like Mira.

I certainly admire Mira. When people were so orthodox that they wouldn't step out [of *parda*] at all, she had the guts to step out. Maybe because I can't step out, I admire her so. She was not a *pativrata*; she was devoted to Krishna. So, we don't consider her an ordinary Rajput woman . . .

———*Comments of four noblewomen*

The human exemplars examined to this point are all protectors of their husbands' welfare, honor, and duty. They show that heroism entails an inversion of *pativrata* norms in serving its aims. Thus, Padmini and the others physically transgress the *zanana* boundary and logically tran-scend the *pativrata* category but are *pativrata*s nonetheless.

Mira Bai is a different matter.[1] Although Rajput women list Mira as one of the two women they most admire, they are aware that she radically and finally departs from the pattern that the military heroines establish. On the one hand, they say that they admire Mira as a Rajput woman because of her exceptionally good character. As we have seen, Rajput women understand a woman of good character as a *pativrata*. On the other hand, they assess Mira as an exemplar of good character who is not a *pativrata*.[2] The reason: rather than serve her (human) husband, Mira opts to dedicate herself to God. She is a devotee, a *bhakt*, of Lord Krishna. Many Rajput women celebrate her even though or perhaps because she radically oversteps the limits of the *pativrata* paradigm.[3] Appreciating the dramatic nature of Mira's transgression requires a good look at the way her story is told in Rajasthan. The account here is the standard variation known to women I interviewed.[4]

THE STORY OF MIRA BAI

Mira was born a princess in the Mertiya branch of the Rathaur clan. As a child, she adored the cowherd god, Krishna, an image of whom she treated as a doll. One day, while watching a wedding procession Mira asked her mother, "Who will be my bridegroom?" Caught by surprise and unsure what to say, her mother replied, "Lord Krishna."

Having matured into an attractive young woman, Mira was married to Mewar's heir apparent.[5] Her love for Krishna undiminished, she set off for her new home at Chitor. Soon after she arrived, her in-laws began to pressure her to abandon her affection for Krishna and to venerate Ekling Ji (the incarnation of Shiv associated with the royal household) as well as the royal *kuldevi*. As a daughter-in-law Mira was supposed to revere the deities of her husband's family; even so, she cared only for Krishna. She spent her days composing love songs for Krishna and dancing for him in a temple she had persuaded her husband to build.

1. Because Mira's behavior is difficult to explain, it simply produces more voluntary and detailed exegesis than the behavior of other heroines, as will become apparent.
2. A few women accord to Mira the title of *pativrata* but, they specify, not in the usual sense.
3. As the first quotation above illustrates, being a *bhakt*, Mira sings and dances in the street, behavior thought appropriate for courtesans, not proper Rajput ladies; even dancing for God has seductive associations. For a vivid example of the tension between *pativrata* devotion and *bhakti*, see Bennett, *Dangerous Wives*, 221–25; also Marglin, *God-King*.
4. It generally agrees with the biography in A. J. Alston, *The Devotional Poems of Mīrābāī* (Delhi: Motilal Banarsidass, 1980), 4–7.
5. Although women never named him, many local people identify this person as Bhoj Raj.

Mira's impudence enraged the household. Adding insult to injury, Mira denigrated her marriage by speaking of Krishna as her true husband and refraining from sexual contact with her human husband, whom she regarded as a brother. Thus not only did Mira reject wifely duties, she refused to be a wife at all. Some women say her husband was infuriated by her behavior. Others say he did not mind; he hardly ever interfered with her *puja*.

Mira's husband died young and heirless. Later, when her father-in-law died, her husband's younger brother (*devar*) came to the throne. The *devar* resented Mira's attitudes, particularly her unwillingness to act as a widow on the grounds that her true husband, Lord Krishna, was alive. Having failed to induce the princess to behave properly, the *devar* plotted to have her killed. First he ordered her nightly drink to be laced with poison. The princess drank this down, but Krishna rendered the poison harmless. Undiscouraged, the king sent Mira a basket of fruit in which a cobra was concealed. Once again Mira escaped injury. Some say Krishna turned the snake into a flower garland. Others say the snake bit her, but its poison became ambrosia.

At this point Mira thought it prudent to leave Chitor. Taking up the life of a mendicant ascetic, she communed with male ascetics (*sadhu*s or yogis)[6] and as she traveled, danced and sang for Krishna along the roadways and in the woods. In time she arrived at Brindavan, the forest home of Krishna's youth.

After some time Mira traveled to Dvaraka, Krishna's home in his later years. There she spent her days attending Krishna at one of his temples. By this point, much to the royal family's dismay, Mira had gained widespread fame as a *bhakt*. At the same time that her reputation was spreading, Mewar was suffering from various problems, some political, some military. Many felt that these problems were either caused or aggravated by the shame that the errant princess was bringing the royal family. They viewed her activities as robbing the king and so his kingdom of dignity and strength. To rectify the situation the Maharana dispatched a retrieval party.[7] When the party members arrived in Dvaraka and entered the temple where Mira served Krishna, they discovered that Mira had disappeared into Krishna's icon. Her sari, draped on the icon, was all that remained to testify to the miracle.

6. Rajput women use these words interchangeably to refer to wanderers seeking enlightenment.
7. This detail is at odds with Priyadas's account, in which the Maharana sends for her because he begins to appreciate Mira's greatness; see the *Bhaktirasasambodhini* (cited in John Stratton Hawley and Mark Juergensmeyer, *Songs of the Saints of India* [New York: Oxford University Press, 1988], 126).

Recounting this story and reflecting on Mira's character, many women emphasize her courage. Mira had to be brave, they say, in order to withstand social criticism and cruelty from her husband's household.[8] Moreover, she had to be brave in order to leave the security of even an unpleasant *sasural* in order to search for Krishna.[9] Several women compare Mira to Padmini on this point. They believe that Mira's courage allowed her to seek God, just as Padmini's courage allowed her to liberate her husband.

Such a comparison ought not to obscure a crucial distinction that Rajput women perceive. Mira's courage does not arise from her life as an ordinary *pativrata*—a woman devoted to the man she has married. Rather, her courage originates from God and is sustained by her love for God. Because Mira sees herself as God's wife, she is able to abandon her family. This distinction is the basis for the crucial qualification mentioned above: although Rajput women tend to think that as a *bhakt* saint Mira had good character, they also think that Mira was not a *pativrata*. Some were quite frank about their difficulty in understanding her behavior; others looked uncomfortable when narrating her departure from conventional norms. While admiring Mira, women clearly recognize her unmistakable, even shocking, deviation from the female role they aspire to fulfill. As one young noblewoman expressed her reservations: "I like Mira because of her dedication to Krishna. Just the dedication I like—she wasn't a *pativrata*. She was married to such a handsome man, but still she wasn't a *pativrata*!" Another said, "Mira was stubborn and caused trouble in her marriage. *Bhakti* is a high calling, but Mira was married. After marriage it is wrong to leave and become a *bhakt*." This woman ultimately concluded, as two others did, that she could not even admire Mira.[10] Her reaction, however, is exceptional: an overwhelming number of women mentioned Mira as a woman they admired. To understand this admiration tempered with consternation, let us examine the disjunctions and confluences Rajput

8. One woman said the main reason she admired Mira was "because of what she [Mira] bore from her in-laws." This woman seemed to think this detail was crucial in revealing good character.

9. Cf. John Stratton Hawley, "Morality Beyond Morality in the Lives of Three Hindu Saints," in *Saints and Virtues* (Berkeley: University of California Press, 1987), 55–59.

10. Another gave the same reason for not admiring Mira even though she was a descendant of Mira's family: "I feel that if she was a devotee following Krishna, she shouldn't have got married. Once she was married, she should have performed her duties as a wife and *rani*. I don't admire her." A third said, "Mira served Krishna but in the Rajput community, one has to marry [a mortal]."

women perceive between performance of *pativrata* duty and contempla-
tion of the divine.

As one might suspect from the tenor of the young *thakurani*'s remark, although Rajput women admire Mira's courage they cannot say
that they would have done what she did. They believe that an ordinary
Rajput woman should aspire to be a *pativrata* by performing *pativrata*
duties and not aim to be a great *bhakt*, which mandates renunciation of
pativrata duties. In the words of another noblewoman, "Mira was
above the Rajput rules and regulations. That's okay only if you're a
saint."

These comments (and Mira's disobedience) notwithstanding, Rajput
women say that Mira's bravery springs from her constitution as a Rajput woman. One noblewoman remarked, "There was only one Mira. It
was difficult to produce even one Mira. Only in the Rajput community
was that possible. Because she was a Rajput, she had strength of character." Hence most Rajput women are proud that Mira is one of them
and feel that because she is one of them she was able to accomplish what
she did (fig. 26). According to another woman, the courage Mira demonstrates in rejecting Rajput custom compares to the courage enabling
the ordinary Rajput woman to suffer the pains and deprivations en-
demic to life as a *pativrata*. Rajput women are able to admire and aspire
after the courage Mira possesses while rejecting for themselves the
course of action it enables her to take.

In other words, Rajput women who admire Mira emulate her as a
moral exemplar, but they do so obliquely. They wish to be *pativrata*s as
Mira is a *bhakt*. This oblique emulation is very different from women's
emulation of *kuldevi*s and *satimata*s. To the extent that Rajput women
emulate *kuldevi*s and *satimata*s, they do so because they have vowed to
protect their husbands to the utmost of their ability, though of course
they cannot perform the superhuman acts of protection of which *kuldevi*s and *satimata*s are capable. By contrast, when women emulate Mira
obliquely, they feel not simply that they could not but rather that they
should not do what she did. One woman neatly summarized the situation: "Mira was a *bhakt*. Whatever she did she did because of God; she
didn't like her husband. She got *moksh*, which was good for her, but it
is good for us to do everything for the husband."

What then of the question of contingent emulation? Would a Rajput
woman do what Mira did if she were in Mira's exact position? We have
seen that most women believe ordinary women should not try to follow
Mira's example by leaving their families, even if they wish to search for

26. Mira Bai dances for Krishna (cover of a devotional pamphlet).

God. As a few women noted, although Mira was truly a great woman, they could not be like her because they would never be in Mira's unique situation. Many factors brought Mira to it: the childhood betrothal to Krishna, the persecution by in-laws, the death of her husband, heartless relatives, and so forth. Not being stereotypical, it is very different from the situation of a *sativrata* who, like many women throughout history, must decide whether to die with or live without her husband. Mira does not, then, play out a scenario. She creates an incomparable and intensely personal relationship with God. Thus, her behavior cannot be measured against our merely human standards. Her devotion to God has taken her out of the social realm, the realm of norm and custom. In the words of one woman, "Mira we can't say was just human; she was something superhuman." The implied question: so how are we to judge her?

Echoing this woman's sentiments, most Rajput women would never condemn Mira for acting as she did, yet they certainly feel they would be reprehensible for acting now as she did then. They point out that even though Mira's situation was intolerable—she was mercilessly persecuted by her in-laws—still, ordinary *pativrata*s in harsh conditions should concentrate, even meditate, on their devotion to their husbands or, if widowed, to their husbands' memories. Nonconformity is the privilege of saints. For ordinary Rajput women, it is better to aspire to be *pativratas* rather than great *bhakt* saints. As one woman who admires Mira remarked, "Mira only did *bhakti*; she had no faith in society. She didn't like Rajput society, only *puja*, *bhakti*. She cut off all her social relationships. In general I don't think that is a good thing; it's better to be a *pativrata* . . . "

Closely related to the matter of emulation is the question of how women mediate the disparity between Mira's good character and her actions. This mediation appears to be accomplished symbolically. Once again, Rajput women focus on her intention revealed by death. As the story says, Mira's life ends through absorption into Krishna. As in the case of other heroines, Mira's death validates her motivations and sanctions her objectives. When Mira melds with Krishna's image, she attains her life's purpose, union with God. She shows that she has lived as a human being but that she has done so in the context of a transcendent mystical association with God. Because her death is miraculous, her character cannot be judged by mundane criteria.

In addition to validating her character, Mira's death confirms her claims of divine marriage, for it certainly connotes *sati* immolation. The *sati*'s ashes commingle with those of her husband, and so the *sati* unites with him in a way not possible during life. When Mira's body dissolves into stone, she also unites with her beloved in a miraculous manner. In both cases, a wife partakes of her husband's essence and destiny. One woman makes this association in her comment that "a *sati* dies in a fire, but Mira disappeared!" Her point is that Mira's death is not just equivalent to *sati* immolation; it is even more impressive as testimony to her greatness.

Moreover, the dissolving of Mira's body into stone recalls commemorative *sati* stones. In Rajasthan, many of these memorials depict *satis* standing alongside their heroic husbands. What joins the spouses physically and symbolizes their shared destiny is the stone itself. Just such a union is indicated by the embrace of Mira's sari and Krishna's image.

David Shulman cites a parallel instance, that of a Tamil princess who merges with a stone image of God after she has been wed to him by the king whom her father had intended for her husband. The image, a *ling*, absorbs her body, except for her hand, which continues to protrude. Shulman posits a correspondence between this hand and the hand insignias found on *sati* stones: "The woman's hand emerging from the *linga* has an iconic analogue in the *sati* stone. Sometimes these stones show an arm bedecked with bangles emerging from a pillar; the bangles suggest a woman whose husband is still alive."[11]

Though Mira is a *bhakt*, not a *pativrata* (at least as this term is normally understood) like the Tamil princess, she is transcendently vindicated. The validation of her intention to love only God makes it possible for women to admire her and to emulate her obliquely. Being a transcendent validation, however, it emphasizes the chasm between the transcendent world of the saint versus the ordinary world of the Rajput woman. Hence in speaking of Mira, Rajput women can say that loving God does not legitimize leaving a family, for one should never leave a family. Rather, loving God legitimizes loving a husband.

In affirming a form of behavior that she explicitly violates, then, Mira resembles Padmini, though only to a certain point. Comparing affirmations of the *pativrata* role reveals the limits of Padmini's transgression and the limitlessness of Mira's transgression. Comparison also discloses the nature and place of *bhakti* in the lives of ordinary women.

11. Shulman, *Tamil Temple Myths*, 64.

MIRA AND PADMINI: A COMPARISON

Mira resembles Padmini in at least three significant ways. Both Mira and Padmini violate the convention of *parda*, take on male roles, and demonstrate unequivocal devotion. But they differ in the extent of and reasons for their transgressions, as we shall see. In the first instance, they cross out of *parda*, which is the basis of household organization and gender identity. A Rajput woman is and should be an insider; she performs *pativrata* duties inside the women's quarters, which are inside the household. Outside it men work as performers of caste functions; by tradition, Rajput men are conquerors, rulers, and defenders of territories. Nevertheless, Padmini leaves the *zanana* to launch a military offensive that will liberate her husband. Mira leaves the *zanana* to travel the road leading to God. In both instances, boundary symbolism is clearly critical. Both departures signal a crossing out of social convention and into arenas where danger is to be encountered and distinction becomes possible. When Padmini leaves *parda*, however, she clearly intends to die. Her body becomes hot with *sat*, which states that her intentions are chaste and suggests that if she lives through the ambush, she will return to the palace to die properly, as a *sati*. Padmini's exit, then, begins the first half of a circle that her return and death complete.

Mira also risks her reputation but does so without an intention to return. In fact, when she leaves the palace for the road she abandons her reputation.[12] As this chapter's epigraphs indicate, she rejects *parda* and sings "in the streets."[13] She further disgraces her family by unabashedly mixing with male ascetics. A woman who withdraws from supervision, even a woman who does so in order to seek God, draws to herself the suspicions of those who remain in the household and so continue to observe social norms and mores. In going outside, she rejects a fundamental norm. Such an unsupervised woman is thought to be (as we might say in English) a "loose woman," a "public woman," a "streetwalker."[14] Of course, such suspicions lead to damaged reputations: Mi-

12. Many poems attributed to Mira focus on this: for example, P. Chaturvedi's *Mīrāṃbāī kī Padāvalī* poem 93 (English trans. in Alston, *Devotional Poems*, 72).

13. Carstairs reports that the people in the village he studied found a film about Mira sexually suggestive. It was shown by a traveling cinema on three successive evenings. Carstairs says: "The film was 'Mirabai' . . . and it was noticeable here, as in Udaipur, that it was the singing and dancing which most powerfully gripped the audience's attention: and both of these were at once religious and sensual . . . many of the villagers went each night to see the three-hour film over again" (*Twice-Born*, 95).

14. For comparative insights on female imagery of binding and loosening, see (1) Alf Hiltebeitel, "Draupadī's Hair," *Puruṣārtha* 5 (1981); (2) Gananath Obeyesekere, *Medusa's Hair* (Chicago: University of Chicago Press, 1981); and (3) Holly Baker Reynolds,

ra's reputation and because of hers, the reputations of Mira's husband and his family. Therefore although Mira's admirers think of her as beyond reproach, they note that she did harm her husband and *sasural* at the time.[15] A bad reputation always diminishes family honor, which Rajputs are particularly keen to preserve.

Her behavior elicits two further criticisms. Mira is a widow and has therefore failed to perform a *pativrata*'s primary purpose, protection of her husband. Worse, she is a widow who refuses to act as a widow. Having rejected the role of wife, she then refuses to think of herself as a widow when her husband dies. As one woman said rather heatedly, "Even when she was a widow, she continued to wear *suhag* [*pativrata*] clothes!"[16] Here we encounter a situation that resembles that of the *sativrata*. Mira both is and is not a widow. As a widow, she violates *parda*. But from the transcendent perspective she does not understand herself as married to her prince and cannot violate *parda*, for God lives everywhere. Therefore Rajput women both call Mira the prince's wife (then widow) and deny that she is the prince's wife (then widow); both statements are true from distinct but valid perspectives.

In this sense, then, Mira's shifting identity as wife–not wife and later as widow–not widow recalls the way in which the *sativrata* procession both symbolizes and denies widowhood. Mira has left home but has not yet found God. Having left the palace and taken to the road, she crosses out of society and its constraints. She drifts from place to place seeking salvation in the form of a lasting union with God.

"An Auspicious Married Woman," in *The Powers of Tamil Women*, ed. Susan Snow Wadley (Syracuse: Syracuse University, 1980). On this theme and Mira's behavior, see Lindsey Harlan, "Abandoning Shame" (paper presented at the conference, Representations of India's Past, Varanasi, India, December 1989).

15. All accounts cite the bad fortune of Chitor as reason for her attempted retrieval but specify no problems. One noblewoman from Jaipur said that because of this bad fortune Mewari women still tend not to respect Mira and that in Udaipur Rajput women will not even sing her *bhajan*s; she said in Udaipur only common people sing Mira's songs, but in Jaipur and Jodhpur everybody does. Only one other woman mentioned such resentment against Mira in Udaipur. I found no evidence that Mira is especially disliked in Mewar, and the Ban Mata temple in the Udaipur City Palace is adorned by a series of large Mira paintings. Moreover, I found concern about Mira's bad behavior distributed among women in all parts of Rajasthan. The Mira *bhajan*s many women know these days in Udaipur and elsewhere they have learned from the radio. In the village where I worked, few people are familiar with Mira Bai's story; they consider it something only educated people would know.

16. Another woman noted how strange Mira's reaction to widowhood is, even by contemporary standards: "Mira was a widow; widows are like vegetables. They're not supposed to take part in merrymaking. They're supposed to wear black, white, or maroon [drab colors]."

The road leading away from society takes Mira into the forest, where she associates with *sadhu*s, men who have utterly renounced the social order. The classic (Sanskritic) Indian notion of social order is summed up by the concept of *varnashramadharma*. At its core, *varnashrama-dharma* explains the caste system's division of labor and sets out four stages of life for high-caste men.[17] Ideally, during the first two stages of life a man lives as a chaste student (*brahmacarin*) and then, having finished his studies, becomes a householder (*grihastha*), an upholder of society and a contributor to social order. He raises a family and performs his caste occupation to support that family. Then when his children are grown, alone or perhaps accompanied by his wife, he leaves his household to become a forest dweller (*vanaprastha*). This third stage of life is a prelude to complete withdrawal from wife and society in the final stage. When the forest dweller feels ready, he becomes a full-fledged renouncer (*sannyasi*). He lives alone in the forest that he might devote himself to undistracted absorption in spiritual matters.

As the traditional stages of life make clear, the forest is understood as the traditional place of meditation and its concomitant, asceticism. There live men in the last stages of life. Moreover, within it men of any age can escape all the stages of life. In other words, men can become renouncers without first going through the three *dharm* stages. All they need do is leave society and head for the road and the forest.

When Mira, a widow without children and so a woman devoid of primary family responsibilities, goes into the forest, she declares herself a renouncer, a *sannyasi* or *sadhu*, for the forest is the abode of the *sadhu*s. When she leaves *parda*, according to one woman, she renounces absolutely everything and lives without attachment. She then pursues an ascetic discipline of *bhakti*. This perspective is summed up in the following lines from one of Mira's poems addressed to Krishna, himself an ascetic:

> I'll take up your yogic garb—
> your prayer beads,
> earrings,
> begging-bowl skull,
> tattered yogic cloth—
> I'll take them all
> And search through the world as a yogi does
> with you—yogi and yogini, side by side.[18]

17. They represent the ideal life pattern in the classic legal texts, the *dharmashastra*s; most men pass up the final two stages of increasing asceticism.
18. Chaturvedi, in Hawley and Juergensmeyer, *Songs*, 139.

In sum, Mira's sojourn in the forest symbolically states her development into a wholly committed *bhakt*. Both the forest and the road on
which she travels represent the renunciation of domesticity essential to
complete religious transformation. Taking up an ascetic life demonstrates Mira's commitment to God and her freedom from social norms,
which only interfere with her commitment to God.

Women are not only concerned by the fact that Mira was a renouncer
of the responsibilities and values they uphold. They are also troubled
that she kept the company of (male) renouncers. It was bad enough
that she entertained *sadhu*s at the palace, as some believe she did.
But when she traveled with them unchaperoned, she truly behaved
outrageously. One woman remarked, "Once the Maharana died, she
sang, ate, and lived with the *sadhu*s!" Another said that "as her husband died when she was young, she did *mala* [rosary], sang *bhajan*s
[hymns], and performed *puja* while she kept the company of *sadhu*s!"
A third observed that "people spoke badly of her going around with
*sadhu*s. There were rumors." And a fourth explained that "the Rajputs didn't like it when she went around with the *sadhu*s. Royalty
doesn't put up with that sort of thing. The family thought it was dis-
graceful."

That the rumors about "that sort of thing" are sexual is made explicit
in the well-known story of how one of Mira's *sadhu* companions tried
to persuade her to have sex with him. He said that, as a holy man and
representative of God, he had the right to demand her sexual favors. She
consented with the caveat that their union be consummated in front of
Krishna's image so God could witness her "offering" to him. Wary of
God's wrath, the *sadhu* lost his nerve and ran away. This lustful *sadhu*
story illustrates the understanding widely held in India that ascetics,
who have repressed their sexual instincts for long periods, can be particularly lascivious if tempted by unsupervised women, especially women
alone in the woods.[19]

The life of a renouncer is thought not really appropriate for women.
Renouncing women are generally thought susceptible to seduction in
the woods, which makes their stay there problematic; they are also
thought to enact a role fundamentally male. Just as the system of *varnashramadharma* applies to men—men become students, men perform
caste functions as householders, and so forth—so does its renunciation.

19. See O'Flaherty, *Śiva*, esp. on Rishyashringa and the pine forest sages. The traditional complementarity of ascetic-courtesan gives strength to the streetwalking associations of Mira's renunciation.

Interview

1. Name
2. Father's family: place (state, *thikana*, or village); genealogy (*vamsh, kul, shakh, khamp, nak*); father's title
3. Mother's family (questions as above)
4. Husband's family (questions as above)
5. Birth date
6. Marriage date
7. Education
8. Work experience
9. Introductory questions (open-ended "warm-up" questions)
   a. What does it mean to be a Rajput woman? How would you describe a Rajput woman to someone who has never met one?
   b. What about Rajput men? What are they like and how would you describe them? These days who keeps up the Rajput traditions: women, men, both?
10. The traditions
    a. *Kuldevi*s
       1. What do you know about the *kuldevi* of your father's family? Do you know any stories about her? How is she worshiped? Are there *ratijaga*s? For what reasons? When and for what reasons is *dhok* given? Where is she worshiped?
       2. What do you know about the *kuldevi* of your mother's family? (questions as above)
       3. What do you know about the *kuldevi* of your husband's family? (questions as above)
    b. Bherus
       1. Is there a Bheru Ji worshiped by your father's family? Do you know any stories about him (them)? How is he (are they) wor-

shiped? Is he (are they) connected with *ratijaga*s? When and why is *dhok* given? Where is he (are they) worshiped?

2. Is there a Bheru Ji worshiped by your mother's family? (questions as above)
3. Is there a Bheru Ji worshiped by your husband's family? (questions as above)

c. *Satimata*s

1. Is there a *satimata* in your father's family? Do you know any stories about her? How is she worshiped? Is she connected with *ratijaga*s? When and why is *dhok* given? Are there any *shrap*s associated with this *satimata*? What about *ok*s? Where is she worshiped?
2. Is there a *satimata* in your mother's family? (questions as above)
3. Is there a *satimata* in your husband's family? (questions as above)

d. *Jhumjhar*s

1. Is there a *jhumjhar* in your father's family? Do you know any stories about him (them)? Is he (are they) connected with *ratijaga*s? When and why is *dhok* given? Where is he (are they) worshiped?
2. Is there a *jhumjhar* in your mother's family? (questions as above)
3. Is there a *jhumjhar* in your husband's family? (questions as above)

e. *Purvaj*s

1. Is there a special *purvaj* (or are there special *purvaj*s) worshiped in your father's family? Do you know stories about him (her/them)? Is he (is she/are they) connected with *ratijaga*s? When and why is *dhok* given? Where is he (is she/are they) worshiped?
2. Is there a special *purvaj* (are there special *purvaj*s) worshiped in your mother's family? (questions as above)
3. Is there a special *purvaj* (are there special *purvaj*s) worshiped in your mother's family? (questions as above)

f. *Ishtadevta*s

1. What is your *ishtadevta*? Do you have other *ishtadevta*s? If so, who?
2. What is your father's *ishtadevta*? Others?
3. What is your mother's *ishtadevta*? Others?
4. What is your husband's *ishtadevta*? Others?

11. Information on exemplars. Looking back over Rajput history, which women do you think exemplify what it means to be a good Rajput woman? Why were these women great? What was their character like?

12. I understand that unlike other people, Rajputs are allowed to eat meat and drink wine. Do you eat meat? If so, why? If not, why not? Do you drink wine? If so, why? If not, why not?

13. Do you keep any *vrat*s? Do you keep any weekly ones? Which ones? How about monthly *vrat*s? Which ones? Annual *vrat*s? Which ones?

14.   General closing questions
   a. When you were growing up, who told you stories? What kind of stories? Do you have children? Does anyone tell them stories? What kind of stories?
   b. How did you learn to be a good wife? Did anyone teach you at your father's house? What about at your husband's house, did anyone teach you there?
   c. Have I left anything out? Are there important parts of your religious tradition that I have left out?
   d. Would it be possible to see the *mandirs* and *thapanas* of this house (*thikana*)?

Glossary

Many of these words are pronounced differently in the various Rajasthani dialects. To avoid chaos and confusion, I use the standard Hindi spelling and drop unpronounced final *a*. Rajasthani words that have no equivalent in Hindi retain their Rajasthani endings. Where the Rajasthani and the Hindi spellings differ, the Hindi and Sanskrit entries appear in parentheses.

Ad Mata [Ād Mātā]	Jhala *kuldevi*
Ashapura [Āśāpūrā]	Cauhan *kuldevi*
ashram [āśram]	spiritual retreat
asur [asur]	demon, e.g., Mahishasur, the Buffalo Demon defeated by the goddess Durga
bahadur [bahādur]	brave; valiant
Bala Satimata [Bālā Satīmātā]	living *satimata* who resided in northwestern Rajasthan
balidan [balidān]	sacrifice, usually a blood sacrifice
baniya [baniyā]	merchant; refers to a person in one of a number of business castes
Ban Mata [Bāṇ Mātā]	Sisodiya *kuldevi*
Bappa Rawal [Bāppā Rāval]	illustrious forefather of the Sisodiyas of Mewar
Bara Battis Thikana [Baḍa Battīs Ṭhikāṇā]	Big Thirty-two Thikana; a thikana belonging to the group of Mewari estates with status lower than the Solah Thikanas and higher than the Chota Battis Thikanas

bhakt [bhakt]	devotee of a deity; lover of God
bhakti [bhakti]	emotional commitment to a deity; devotional love
Bhat [Bhāṭ]	genealogist caste
bhav [bhāv]	possession; influence
Bheru [Bherū]	(Hindi and Sanskrit, Bhairava) guardian deity; each Rajput *kuldevi* is associated with a Bheru
Bhil [Bhīl]	tribe famed for archery skills; the blood brothers of Guha
bhopa [bhopā]	medium who is possessed by various deities
bolma [bolmā]	vow to perform a stated service for a deity if the deity first grants a devotee's desires
Bukh Mata [Būkh Mātā]	the Hungry Goddess; epithet of Ban Mata, *kuldevi* of the Sisodiyas of Mewar
cabutra [cabūtrā]	platform marking a sacred place; square on which a cenotaph (*chatri*) is sometimes mounted
camatkar [camatkār]	miracle; confirmation of superhuman power
Caran [Cāraṇ]	bard caste
caritra [caritra]	character, nature
Cauhan [Cauhāṇ]	a Rajput *kul*
Chitor [Citoḍ or Citauḍ]	a former capital of Mewar
chota bhai Rajput [choṭā bhāī Rājpūt]	little brother Rajput; a village Rajput, who claims descent from a younger brother of a ruler
Chota Battis Thikana [Choṭā Battīs Ṭhikāṇā]	Little Thirty-two Thikana; a thikana belonging to a group of Mewari estates ranked just below the Bara Battis Thikanas
cil [cīl]	kite, bird of prey
cita [citā]	funeral pyre
Daroga [Dārogā]	offspring of a Rajput father and a lower-caste consort
darshan [darśan]	auspicious sight of a Hindu deity, a revered person, or a sacred place
Dashamata [Daśāmātā]	Mother of Fate; name of a goddess worshiped in Rajasthan and for whom ten (*das*) stories are told illustrating the benefits of keeping an annual vow for her
Dashara [Daśharā]	festival celebrating the victory of Rama, hero of the *Ramayan*, over his demon nemesis Ravana
devar [devar]	younger brother-in-law
devi [devī]	goddess, term often applied to the Sanskritic Goddess (Devi)

Devimahatmya
[Devīmāhātmya]   part of the Markandeya Upanishad; text praising the Goddess, who is seen as ultimate reality; translated in Hindi as the *Durga Path* (lesson of Durga)

dharm [dharm]   duty; law; custom; order

dharmashastra
[dharmaśāstra]   Sanskritic legal text

dhok [dhok]   respect paid a Hindu deity

Dholi [Ḍholī]   drummer caste

doha [dohā]   short couplet, often championing heroic virtues

Durga [Durgā]   Sanskritic goddess worshiped especially on Navratri

Ekling Ji [Ekliṅg Jī]   incarnation of Shiv associated with the ruling family of Mewar

ghunghat [ghūṅghaṭ]   women's practice of covering their faces to preserve modesty in front of men and sometimes senior women in their conjugal households

gotra [gotra]   group of people claiming spiritual descent from a common preceptor

Guha [Guhā]   founder of the Guhil *kul* of Mewar

Guhil [Guhil]   *kul* to which the Sisodiyas belong

Gujar [Gujar]   agrarian caste

gun [guṇ]   quality; one of the three qualities, which are *sattva*, *rajas*, and *tamas*

Hari Rani
[Hāḍī Rānī]   Rajput heroine who sliced off her head to give to her husband as a memento when he went off to war

Harit [Hārīt]   divine sage, Bappa Rawal's spiritual teacher

haveli [havelī]   traditional urban household that a Rajput nobleman used when he came to the state capital to serve in the king's court

ishtadevta [iṣṭadevtā]   chosen deity; god or goddess chosen by an individual or family as a guardian deity

itihas [itihās]   history

Jamvai Mata
[Jamvāī Mātā]   Kachvaha *kuldevi*

Jat [Jāṭ]   agrarian and martial caste especially numerous in Panjab

jati [jāti]   literally, kind or genus; birth group, caste, or caste group

jauhar [jauhar]   (Hindi, jauhar) woman's self-immolation to avoid capture by enemy forces; jewel; proof; quality; ritual revenge taken against an enemy

Jhala [Jhālā]	a Rajput *kul*
jhumjhar [jhūṃjhār]	literally, struggler; hero who, having been decapitated in battle, exacts revenge for his death by killing many enemies before his body falls to the ground
Kachvaha [Kachvāhā]	a Rajput *kul* whose members include the rulers of Jaipur
Kali [Kālī]	the Black Goddess; conqueror of demons in the *Devimahatmya*
Karni Mata [Karnī Mātā]	*kuldevi* of a Caran *kul*
Kayasth [Kāyasth]	scribe caste
khamp [khāṃp]	twig; kinship unit between the *shakh* and *nak*
Krishna [Kṛṣṇa]	cowherd god, charioteer in the *Bhagavad Gita*; incarnation of Vishnu
Krittikas [Kṛttikās]	mothers of Kartikeya, the Sanskritic war god
kshatriya [kṣatriya]	member of any warrior caste
kul [kul]	kinship unit comprising the lesser segmentary units *shakh*, *khamp*, and *nak*
kuldevi [kuldevī]	goddess of a *kul* or some lesser kinship unit
Kumbhalgarh [Kumbhalgaḍh]	a former capital of Mewar; a fortress constructed in rugged hill country in the fifteenth century by Maharana Kumbha
laj [lāj]	modesty, shame
madaliyau [mādaliyau]	bracelet worn on the upper arm
Mahabharat [Mahābhārat]	great epic relating the adventures of the Pandava brothers
Maharaja [Mahārājā]	great king; title used by rulers of most large Rajasthani states; title used by a younger brother in the royal family of Mewar
Maharana [Mahārāṇā]	great king; title used by the ruler of Mewar
mahasatiyam [mahāsatiyāṃ]	cremation ground in which the cenotaphs of *sati*s are found
Mahish [Mahiṣ]	(Sanskrit, Mahisha) the Buffalo Demon whose death at the hands of the goddess Durga is told in the *Devimahatmya* and celebrated on the festival of Navratri
malipanau [mālīpaṇau]	shiny foil used to adorn religious icons
mandir [mandir]	Hindu temple

manvar [manvār]   ritual toast or giving of honor; in traditional Rajput weddings it can involve ritual sharing of alcohol and sometimes of opium

mardana [mardānā]   male quarters in a traditional Rajput household

Marwar [Marvāḍ]   state in northwestern Rajasthan ruled by the Rathaurs

mata [mātā]   mother; epithet of goddesses

mela [melā]   religious festival, fair

Mewar [Mevāḍ]   state in southwestern Rajasthan ruled by the Sisodiyas

Mina [Mīnā]   tribal group defeated by the Kachvahas on their arrival in the Jaipur area

Mira Bai [Mīrā Bāī]   Mewari princess who left Chitor to become a devotee of Krishna

moksh [mokṣ]   enlightenment

Naganecha Ji
[Nāgānechā Jī]   Rathaur *kuldevi*

Nai [Nāī]   barber caste

nari [nārī]   woman

Navratri [Navrātrī]   festival celebrating the defeat of Mahish, the Buffalo Demon, by the goddess Durga

ok [ok]   observance; prohibition established by a *sativrata*

Padmini [Padminī]   queen who immolated herself with other Rajput women in the vaults of a palace of Chitor

pala [pālā]   literally, protector; embossed pendant bearing a divine image and worn by women to protect their husbands

parakiya [parakīyā]   the wife of another

parda [pardā]   literally, curtain; seclusion of women

Parvati [Pārvatī]   a Sanskritic goddess, wife of Shiv

pativrata [pativratā] woman who has taken a vow (*vrat*) of devotion to her husband (*pati*); a word often used to describe any wife whose husband is alive

pitr [pitṛ]   male ancestor

pitrani [pitrānī]   female ancestor

puja [pūjā]   worship; devotional service to a deity at a temple or shrine

pujari [pujārī]   priest who performs devotional services

purana [purāṇa]   type of text, generally in Sanskrit, that tells of "ancient" matters, including many myths about the gods

purohit [purohit]   Brahmanical religious advisor to a Rajput family

purvaj [pūrvaj]   ancestor

putli [putlī]   embossed pendant worn around the neck; see *pala* above raja [rājā]   king, title used by rulers of both independent states and *thikana*s

Rajput [Rājpūt]   son of a king; member of a military caste

Ram [Rām]   hero of the epic, the *Ramayan*; an incarnation of Vishnu

Ramayan [Rāmāyaṇ]   epic celebrating the deeds of King Ram

Ranimanga
[Rāṇīmaṅgā]   genealogist who records the births and marriages of Rajput women

Rani of Jhansi
[Jhānsī kī Rānī]   Maratha queen who died fighting the British

Rathaur [Rāṭhauḍ]   Rajput *kul* whose members include the rulers of Marwar

ratijaga [rātijagā]   night wake in which songs to various family deities are sung

rup [rūp]   form, shape; incarnation (of a deity)

Ruthi Rani
[Ruṭhī Rānī]   the Angry Queen, who felt insulted by her husband's attentions to dancing girls but ultimately died a *sati*

sadhu [sādhu]   holy man; world renouncer

saka [sākā]   cutting down; entering into battle with no expectation of success or survival; sacrifice (*balidan*)

sannyasi [sannyāsī]   world renouncer; one whose goal is liberation from rebirth

Saptamatrikas
[Saptāmatṛkās]   the Seven Mothers associated with the Pleiades in Sanskritic tradition

sasural [sasurāl]   husband's household

sat [sat]   goodness, purity, truth; character

sati [satī]   good woman; a woman who dies on her husband's funeral pyre

satimata [satīmātā]   *sati*; a guardian of family fate and fortune

sativrata [satīvrātā]   woman who has taken a vow to join her husband in the afterlife

sattvic [sattvic]   characterized by *sat*

seva [sevā]   worship, service of a god or husband

shakh [śākh]   branch; kinship unit between *kul* and *khamp*

shakti [śakti]   power, strength associated with women and goddesses; consort goddess; epithet of the Goddess (Shakti)

sharam [śaram]   modesty, shyness

Shila Mata
[Śilā Mātā]   goddess whose shrine in Amber is patronized by the
                               ruling family of Jaipur
Shiv [Śiv]   Sanskritic deity, husband of Parvati
shrap [śrap]   (Hindi and Sanskrit, shāp) curse
sindur [sindūr]   vermilion
Sisodiya [Sīsodiyā]   Rajput *kul* among whose members are the rulers of
                               Mewar
Skand [Skand]   Kartikeya, god of war
Solah Thikana
[Solah Ṭhikānā]   Sixteen Thikana; a thikana belonging to the group of
                               Mewar estates ranked highest
Soni [Sonī]   metalsmith caste
suhagin [suhāgin]   *pativrata*; a woman whose husband is alive
Suryavamsh
[Sūryāvaṃś]   family (*vamsh*) of the sun, the one to which the Siso-
                               diya Guhils belong
svakiya [svakīya]   one's own wife
tapas [tapas]   heat generated by ascetic penances
taqlif [taḵliph]   trouble, difficulty
thakur [ṭhākur]   nobleman, king
thakurani [ṭhakurānī]   noblewoman, queen
thapana [thāpaṇā]   (Hindi, sthapana) place; simple shrine to a deity
thikana [ṭhikāṇā]   estate ruled by a nobleman
trishul [triśul]   trident, associated with goddesses and Shiv
Umca Satimata
[Uṃcā Satīmātā]   living *satimata* from southwestern Rajasthan
upanayan [upanāyan]   initiation ceremony for high-caste Hindu men; spiri-
                               tual rebirth
vaishya [vaiśya]   member of any one of a number of agricultural or mer-
                               chant castes
vamsh [vaṃś]   family; the largest Rajput kinship group, which com-
                               prises various *kuls*
varnashramadharma
[varṇāśramadharma]   Sanskritic code of duties articulated in dharmashastric
                               literature and pertaining to caste and the stages of life
                               for high-caste men
vir [vīr]   hero
virgati [vīrgati]   literally, the goal of heroes, warrior heaven
vrat [vrat]   vow
zanana [zanānā]   women's quarters in a traditional Rajput household

Bibliography

BOOKS AND ARTICLES

Abu-Lughod, Lila. *Veiled Sentiments: Honor and Poetry in a Bedouin Society.* Berkeley: University of California Press, 1986.

Agni Purāṇaṃ. Trans. Manmatha Nath Dutt Shastri. 2 vols. Chowkhamba Sanskrit Series, no. 54. Varanasi: Chowkhamba Sanskrit Studies Office, 1967.

Allen, Charles, and Sharada Dwivedi. *Lives of the Indian Princes.* London: Century Publishing, 1984.

Alston, A. J. *The Devotional Poems of Mīrābāī.* Delhi: Motilal Banarsidass, 1980.

Apte, Vaman Shivram. *The Practical Sanskrit-English Dictionary.* Rev. ed. Delhi: Motilal Banarsidass, 1978.

Bakshi, Rajni. "Shame!" *The Illustrated Weekly of India*, 4 October 1987, 20–23.

Beck, Brenda. *Peasant Society in Koṅku: A study of right and left subcastes in South Asia.* Vancouver: University of British Columbia Press, 1972.

———. *The Three Twins: The Telling of a South Indian Folk Epic.* Bloomington: Indiana University Press, 1982.

Beech, Mary Higdon. "The Domestic Realm in the Lives of Hindu Women in Calcutta." In *Separate Worlds: Studies of Purdah in South Asia*, ed. Hanna Papanek and Gail Minault, 110–38. Delhi: Chanakya Publications, 1982.

Bennett, Lynn. *Dangerous Wives and Sacred Sisters: Social and Symbolic Roles of High-Caste Women in Nepal.* New York: Columbia University Press, 1983.

Berreman, Gerald. *Hindus of the Himalayas: Ethnography and Change.* Berkeley: University of California Press, 1972.

Bhadvar, Inderjit. "Militant Defiance." *India Today*, 31 October 1987, 18–20.

Bhattacharya, France. "La déesse et le royaume, selon le Kālaketu Upākhyāna du Caṇḍī Maṅgala." *Puruṣārtha: Sciences Sociales en Asie du Sud* 5 (1981): 17–53.

Biardeau, Madeleine, and Charles Malamoud. *Le sacrifice dans l'Inde ancienne.* Paris: Presses universitaires de France, 1976.

Callewaert, Winand M. "Dadu and the Dadu-Panth: The Sources." In *The Sants: Studies in a Devotional Tradition of India,* ed. Karine Schomer and W. H. McLeod, 181–89. Delhi: Motilal Banarsidass, 1987.

Carstairs, G. Morris. *The Twice-Born: A Study of High-Caste Hindus.* Bloomington: Indiana University Press, 1967.

Chaturvedi, Mahendra, and B. N. Tiwari. *A Practical Hindi-English Dictionary.* 10th ed. Delhi: National Publishing House, 1983.

Chauhan, Brij Raj. *A Rajasthan Village.* Delhi: Vir Publishing House, 1967.

Coburn, Thomas B. *Devī Māhātmya: The Crystallization of the Goddess Tradition.* Columbia, Mo.: South Asia Books, 1985.

Coccari, Diane. "The Bir Babas of Banaras: An Analysis of a Folk Deity in North Indian Hinduism." Ph.D. dissertation, University of Wisconsin, Madison, 1986.

Courtright, Paul. *The Goddess and the Dreadful Practice.* London: Oxford University Press (forthcoming).

Cutler, Norman, and Joanne Punzo Waghorne, eds. *Gods of Flesh, Gods of Stone: The Embodiment of Divinity in India.* Chambersburg, Pa.: Anima Books, 1985.

Das, Veena. "Gender Studies, Cross-Cultural Comparison, and the Colonial Organization of Knowledge." *Berkshire Review* (1986): 58–79.

———. "The Goddess and the Demon: An Analysis of *The Devī-Māhātmya.*" Unpublished paper, 1986.

———. "Strange Response." *The Illustrated Weekly of India,* 28 February 1988, 30–32.

Datta, V. N. *Sati: A historical, social, and philosophical enquiry into the Hindu rite of widow burning.* Delhi: Manohar, 1988.

Davis, Marvin. *Rank and Rivalry: The Politics of Inequality in Rural West Bengal.* New York: Cambridge University Press, 1983.

Devi, Gayatri, of Jaipur, and Santha Rama Rau. *A Princess Remembers: The Memoirs of the Maharani of Jaipur.* Delhi: Vikas, 1976.

Dirks, Nicholas. *The Hollow Crown.* Cambridge: Cambridge University Press, 1987.

Eck, Diana. *Darśan: Seeing the Divine Image in India.* Chambersburg, Pa.: Anima Books, 1981.

Filliozat, Pierre. "The After-Death Destiny of the Hero According to the Mahābhārata." In *Memorial Stones: A Study of Their Origin, Significance, and Variety,* ed. S. Settar and Gunther D. Sontheimer, 3–8. Dharwad: Institute of Art History, Karnatak University and Heidelberg: South Asia Institute, University of Heidelberg, 1982.

Fox, Richard G. *Kin, Clan, Raja, and Rule: State-Hinterland Relations in Pre-industrial India.* Berkeley: University of California Press, 1971.

Fruzetti, Lina M. *The Gift of a Virgin: Women, Marriage, and Ritual in a Bengali Society.* New Brunswick, N.J.: Rutgers University Press, 1982.

Fuller, C. J. "The Hindu Pantheon and the Legitimation of Hierarchy." *Man: Journal of the Royal Anthropological Institute*, n.s., 23, no. 1 (March 1988): 19–39.

————. *Servants of the Goddess: The Priest of a South Indian Temple.* Cambridge: Cambridge University Press, 1984.

Galey, Jean-Claude. "Totalité et hiérarchie dans les sanctuaires royaux du Tehri-Garhwal." *Puruṣārtha: Sciences Sociales en Asie du Sud* 10 (1986): 55–95.

Gaur, Meena. *Sati and Social Reforms in India.* Jaipur: Publication Scheme, 1989.

Geertz, Clifford. *The Interpretation of Cultures.* New York: Basic Books, 1973.

Gold, Ann Grodzins. "Cow Worship, Goat Talk: Women's Play and the Sexual Reversal of Death." Paper presented at the American Anthropological Association, Annual Meeting, Denver, November 1984.

————. *Fruitful Journeys: The Ways of Rajasthani Pilgrims.* Berkeley: University of California Press, 1988.

————. "Stories of Shakti: Interpreting Female Violence in Some Rajasthani Traditions." Paper presented at the Association for Asian Studies, Annual Meeting, Washington, D. C., March 1989.

Goldman, Robert. "Fathers, Sons, and Gurus: Oedipal Conflict in the Sanskrit Epics." *Journal of Indian Philosophy* 6 (1978): 325–92.

Hanchett, Suzanne. "Ritual Symbols—Unifying or Divisive: Observations on the Relation Between Festivals and Political Processes in South Asia." In *Religion in Modern India*, ed. Giri Raj Gupta, 131–50. Delhi: Vikas, 1983.

Hansen, Kathryn. "The Virangana in North Indian History: Myth and Popular Culture." *Economic and Political Weekly*, 30 April 1988, 25–33.

Harlan, Lindsey. "Abandoning Shame." Paper presented at the conference, Representations of India's Past, Varanasi, India, December 1989.

————. "Kuldevi Tradition among Rajput Women." Paper presented at the conference, Women's Rites, Women's Desires, Harvard University, April 1988.

————. "Sati Veneration." In *New Light on Sati*, ed. John Stratton Hawley (forthcoming).

————. "Social Change and Rajput Tradition." Paper presented at the Conference on Modern South Asian Religion, Social Science Research Council, Amherst, August 1987.

Harman, William. *The Sacred Marriage of a Hindu Goddess.* Bloomington: Indiana University Press, 1989.

Hawley, John Stratton. "Morality Beyond Morality in the Lives of Three Hindu Saints." In *Saints and Virtues*, 52–72. Berkeley: University of California Press, 1987.

————, ed. *Saints and Virtues.* Berkeley: University of California Press, 1987.

Hawley, John Stratton, and Mark Juergensmeyer. *Songs of the Saints of India.* New York: Oxford University Press, 1988.

Heesterman, Jan. *The Inner Conflict of Tradition: Essays on the Indian Ritual, Kinship, and Society.* Chicago: University of Chicago Press, 1985.

Herrenschmidt, Olivier. "Le sacrifice du buffle en Andhra cotier: le «culte de village» confronté aux notions de sacrifiant et d'unité de culte." *Puruṣārtha: Sciences Sociales en Asie du Sud* 5 (1981): 137–77.

Hess, Linda. "The Poet, the People, and the Western Scholar: Influence of a Sacred Drama and Text on Social Values in North India." *Theatre Journal* 40, no. 2 (May 1988): 236–53.

Hiltebeitel, Alf. *The Cult of Draupadī.* Vol. 1: *From Gingee to Kuruksetra.* Chicago: University of Chicago Press, 1988.

———. "Draupadī's Hair." *Puruṣārtha: Sciences Sociales en Asie du Sud* 5 (1981): 179–214.

———. *The Ritual of Battle: Krishna in the Mahābhārata.* Ithaca: Cornell University Press, 1976.

Hitchcock, John T. "The Idea of the Martial Rājpūt." In *Traditional India: Structure and Change,* ed. Milton Singer, 10–17. Austin: University of Texas Press, 1959.

Hudson, Dennis. "Examples of the Ritual Act of Sati." Manuscript compilation, n.d.

Hyde, Janice S. "Women's Village Networks: Marriage Distance and Marriage Related Folksongs." Paper presented at the Conference on Preservation of the Environment and Culture in Rajasthan, Rajasthan University, Jaipur, India, December 1987.

Inden, Ronald. *Marriage and Rank in Bengali Culture.* Berkeley: University of California Press, 1976.

Jacobson, Doranne, and Susan Snow Wadley. *Women in India: Two Perspectives.* Delhi: Manohar, 1977.

Jeffery, Patricia. *Frogs in a Well: Indian Women in Purdah.* London: Zed Press, 1979.

Jeffry, May Pauline. *Ida S. Scudder of Vellore: The Life Story of Ida Sophia Scudder of Vellore.* Mysore City: 1951.

Kakar, Sudhir. *The Inner World: A Psycho-Analytic Study of Childhood and Society in India.* New York: Oxford University Press, 1981.

Khare, R. S. "From Kanyā to Mātā in Aspects of the Cultural Language of Kinship in North India." In *Concepts of Person: Kinship, Caste, and Marriage in India,* ed. Akos Ostör, Lina Fruzetti, and Steve Barnett, 143–71. Cambridge, Mass.: Harvard University Press, 1982.

Kinsley, David. *Hindu Goddesses: Visions of the Divine Feminine in the Hindu Religious Tradition.* Berkeley: University of California Press, 1986.

Kolff, Dirk H. A. "The Rajput of Ancient and Medieval North India: a warrior ascetic." Paper presented at the Conference on Preservation of the Environment and Culture in Rajasthan, Rajasthan University, Jaipur, India, December 1987.

Kothari, Komal. "Epics of Rajasthan." Paper presented at the Conference on Oral Epics, University of Wisconsin at Madison, July 1982 [Revised version published as "Performers, Gods, and Heroes in the Oral Epics of Rajasthan." In *Oral Epics in India,* ed. Stuart H. Blackburn, Peter J. Claus, Joyce B.

Flueckiger, and Susan S. Wadley, 102–17. Berkeley: University of California Press, 1989].

Lalas, Sitaram. *Rājasthānī Sabd Kos.* Vol. 4, pt. 3. Jodhpur: Caupasni Shiksha Samiti, 1978.

Luschinsky, Mildred S. "The Life of Women in a Village in North India." Ph.D. dissertation, Cornell University, 1962.

McGee, Mary. "Feasting and Fasting: The Vrata Tradition and Its Significance for Hindu Women." Ph.D. dissertation, Harvard Divinity School, 1987.

Mandelbaum, David G. *Women's Seclusion and Men's Honor: Sex Roles in North India, Bangladesh, and Pakistan.* Tucson: University of Arizona Press, 1988.

Mani, Lata. "Multiple Mediations: Feminist Scholarship in the Age of Multi-National Reception." *Inscriptions: Special Issue on Predicaments of Theory,* 1–21. Santa Cruz: University of California, 1989.

Marglin, Frédérique Apffel. "Types of Sexual Union and Their Implicit Meanings." In *The Divine Consort: Rādhā and the Goddesses of India,* ed. John Stratton Hawley and Donna Marie Wulff, 298–315. Berkeley: University of California Press, 1982.

———. *Wives of the God-King: The Rituals of the Devadasis of Puri.* Delhi: Oxford University Press, 1985.

Marriott, McKim, and Ronald B. Inden. "Towards an Ethnosociology of South Asian Caste Systems." In *The New Wind: Changing Identities in South Asia,* ed. Kenneth David, 227–38. The Hague: Mouton, 1977.

Mayer, Adrian C. *Caste and Kinship in Central India: A Village and Its Region.* Berkeley: University of California Press, 1970.

Mehta, Rama. "Purdah Among the Oswals of Mevar." In *Separate Worlds: Studies of Purdah in South Asia,* ed. Hanna Papanek and Gail Minault, 139–63. Delhi: Chanakya Publications, 1982.

Meister, Michael. "Regional Variations in Mātṛkā Conventions." *Artibus Asia* 47, nos. 3–4 (1986): 233–46.

Meyer, Eveline. *Aṅkāḷaparmēcuvari: A Goddess of Tamilnadu, Her Myths and Cult.* Stuttgart: Steiner Verlag, 1986.

Minturn, Leigh, and John Hitchcock. *The Rājpūts of Khalapur, India.* New York: John Wiley and Sons, 1960.

M. N. M. *The Hind Rajasthan.* Privately published tribute to H. H. Maha Raol Shri Pratabsingh Gulabsinghji, Bansda, 1896.

Nainsī rī Khyāt. Ed. Acarya Jinvijay Muni. Vol. 1. Jodhpur: Rajasthan Oriental Research Institute, 1960.

Nandy, Ashis. "The Human Factor." *Illustrated Weekly of India,* 17 January 1988, 20–23.

Narayana Rao, Velcheru. "Epics and Ideologies: Six Telegu Epics." In *Another Harmony: New Essays on the Folklore of India,* ed. Stuart H. Blackburn and A. K. Ramanujan, 131–64. Berkeley: University of California Press, 1986.

Obeyesekere, Gananath. *The Cult of the Goddess Pattini.* Chicago: University of Chicago Press, 1984.

———. *Medusa's Hair: An Essay on Personal Symbols and Religious Experience.* Chicago: University of Chicago Press, 1981.

O'Flaherty, Wendy Doniger. *Śiva: The Erotic Ascetic*. Oxford: Oxford University Press, 1973.

———. *Women, Androgynes, and Other Mythical Beasts*. Chicago: University of Chicago Press, 1980.

Ojha, Gaurishankar Hirachand. *Rājpūtāne kā Itihās*. Vol. 2. Ajmer: Vedic Yantralaya, 1932.

Ortner, Sherry. "On Key Symbols." *American Anthropologist* 75 (1973): 1338–46.

Papanek, Hanna, and Gail Minault, eds. *Separate Worlds: Studies of Purdah in South Asia*. Delhi: Chanakya Publications, 1982.

Pocock, David F. *Kanbi and Patidar: A Study of the Patidar Community of Gujarat*. London: Oxford University Press, 1972.

Rajan, Rajeshwari Sundar. "The Subject of Sati, Pain, and Death in the Contemporary Discourse on Sati." *Yale Journal of Criticism*, Vol. 3, no. 2, Spring 1990.

Ramanujan, A. K. *Speaking of Śiva*. Middlesex: Penguin Books, 1973.

———. "Two Realms of Kannada Folklore." In *Another Harmony: New Essays on the Folklore of India*, ed. Stuart H. Blackburn and A. K. Ramanujan, 41–75. Berkeley: University of California Press, 1986.

———. "On Women Saints." In *The Divine Consort: Rādhā and the Goddesses of India*, ed. John Stratton Hawley and Donna Marie Wulff, 316–24. Berkeley: University of California Press, 1982.

Reinich, Marie-Louise. *Les dieux et les hommes: Etudes des cultes d'un village du Tirunelveli, Inde du Sud*. Cahiers de l'homme, n.s. 18: Ethnologie-Géographie-Linguistique. Paris: Mouton, 1975.

Reynolds, Holly Baker. "An Auspicious Married Woman." In *The Powers of Tamil Women*, ed. Susan Snow Wadley, South Asia Series, no. 6, 35–60. Syracuse: Syracuse University, 1980.

Roghair, Gene H. *The Epic of Palnāḍu: A Study and Translation of Palnāṭi Vīrula Katha, a Telugu Oral Tradition from Andhra Pradesh India*. Oxford: Clarendon Press, 1982.

Roy, Manisha. *Bengali Women*. Chicago: University of Chicago Press, 1975.

Rudolph, Susanne Hoeber, and Lloyd I. Rudolph. "The Political Modernization of an Indian Feudal Order: An Analysis of Rajput Adaptation in Rajasthan." In *Essays on Rajputana: Reflections on History, Culture, and Administration*, 38–78. Delhi: Concept Publishing, 1984.

———. "Rajput Adulthood: Reflections on the Amar Singh Diary." In *Essays on Rajputana: Reflections on History, Culture, and Administration*, 177–210. Delhi: Concept Publishing, 1984.

———. "Rajputana under British Paramountcy: The Failure of Indirect Rule." In *Essays on Rajputana: Reflections on History, Culture, and Administration*, 3–37. Delhi: Concept Publishing, 1984.

Sangari, K., and S. Vaid. "Sati in Modern India: A Report." *Economic and Political Weekly*, 1 August 1981, 1285–88.

"Sati: A Pagan Sacrifice." *India Today*, 15 October 1987, 58–61.

Sax, William. *Mountain Goddess: Gender and Politics in a Himalayan Pilgrimage*. Oxford: Oxford University Press, forthcoming.

———. "Village Daughter, Village Goddess: Residence, Gender, and Politics in a Himalayan Pilgrimage." Paper presented at the conference, Women's Rites, Women's Desires, Harvard University, April 1988.

Sharma, Arvind. *Sati: Historical and Phenomenological Essays.* Delhi: Motilal Banarsidass, 1988.

Sharma, Dasaratha. *Rajasthan through the Ages.* Bikaner: Rajasthan State Archives, 1966.

Sharma, G. N. *Social Life in Medieval Rajasthan [1500–1800 A.D.].* Agra: Lakshmi Narain Agarwal, 1968.

Shulman, David Dean. *The King and the Clown in South Indian Myth and History.* Princeton: Princeton University Press, 1985.

———. *Tamil Temple Myths: Sacrifice and Divine Marriage in the South Indian Śaiva Tradition.* Princeton: Princeton University Press, 1980.

Shyamaldas, Kaviraj. *Vīr Vinod.* 4 vols. Udaipur, privately published by the Mewar darbar [ca. 1884] [Reissued. Delhi: Motilal Banarsidass, 1986].

Singer, Milton. "The Great Tradition in a Metropolitan Center: Madras." In *Traditional India: Structure and Change,* 141–82. Austin: University of Texas Press, 1959.

Somani, Ram Vallabh. *History of Mewar (From earliest times to 1751 A.D.).* Jaipur: C. L. Ranka, 1976.

Sontheimer, Gunther D. "Hero and Satī-stones in Maharasthra." In *Memorial Stones: A Study of Their Origin, Significance, and Variety,* ed. S. Settar and Gunther D. Sontheimer, 261–81. Dharwad: Institute of Art History, Karnatak University and Heidelberg: South Asia Institute, University of Heidelberg, 1982.

———. *Pastoral Deities in Western India,* trans. Anne Feldhaus. Oxford: Oxford University Press, 1989.

Stangroom, Cynthia Packart. "The Development of the Medieval Style in Rajasthan: Ninth and Tenth Centuries." Ph.D. dissertation, Harvard University, 1988.

Stern, Henri. "Le temple d'Eklingji et le royaume du Mewar (Rajasthan), (rapport au divin, royauté et territoire: sources d'une maîtrise)." *Puruṣārtha: Sciences Sociales en Asie du Sud* 10 (1986): 15–30.

Tambiah, S. J. "From Varna to Caste through Mixed Unions." In *The Character of Kinship,* ed. Jack Goody, 191–229. Cambridge: Cambridge University Press, 1973.

Tarabout, Giles. *Sacrifier et donner à voir en pays Malabar: Les fêtes de temple au Kerala (Inde du Sud).* Paris: Ecole Française d'Extrême-Orient, 1986.

Thapar, Romila. "Death and the Hero." In *Mortality and Immortality: The Anthropology and Archaeology of Death,* ed. S. C. Humphries and Helen King, 293–315. London: Academic Press, 1982.

———. "In History." *Seminar* 342, "Sati: a symposium on widow immolation and its social context" (February 1988): 14–19.

Thurstan, Edgar. *Castes and Tribes of Southern India.* 7 vols. Madras: Government Press, 1909.

Tod, James. *Annals and Antiquities of Rajasthan.* 2 vols. 1829. Reprint. Delhi: M. N. Publishers, 1978.

Turner, Victor. "Betwixt and Between: The Liminal Period in Rites de Passage."
    In *The Forest of Symbols: Aspects of Ndembu Religion*, 93–111. Ithaca:
    Cornell University Press, 1967.
————. "Symbols in Ndembu Ritual." In *The Forest of Symbols: Aspects of
    Ndembu Religion*, 19–47. Ithaca: Cornell University Press, 1967.
van Buitenen, J. A. B. *The Bhagavadgītā in the Mahābhārata*. Chicago: Univer-
    sity of Chicago Press, 1981.
Vidal, Dennis. "Le puits et le sanctuaire. Organisation cultuelle et souveraineté
    dans une ancienne principauté de l'Himalaya occidentale." *Puruṣārtha: Sci-
    ences Sociales en Asie du Sud* 10 (1986): 31–54.
Wadley, Susan Snow. "Power in Hindu Ideology and Practice." In *The New
    Wind: Changing Identities in South Asia*, ed. Kenneth David, 133–55. The
    Hague: Mouton, 1977.
————. *Shakti: Power in the Conceptual Structure of Karimpur Religion*. Chi-
    cago: Department of Anthropology, University of Chicago, 1975.
————, ed. *The Powers of Tamil Women*. South Asia Series, no. 6. Syracuse:
    Syracuse University, 1980.
Weisman, Steven R., "Indian Widow's Death at Pyre Creates Shrine," *New York
    Times*, 19 September 1987.
Yalman, Nur. *Under the Bo Tree: Studies in Caste, Kinship, and Marriage in the
    Interior of Ceylon*. Berkeley: University of California Press, 1967.
Zaehner, R. C. *Hindu Scriptures*. London: Dent, 1966.
Ziegler, Norman. "Action, Power, and Service in Rajasthani Culture: A Social
    History of the Rajpūts of Middle Period Rajasthan." Ph.D. dissertation, Uni-
    versity of Chicago, 1973.

FILMS

An Indian Pilgrimage: Ramdevra. Madison: University of Wisconsin [1977].
Sitala in Spring. Joint venture of Shape Films and University of Wisconsin. Cal-
    cutta: Shape Films [1987].

PAMPHLETS

Anil, Rajkumar. *Rājasthān ke Durg*. Delhi: Sahitya Prakashan, 1984.
Catursen, Acarya. *Rājpūt Nāriyāṃ*. Delhi: Prabhat Prakashan, 1984.

PERIODICALS

Manushi, nos. 42–43, special double issue, September–December 1987.
Seminar 342, "Sati: a symposium on widow immolation and its social context"
    (February 1988).

Index

Compositor:	Princeton University Press
Text:	Sabon 10/13
Display:	Sabon
Printer:	Princeton University Press
Binder:	Princeton University Press